Independence and Nationhood

Scotland 1306 – 1469

Independence and Nationhood

Scotland 1306 – 1469

Alexander Grant

Edinburgh University Press

© Alexander Grant 1984

First published 1984 in The New History of Scotland series by Edward Arnold
(Publishers) Ltd and reprinted 1991 and 1992 by
Edinburgh University Press
22 George Square, Edinburgh Ltd

Printed and bound in Great Britain by The Cromwell Press Limited

British Library Cataloguing in Publication Data
Grant, Alexander
Independence and nationhood: Scotland 1306-1469—
(The new history of Scotland; 3)
1.   Scotland — History — 1057-1603
I.   Title   II.   Series
941.103 DA783

ISBN 0 7486 0273 9

Contents

Acknowledgements

Many people have helped me with this book. The most important is my wife, without whose constant encouragement and forbearance it would never have been finished. Then I must acknowledge my debt to friends and colleagues in the Conference of Scottish Medieval History and in the History Departments at Queen's University, Belfast and at Lancaster University. I am especially grateful to my fellow Scottish historians at Lancaster, Dr K.J. Stringer (who read the entire typescript), Dr M.H. Merriman and Dr I.D. Whyte; I pestered them mercilessly, and benefited greatly from their assistance and criticisms. I am similarly indebted to my editor Dr Jenny Wormald, who had to wrestle with the problems of this book almost as much as I had to myself; and to the following: Professor G.W.S. Barrow, Dr A.L. Beier, Mr J. Campbell, Professor E.J. Cowan, Mr C.H.W. Gane, Rev. G.V.R. Grant, Dr J.A. Green, Dr R.J. Lyall, Mr H.L. McQueen, Mr M. Mullett, Dr A.L. Murray, Mrs F. Riddy, Mr W.W. Scott, Mr W.D.H. Sellar, Professor D.E.R. Watt, and Mr B. Webster. My warmest thanks to them all. I must add, of course, that while their assistance was invaluable, the opinions and arguments expressed in the book, and the slips and oversimplifications that have no doubt been perpetrated, remain entirely my own responsibility.

Sandy Grant
Lancaster
March 1984

Late-Medieval Scotland : 'Provincial' Earldoms and Lordships, Sheriff-doms, Burghs, Battles

I

Wars of Independence

1

Bruce, Balliol and England

I

The dominant feature of Scottish history in the period of this book is war with England. The conflict with England had opened with the English attempt at conquest in 1296, and dragged on – though from the later fourteenth century in a much less virulent form – right up until the Reformation in the mid sixteenth century. It was, however, a conflict with several distinct phases, or wars within the war. First there was the 'Edward I phase', a straightforward contest for control of Scotland between the English under Edward I, and the Scots fighting on behalf of their absent king, John Balliol. In 1296 Edward I had made King John abdicate, and then imprisoned and later exiled him, but the abdication was not recognized in Scotland. During John's imprisonment and exile the procedures developed for dealing with the interregnum after Alexander III's death in 1286 were again employed. The government was headed by guardians, and the concept of 'the community of the realm', representing Scottish society as a whole, was used to give responsibility and sanction to their actions. Various guardians kept the war going for eight years, but they often quarrelled, and provided a poor substitute for the leadership of an active king. Since the community of the realm contained a host of individuals who could act collectively if led and organized, but who could not lead or organize on their own, if the leadership collapsed the community's efforts also failed. That happened in 1304 during a massive campaign by Edward I. 'The force, violence and manifold fears which can strike even the most steadfast' (as the Scottish clergy expressed it in 1309) made the Scots leaders, and therefore the community, give in. There were widespread submissions to Edward I and much collaboration with his regime, especially by the leading men of the kingdom. Scotland became a conquered country. Edward I described it not as a kingdom but as a 'land', and began to establish 'direct rule from Westminster' over it.

But while the 1304 collapse ended the first phase of the war, the whole conflict was far from finished. Scottish acquiescence in English conquest proved no more permanent after 1304 than it had been after 1296. Fresh resistance started in 1305, and early in 1306 a full-scale revolt broke out under Robert Bruce earl of Carrick, who soon had himself crowned as Robert I. This was one of the great turning-points of Scottish history, leading to the triumphant restoration of Scottish independence under the Bruce–Stewart line of kings. In the short term, however, Bruce's revolt seriously divided the Scots, and indeed dangerously weakened the Scottish independence movement.

To Robert Bruce, grandson and heir of John Balliol's chief opponent in the 1292 contest for the throne, the Scottish collapse must have demonstrated that the independence struggle could no longer be maintained by guardians, that the cause of Balliol was doomed, and that the time was ripe for his own bid for the throne, especially since Edward I was unlikely to live much longer. With hindsight we can see he was right, but at the time things were not so clear. When Robert I became king he usurped the throne, deposing the existing absentee king, John Balliol. Moreover at the beginning of his revolt he murdered his main rival within Scotland, John Comyn lord of Badenoch. John Comyn had been head of the family of Comyn, which with its adherents was the major political grouping in Scotland; he was also King John's nephew, and the Comyns were committed to the Balliol kingship. Bruce's murder of John Comyn and his seizure of the throne made the Comyns his implacable enemies. From 1306 there was civil war between the Bruce and the Balliol–Comyn factions, which coincided with the Anglo-Scottish war. To Robert I's Scottish enemies, English overlordship was a lesser evil than Bruce kingship, and so the Balliol–Comyn faction, hitherto prominent upholders of Scottish independence, allied with the English. Scots who were uncommitted to either faction now faced a cruel dilemma. To support the patriotic cause meant supporting a usurper against the legitimate king, to support the legitimate king meant supporting the allies of the English against those who were fighting for independence.

In 1306, therefore, a second phase of the Anglo-Scottish conflict began. It was characterized by the Bruce–Balliol civil war, and lasted much longer than the first. It did not end with Robert I's triumphs, either military in 1314 or diplomatic in 1328, but continued well into the reign of his son David II. Only in the late 1340s can the Bruce–Balliol civil war be said to have ended, and the Balliol–Comyn faction to have ceased to play a major part in the conflict as a whole. That gives the period from 1306 to the late 1340s a distinct unity within the Anglo-Scottish conflict: it is the 'Bruce–Balliol phase'.

II

The 'Bruce–Balliol phase' can be subdivided into a number of separate parts. Initially the Bruce cause suffered disaster in 1306. Robert Bruce's revolt was not a national rising backed by 'the community of the realm'. Because of that, there could be no collective decision on whether or not to join him; it had to be made by individuals, according to individual factors. Those who revolted did so for various reasons, including personal and territorial ties and particular grudges against the English administration, as well as genuine patriotism. Analysis of over 100 landowners known to have revolted shows that Robert had an impressive but far from national following. Less than a third of the magnates sided with him, and more were actively hostile; his support among the lesser nobility was hardly greater. Most people presumably preferred to await events – which were, in summer 1306, two crushing defeats for King Robert, first by an English army and then by the forces of the lord of Argyll, a kinsman of the Comyns.

These defeats made Robert I flee from the Scottish mainland; he probably finished up on Rathlin island, off the north coast of Ireland. Most of his supporters surrendered or were captured. Reversing what had been a mainly conciliatory policy, Edward I had many of the captives executed. The change of policy, which was later to backfire, doubtless made sense at the time. When the country was relatively united, executing opponents would have made it difficult for the English to obtain collaboration; but in 1306 Edward I was assured of Scottish support from the Balliol–Comyn faction, irrespective of his actions towards their common enemies, and so those who revolted with Robert I could be treated with the utmost harshness in the hope of crushing the Bruce faction once and for all. The policy nearly succeeded: Robert I's family and friends were almost wiped out, and he himself was fortunate to avoid capture and execution. Had that happened, the independence cause might have died with him. As it was, the civil war seemed over almost as soon as it had begun, with victory for the Balliol–Comyn faction – which was also victory for the English. In 1306 the immediate consequence of Robert Bruce's revolt was to bring the English close to achieving their aim of asserting effective dominion over Scotland.

III

The second part of the 'Bruce–Balliol phase' lasted from 1307 to 1309. In it Robert I carried out one of the most remarkable military achievements in British history. Early in 1307 he returned to his own earldom of Carrick. After initial setbacks he gathered a small army in the south-west, and in May 1307 defeated an English force at Loudon in Ayrshire. That enabled him to break out of the south-west and move north, to attack the leaders of the Balliol–Comyn faction, the earls of Buchan and Ross and the lord of Argyll. During the next two years he defeated these in turn. The earl of Buchan and the lord of Argyll fled to England; the earl of Ross submitted to Robert I. So by late 1309 the tables had turned in the civil war. The Balliol–Comyn faction was defeated and leaderless, while Robert I controlled most of Scotland north of the Forth and much of the south-west.

The transformation in Robert I's fortunes was largely due to the outstanding military skill he showed from 1307. He learned from his early defeats to forsake conventional for guerrilla warfare, at which he proved a genius. His strategy was based on swift, small-scale operations in which he kept the initiative. He fought only on his own ground and preferably from ambush, he avoided major pitched battles, and he always dismantled rather than garrisoned strongholds which fell into his hands.

Several other factors also contributed to Robert's success in this part of the war. Chief among them was the death of Edward I of England in July 1307 – something Robert had probably been anticipating the previous year. The new English king, Edward II, had the same uncompromising attitude to Scotland but lacked his father's drive and ability; he also faced severe political problems within England. After Edward II's accession English activity in

Scotland diminished. Their armies no longer harried Robert I, and this enabled him to concentrate on the civil war within Scotland.

In the civil war the territorial structure of Scottish lordship, in which magnates' power and authority were concentrated on particular areas, worked to Robert's advantage. His enemies in the north, the earls of Buchan and Ross and the lord of Argyll, were supreme in their own provinces but relatively unimportant elsewhere. Moreover their territories were separated by the province of Moray, where there was no earl to organize resistance to Robert I, and where the population had been prominent in the independence struggle ever since 1296. In Moray Robert appealed directly to the lesser men, who responded well, providing the bulk of his support at this time. The province also had great strategic importance; it gave Robert internal lines of communication from which to strike at each of his enemies in turn, making them defend their own lands and preventing them from uniting against him. Thus although Robert I would have been outnumbered by his enemies' full force, he was never confronted by more than a fraction of it. He was even able to send part of his own army back to the south-west to deal with John Balliol's old lordship of Galloway, the other main centre of opposition.

The attitude of the Scottish Church was also significant at this time. Most of the bishops were staunch nationalists, who had stocked their dioceses with like-minded relatives and dependants. Not all of them actively supported Robert I, but few were directly hostile. On the whole the Scottish Church, unlike the nobility, attached more importance to the national cause than to the way Robert had seized the throne; it did not censure, let alone excommunicate, him for his sacrilegious murder of John Comyn in a church. In 1306 the bishops of St Andrews and Glasgow were involved in Robert's revolt, and were imprisoned in England as a result. Moreover their subordinates, who mostly had close personal ties with them, would have ensured that the Church in these two great dioceses continued to support Robert I. The bishop of Glasgow stated that fighting for King Robert against the English was the equivalent of fighting on Crusade, and a similar message was preached by the bishop of Moray, whose support was crucial in Robert's northern campaign. Churchmen, too, were behind Robert I's 'propaganda department', whose work culminated in the Declaration of Arbroath of 1320. Its activities are evident as early as May 1307, when Edward I was informed that 'Bruce never had the good will of his followers or of the people generally so much with him as now. It appears that God is with him. . . . The people believe that Bruce will carry all before him, exhorted by "false prophets" from Bruce's army.'

As this indicates, Robert I's military successes naturally increased his popular support. The successful military leader could force opponents to submit; when Robert I devastated Buchan in 1308 it was a terrible warning to other actual or potential enemies. But generally at the popular level coercion was unnecessary after Robert had proved he was no longer a loser and could provide the effective leadership which had been missing since 1303. The 'good will of the people' steadily increased after 1307, despite his enemies' efforts. Once Robert I's fortunes started to improve, the policy of savage repression initiated by Edward I and his Scottish allies in 1306 worked against them. As Edward I realized just before he died, it caused widespread hostility to the English, did not stop men from joining Robert I, and ensured that those who did would die rather than surrender.

With the continuing military success, Robert acted less as partisan leader and more as national monarch. His earliest surviving acts of government date from autumn 1308; in October 1308 he appointed Bernard of Linton chancellor; and in March 1309 he held his first parliament, at St Andrews. The parliament's main business was to legitimize his kingship. That was done through declarations from the clergy and nobility that John Balliol should never have been king but had been wrongfully imposed on the Scots by superior English might, and that Robert Bruce, who was the people's choice, had inherited the best claim to the throne, had conquered his enemies, and had shown the necessary virtues, was the rightful king. These declarations, which contain the first exposition of the myth that Balliol was a puppet forced upon the Scots, were an important step towards consolidating Robert I's rule. It must be stressed, however, that they were produced in a partisan parliament consisting almost entirely of Bruce supporters, especially the survivors of the 1306 rebels. Admittedly the presence of the earl of Ross and some other recent adherents shows Robert's following among the nobility was widening, but many magnates were still conspicuous by their absence. Although the declarations supporting Robert I were probably said to have been made by the community of the realm, another document issued at the parliament describes those present as 'the inhabitants of the whole realm of

Scotland acknowledging allegiance to King Robert'. This awkward terminology is closer to the real situation. Remarkable as
Robert's success had been, much had still to be done to justify his
title 'king of Scots'.

IV

The establishment of Robert I's rule throughout the whole of
Scotland was achieved in the next part of the war, from 1310 to
1314. To do this the strongholds in the south held by the English
and their allies had to be captured. Robert had no siege equipment,
and it was against his general strategy to starve out fortresses by
long sieges. Therefore guerrilla tactics involving surprise attacks
were necessary, as for example at Perth in January 1313 when,
after pretending to lift the siege, Robert personally led a night
assault by wading through the moat and scaling the wall with rope
ladders. Some fortresses were seized while the king and his army
were far distant, when carelessness on the part of the garrisons
allowed local people to take them by surprise. Whenever strongholds were captured, their defences were dismantled to prevent
them from being used against Robert I in the future. The process of
capturing strongholds gathered momentum as confidence and
expertise increased in Robert's army. By summer 1313 only
Lothian was outside Robert's control, and in spring 1314 two of the
greatest castles there, Roxburgh and Edinburgh, were captured by
his chief lieutenants James Douglas ('the good Sir James') and
Thomas Randolph (for whom the earldom of Moray had been
revived in 1312). That left Stirling (due to surrender if not relieved
by midsummer 1314), Bothwell, Dunbar, Jedburgh and Berwick
as the only important strongholds held against Robert I. Otherwise
the conquest of his kingdom was complete.

  This success within Scotland was not achieved in total isolation.
In 1309 the French king, previously an ally of John Balliol, established friendly relations with Robert I (although the full Franco-
Scottish alliance was not revived until 1326). Three years later a
formal treaty – the treaty of Inverness – was made with the king of
Norway. But at this stage of the war Scotland's most vital foreign
ties were with Flanders and north Germany, and were mercantile
rather than diplomatic. The trading links for exporting wool,
leather and timber and importing foodstuffs and manufactured

goods (see chap. 3:iv) survived throughout the war. Strenuous English efforts to destroy them and also to prevent smuggling from English ports failed. The decisive factor in the defeat of the English blockade was the capture of Aberdeen in 1308 by Robert I's forces. While the southern ports were in English hands until much later, Aberdeen, out of range of English attack but with excellent North Sea communications, was Scotland's gateway for supplies from the Continent. Without these supplies – especially weapons and armour – Robert I's military genius and the courage of his forces might in the end have come to nothing.

Apart from attempts at blockade and prohibitions of trade, Edward II did little to oppose Robert I. One abortive expedition to southern Scotland was made in 1310; otherwise the garrisons of the English and their Scottish allies were left to their own devices. Edward was equally unable to protect the north of England when Robert began in 1311 to unleash retaliatory raids. But the agreement of 1313 to surrender Stirling castle at midsummer 1314, if it was not relieved by an English army, was a challenge that not even Edward II could ignore. He invaded Scotland with some 15,000 infantry and 2,500 cavalry, and was confronted near Stirling by Robert I with an army of perhaps around 8,000 infantry. Robert only took the decision to abandon his strategy of avoiding major battles at the last minute. He did keep to his tactics of fighting on his own ground, under the best possible conditions for infantry rather than cavalry. The result, at Bannockburn on 23–4 June 1314, was complete victory for Robert's army, and the greatest humiliation of English arms since the loss of Normandy over a century earlier.

In the Anglo-Scottish war, however, Bannockburn was relatively unimportant; not for 14 years did the English recognize Scottish independence, and then only briefly. The battle's main impact was on the Scottish civil war. To most contemporaries it proved that God and right were on Robert I's side. Also, mo:e prosaically, it made Robert's Scottish opponents recognize that his power in Scotland was now irresistible, and that there was no chance of the tide turning again, even with English help. Most of them, realistically, accepted Robert I as king. The castellan of Bothwell, Walter son of Gilbert (progenitor of the Hamiltons), did so spectacularly: he had admitted English fugitives from Bannockburn to the castle, but once he learned of the Scottish victory he immediately changed sides, and handed them over to King Robert.

The seal was set on Robert I's victory five months later in a parliament held at Cambuskenneth abbey beside the battlefield of Bannockburn. Parliament enacted that those who had not come into King Robert's peace, or whose fathers had died in battle against him, were to be permanently disinherited and treated 'as enemies of the king and kingdom'. The statute was not interpreted strictly – so long as future allegiance was promised Robert always forgave past opposition – and only a few irreconcilables suffered forfeiture. Nevertheless it had important results. First, lands could no longer be held in Scotland *and* England, as Scottish magnates had done in the thirteenth century; allegiance to Edward II, necessary for keeping English lands, was incompatible with allegiance to Robert I, and vice versa. Next, the few who did suffer forfeiture left extensive estates, from which Robert rewarded those who had supported him throughout the conflict or who had joined him at critical moments; this territorial redistribution produced a radical change in the Scottish higher nobility. Finally, Robert's enemies did not accept their disinheritance meekly; they formed an important pressure group in England with strong personal and territorial interests in reversing the Bruce victory.

In this part of the war, as earlier, Robert I's military genius is clear, not only in his own strategy and tactics, but also in his choice and training of lieutenants. Among them his nephew Thomas Randolph and James Douglas are outstanding; his brother Edward, chosen for his position rather than his ability, is the only one with a questionable record. Conversely, Robert's enemies, particularly Edward II, showed little military skill. The difference between Edward II and his father also continued to be important. Edward I had been an awesome person, but few found themselves in awe of Edward II. In England his political opponents were bolder than his father's, and left him little opportunity for invading Scotland; and when he did so he could not cow his enemies into submission as Edward I had done. Had Edward I, not Edward II, been leading the English army in 1314, Robert I would never have dared fight Bannockburn.

In addition to the quality of leadership and the maintenance of the Continental supply-route, the crucial factor in Robert I's successes between 1310 and 1314 was the control over northern Scotland enjoyed since 1309. Without control north of the Forth (the original Scottish kingdom) nobody, Scots or English, could effectively rule Scotland as a whole. It is no coincidence that Edward I's campaigns of 1296 and 1303, the only major English campaigns in the north (both reached the Moray Firth), were followed by general Scottish submissions. None of Edward I's successors realized the significance of the north, but Robert I did, and dominated it by the end of 1309. The north provided him both with a reservoir of man-power and with a refuge from English attacks and invasions. When the English invaded in 1310 he waited without being forced into battle for their inevitable withdrawal, and then continued his task of subduing the south. The English garrisons in the south made this task slow. On the other hand these garrisons were ruinously expen-sive for the English crown, and were purely defensive: they might retard Robert's conquest of southern Scotland, but they could assist neither the king of England nor the Balliol–Comyn faction in reconquering the north. With hindsight we can see that so long as Robert controlled the north, received essential supplies from the Continent via Aberdeen, and avoided being caught and defeated in battle, the south was bound eventually to fall to him. It is hardly surprising that Robert was reluctant to fight at Bannockburn. But paradoxically Bannockburn, no part of his original strategy, brought this part of the war to a much quicker conclusion than would otherwise have been possible.

V

One striking feature of medieval warfare was that the participants hardly ever had sufficient strength or resources to achieve their war aims fully, yet they usually refused to compromise. Edward I's great campaigns in Scotland never gained more than temporary Scottish submissions. And for all its effect on Edward II, Bannock-burn might not have been fought; Edward still claimed to be over-lord of Scotland, and refused to make peace on any other basis. Scottish efforts to make him change this recalcitrant attitude and accept Robert I's triumph in Scotland characterize the next part of the war, which dragged on, less successfully for the Scots, until 1323.

The Scottish aims could only be achieved through military pres-sure on Edward II's dominions. Therefore cross-border raiding was greatly intensified. For 10 years the north of England was harried; Edward II could not defend it effectively, and only pur-chases of immunity from the Scots costing over £20,000 prevented its total devastation. The strategy succeeded with the inhabitants of northern England; most wanted peace, and some even accepted Robert I as their lord. But it was a different matter with respect to the English government. The Scots could not penetrate beyond Yorkshire and Lancashire, and so southern England, which was politically and economically much more important than the north, escaped unscathed. So long as the English government remained unmoved by the sufferings of the north, cross-border raids could not force it to come to terms. The only Scottish gain was the recapture of Berwick, the last piece of territory in English hands, in 1318.

In addition to the raids on the north of England a second front was opened in Ireland. In 1315 Robert's brother and heir-presumptive, Edward, invaded Ulster, and for the next three years Scottish forces campaigned across the Irish Sea. The Scottish invasion seriously weakened English power in Ireland; it also stopped the English use of Irish troops and resources against Scotland. Much more was intended, however. The Scots army was to provide the backbone of a national Irish rising that would drive the English from Ireland just as they had been driven from Scotland. This plan was not completely far-fetched, though Irish disunity was a considerable obstacle. But following Edward Bruce's initial victories, an even grander strategy was conceived. Ireland would be conquered as a kingdom for Edward Bruce, and then used as a base for invading Wales, where the process would be repeated. A great Celtic alliance would be constructed against England, overturning the balance of power in the British Isles. Traditionally this grandiose scheme has been blamed on Edward Bruce's ambition; the contrast between a letter from Robert to the Irish envisaging a Scotto-Irish alliance, and one from Edward to the Welsh envisaging a Bruce lordship over Wales, perhaps bears that out. But Robert wholeheartedly supported his brother in Ireland, and fought there himself in 1317. Despite his military caution, Robert I was a political optimist; to the man who had looked for Comyn support in 1306, and who had continued fighting in the apparently hopeless situation of 1307, the idea of a Bruce conquest of Ireland and Wales might not have appeared impracticable.

For a short time the threat seemed to be proving too much for Edward II's government. But eventually the extension of the original Scottish strategy led to catastrophe. It was even harder for the Scots to conquer Ireland than for the English to conquer Scotland. Geography and logistics were against them, and the situation was made worse by bad weather and famine in 1316–17. The native

Irish were even less united than the Scots had been in 1306, and embroiled Edward Bruce in their internecine struggles. The idea of a Scottish kingdom of Ireland, in which Edward Bruce's main Irish ally, Donal ONeill of Tyrone, would probably be the dominant force, was resisted by many Irish chiefs. The Anglo-Irish had everything to lose from a Bruce victory, and most opposed the Scots vigorously. Finally, Edward II, who would not recognize Robert Bruce as king of Scots, was hardly likely to accept Edward Bruce as king of Ireland. So although Edward Bruce had himself made 'High King of Ireland', and devastated much of the country in two campaigns, he achieved no real political success. His defeat and death near Dundalk in 1318 brought the Scots invasion of Ireland to a disastrous end.

At the beginning of the 1320s, therefore, Robert I was no nearer his goal of winning English recognition of Scottish independence. In addition there was a problem with the papacy. The popes were reluctant to recognize someone who had seized the throne from the legitimate king and killed one of his rivals in a church. Furthermore in 1317 Robert had refused to agree to an Anglo-Scottish truce negotiated by papal envoys that would have prevented the Scots from recapturing Berwick. The papacy wanted peace throughout Europe, to mount a crusade against Islam; increasingly, and particularly because of English propaganda, Robert I appeared as one of the main obstacles. Accordingly in the winter of 1319–20 a series of papal bulls was issued, which excommunicated Robert and his supporters, summoned him and four bishops to the papal court, released his subjects from their allegiance, and placed Scotland under an interdict prohibiting almost all religious activity.

These bulls could not be ignored, and so in May 1320 three answers were sent to Pope John XXII: from the king; from the bishop of St Andrews; and from eight earls, 31 barons, and the rest of the nobility and 'community of the realm' of Scotland. The most important letter was the third, the 'Declaration of Arbroath'. It was designed to do three things: to prove the Scots were fighting a just, legitimate war against unjust English aggression, 'not for glory, nor riches, nor honours, but for freedom alone, which no good man gives up except with his life'; to justify Robert I's kingship, which was supported by the whole united community, but only while he upheld the cause of independence; and to request the pope to urge Edward II to leave the Scots in peace. The Declaration, which had several precedents in other countries, was a piece of political rhetoric intended to defuse a particular diplomatic crisis. It is, nevertheless, a brilliant, inspiring, and justly famous assertion of Scottish independence. But it impressed the pope less than most modern Scots: little pressure was applied on Edward II; the papacy still did not style Robert Bruce 'king of Scots'; and the excommunications and interdict were not relaxed (although they were ignored inside Scotland). The papal attitude did not change until 1328.

In summer 1320 Robert I also faced an internal crisis. A conspiracy to assassinate him and crown William Soules of Liddesdale, son of one of the Competitors of 1291, was discovered. Those accused of treason included five signatories of the Declaration of Arbroath; three of them and three lesser nobles were convicted. This episode is difficult to understand. With hindsight, Robert's position within Scotland after 1314 appears impregnable. Yet, although Bannockburn had made most Scots accept him as king, after the disaster in Ireland it was perhaps not certain at the time that all his subjects would stay loyal, especially when the pope had absolved them from their allegiance. There were security worries in 1318, when seditious rumour-mongering was condemned by parliament, and English sources record Edward II negotiating with certain Scots in 1319. The Soules conspiracy itself may have derived from dissatisfaction at the redistribution of the lands forfeited after 1314. Robert I's patronage was limited to those who had supported him ever since 1306 plus a few who had joined him at important moments; none of those arrested in 1320 had received substantial grants. William Soules must have resented this. He had royal blood, and was the head of what had been one of the greatest houses of early feudal Scotland, whose only equals among surviving 'Norman' families were the Bruces (who had gained the throne) and the Stewarts (who had had extensive grants of land) – yet Soules received little royal patronage. Similar points apply to another of those arrested, David Brechin; he had considerably higher status than many rewarded by Robert. Brechin's crime was not conspiracy but failing to warn the king about the plot after learning of it. That was as much a breach of his feudal obligations as actual conspiracy, and technically counted as treason. But his execution apparently shocked contemporaries. That perhaps suggests Robert I over-reacted; it may be another indication of insecurity in the regime at that time. On the other hand, once the conspiracy had been crushed, Robert's position inside Scotland was of course greatly strengthened.

In the war, 1320 and 1321 were years of truce, which Robert I had accepted once Berwick was secured. In 1322 hostilities resumed, with the Scots hoping to benefit from an outbreak of rebellion in England. In the event a northern English knight, Andrew Harclay, defeated the rebels, and this victory encouraged Edward II to attempt another invasion of Scotland. Robert I successfully countered it with his usual scorched-earth tactics, withdrawal beyond the Forth, and hot pursuit of the English when they retreated. This fiasco led Harclay to take the initiative in 1323 and negotiate his own treaty confirming Scottish independence, 'on behalf of all those in England who wish to be spared and saved from war by Robert Bruce and all his men'. Edward II's reaction to Harclay's peace initiative was to have him executed for treason. But a few months later Edward II did bring the war to a temporary end, by making a 13-year truce with the Scots in May 1323. That stopped the Scottish raids, but did not signify any change in the English government's attitude; at the beginning of the negotiations Edward proposed a truce with 'the people of Scotland', without reference to King Robert, and he eventually concluded it with 'Sire Robert de Brus' and his subjects. To Edward II, the truce was merely a breathing space. Robert I presumably saw it as something more: although he had failed to make the English meet his demands, the fighting had ended with *de facto* independence for Scotland, and he would have hoped that after the 13 years the truce would be extended, perhaps indefinitely.

VI

The 1323 truce brought the first long break in Anglo-Scottish hostilities since 1296. Robert I could now concentrate on consolidating his regime, regularizing the crown's financial position, restoring the machinery of government, and overhauling Scots law. He also concluded a full-scale treaty of alliance with France, sealed at Corbeil (near Paris) in 1326. The treaty of Corbeil, which lasted until the sixteenth century, went much further than earlier Franco-Scottish relationships, providing that the French would aid and counsel the Scots in any Anglo-Scottish war, and that the Scots would attack England in any Anglo-French war. The initiative for the alliance came as much from the French as from the Scots, but the terms placed a heavier obligation on the Scots. Nevertheless the treaty meant Scotland would no longer be isolated in the face of English aggression; this outweighed the heavy Scottish commitment to France, especially in the 1330s.

While the treaty of Corbeil was an insurance in case of fresh war, in the 1320s Robert I was hoping for peace. Until 1327 Anglo-Scottish negotiations continued in their familiar stalemate, but then events inside England transformed the diplomatic situation. Edward II was deposed by his wife Queen Isabella and her lover Roger Mortimer, who took over the English government in the name of Edward II's 14-year-old son, now Edward III. The truce technically lapsed with Edward II's deposition, and the new regime was vulnerable, so Robert I immediately reopened hostilities. This stage of the war was short and sharp. As after Bannockburn, an attack on the north of England (which humiliated a large English army including the young Edward III) was combined with a descent on Ireland. But this time, having exhausted the English defences, Robert mounted a third campaign in which – by besieging strongholds and even granting out land to his followers – he appeared to be annexing Northumberland. Isabella and Mortimer could not resist this final onslaught, and while they, like Edward II, might have allowed the north of England to be ravaged, they could hardly let the Scots conquer it. They therefore sued for peace. At last Robert I had managed to force an English government to agree to his terms. An Anglo-Scottish treaty was concluded at Edinburgh in March 1328, and was ratified by the English king and parliament at Northampton the following May.

By the treaty of Edinburgh the Scots won formal English acknowledgment of Scotland's absolute independence. The treaty was cemented by the marriage of Robert I's son and heir David to Edward III's sister Joan. At the same time the Scots paid £20,000; this could have been seen as compensation for the money extorted from the north of England, but it also gave the near-bankrupt Isabella and Mortimer a financial interest in having the treaty ratified. The treaty and marriage marked the culmination of Robert Bruce's career. Sadly, he did not enjoy his triumph for long: he was already seriously ill in 1327, and he died in June 1329, aged 54.

Although he is not above criticism, Robert I was one of the greatest kings of medieval Europe, and indeed 'one of the big figures of history'.[1] Whether or not the cause of Scottish independence would have survived after 1305 under other leaders is immaterial; the fact is that it did so under Robert I, who achieved something that seemed impossible in the first years of his reign. It was fitting that he died with his kingdom independent and at peace. And although he failed in one vital aspect of medieval kingship by not leaving an adult heir, his five-year-old son David seemed to have entered upon an excellent inheritance. Robert I's success, however, had been essentially personal, deriving from his great qualities of military and domestic leadership. Without his dominating figure, both the Scottish crown and the Bruce regime were immeasurably weakened.

VII

The peace brought by the treaty of Edinburgh only lasted four years. It was condemned as shameful in England. Edward III had tried to obstruct the treaty, and showed his feelings by neither attending his sister's wedding nor giving her a dowry. Opposition to the treaty helped to cause a rebellion against Isabella and Mortimer in 1329, and also, indeed, their eventual overthrow in 1330. The proposal to return the stone of Scone and the relic known as the Black Rood, taken by Edward I in 1296, was foiled by a London mob. Most seriously, 'the disinherited', whose claims were ignored in the peace settlement, still hoped to recover lands in Scotland. These were the men who had forfeited inheritances for preferring Edward II to Robert I after 1314. Most were enemies of Isabella and Mortimer, who gave them no help; but Edward III was sympathetic to them when he came to power. The person who had suffered the greatest disinheritance, King John's son Edward Balliol, was allowed to come to England from his French estates, and while he was not openly encouraged by Edward III to try to regain his father's crown, he was not discouraged. This set the stage for the reopening of the Bruce–Balliol civil war, now with an adult Balliol confronting a child Bruce. In its wake, inevitably, the whole Anglo-Scottish conflict was rekindled.

When the civil war restarted in 1332, the situation in Scotland was very different from the heady days of 1327–8. Not only Robert I but also his chief lieutenants, the earl of Moray and James

[1] G.W.S. Barrow, *Robert Bruce* (2nd edn, Edinburgh, 1976), p. xiii.

Douglas, had died; Douglas in Spain in 1330 while fulfilling the king's last wish to take his heart on Crusade, Moray in 1332 while preparing to meet the impending Balliol attack. Moray's death robbed Scotland of effective leadership; three weeks later Edward Balliol and the disinherited launched a sea-borne invasion which landed in Fife.

The new Scottish leadership could not repel the attack. Instead there was a reversion to the earlier pattern of warfare, in which the fortunes of the Bruce party, upholding the cause of Scottish independence, and those of the Balliol party, which accepted Edward III as overlord and even ceded most of southern Scotland to him in 1334, ebbed and flowed. In 1332 Balliol routed the Scots at Dupplin (near Perth) and was crowned at Scone, but he was driven out later in the year. In 1333, now with the open assistance of Edward III (who repudiated the treaty of Edinburgh), he re-established himself in Scotland following a massive victory by Edward III at Halidon Hill (outside Berwick). David II was sent to France for safety, but his supporters continued to resist. Edward III himself campaigned in Scotland each year from 1333 to 1337, in 1335 with one of the largest armies he ever raised. The Bruce party rode out the storm, however, and eventually regained most of the kingdom. In 1341 they brought King David back to Scotland.

At times in this part of the war the cause of Scottish independence seemed in as much jeopardy as in 1296, 1304–5, and 1306–7. The near collapse of the Bruce regime was brought about by the two crushing military defeats. The nobility suffered heavily; eight earls and many great barons were killed. After Halidon, the English reckoned, there was no one left in Scotland to raise and lead an army. Dupplin and Halidon were disastrous reversals of Robert I's policy of avoiding pitched battles, but there was some reason (besides over-confidence) for fighting them. At Dupplin the intention was to destroy the invaders before they built up strength; at Halidon it was to end the English siege of Berwick, a situation which resulted from Robert I's decision to strengthen rather than dismantle Berwick's fortifications after its capture in 1318. These intentions misfired partly because English tactics had changed dramatically since Bannockburn. Edward Balliol at Dupplin and Edward III at Halidon both fought on the defensive, using dismounted men-at-arms and archers in the deadly combination that was later to have such success in France. But the main reason for the defeats was poor leadership. The Scots were surprised at

Dupplin. The new guardian, Robert I's nephew Donald earl of
Mar, was accused of treachery by other Scots leaders (he had
become closely attached to the homosexual Edward II while a
prisoner in England, and had not returned to Scotland until
Edward's deposition in 1327). They all quarrelled, then charged;
the Scottish vanguard was trampled underfoot by the rest of the
army, causing total confusion and an utter rout. At Halidon the
guardian, now Archibald Douglas (brother of 'the good Sir James'),
bungled an attempt to repeat Robert I's strategy in relieving an
earlier siege of Berwick. He manoeuvred himself into much the
same position as Edward II's at Bannockburn – with much the
same result, too.

David II's supporters had other leadership problems. There was
a rapid turnover of guardians. The earl of Moray died in July 1332,
the earl of Mar was killed in August 1332 at Dupplin, Andrew
Murray of Bothwell (son of Wallace's colleague of 1297, and the
best Scots commander of the period) was captured in October
1332, and Archibald Douglas was killed in July 1333 at Halidon.
There was then no guardian until 1334, when two teenagers,
Robert Stewart (Robert I's grandson and David II's heir-
presumptive), and John Randolph the new earl of Moray, who had
both been prominent already in the resistance, took over the office
jointly. They soon quarrelled; Stewart was probably jealous of
Moray and thought he should be sole guardian because of his
relationship to David II. In September 1335, following Edward
III's great invasion and a direct attack on his own lands by an Irish
army, Stewart submitted briefly to Edward III. At about the same
time Moray fell into English hands.

Not surprisingly, therefore, resistance to Edward III and Balliol
was more often a series of local individual efforts than a coherent
unified movement. And while some individuals resisted others submitted. After Dupplin and Halidon, God could have been said to
have deserted the Bruce cause, while Edward III's invasion of 1335
seemed to show that further resistance was pointless. In 1335, as
'Wyntoun' wrote later, only little children dared say they supported 'King Dawy'. That is an exaggeration – the submissions
were not so extensive as in 1296 or 1304 – but in autumn 1335
Edward III was confident that Scotland was finally conquered. He
dominated the south, while Balliol and his lieutenant David of
Strathbogie seemed to control the north. Negotiations for a final
capitulation were under way with Andrew Murray (who had been

ransomed and was guardian again), and Edward was even considering what land should be settled upon his brother-in-law, David Bruce. But that was the high-point for Edward III and Balliol. In November 1335 Murray defeated and killed Strathbogie at Culblean, in Mar. During the next two years, by effectively following Robert I's strategy of avoiding battles, wasting the countryside, and dismantling strongholds, he regained most of the kingdom for the exiled David II.

Murray's success indicates that given good leadership, David's cause was actually healthier than it appeared in 1332–3. Most of the factors contributing to Robert I's triumph applied again when his strategy was repeated. And although on the English side Edward III was a much greater commander than Edward II, his task in Scotland was even harder than his father's or grandfather's. While the Scottish submissions were serious at the time, on the first signs of success by David II's supporters most of those who had submitted changed sides again. There was in fact little collaboration, probably because the men who recovered inheritances or received lands from Edward III and Balliol would have appeared to the local populations as Anglicized or English intruders, rather than as the native, rightful lords – as the original generation of the Balliol–Comyn faction had been. Edward III and Balliol realized this, and began expropriating many freeholders – which stiffened resistance. They also allowed their armies to pillage friend and foe indiscriminately, and so could not benefit from any native resistance to the scorched-earth policy of Andrew Murray and his colleagues.

The lack of Scottish cooperation meant that to be victorious Edward III and Balliol had to conquer Scotland outright. They might have had more success had there been a network of fortifications from which small garrisons could have dominated surrounding areas. But Robert I had had most strongholds destroyed or damaged, and of those which were still usable several were held for David II. Therefore much refortification was needed, and until that was carried out Scotland could only be controlled by a large army of occupation. The cost of meeting these requirements fully would have been prohibitive. Edward III did not manage nearly enough in either direction, although he spent over £25,000 on wages in his three-month campaign in 1335, and at least £26,000 on fortifications and garrisons in 1336 and 1337. By summer 1337 it was Andrew Murray (who unlike Robert I had excellent siege engines, acquired or built since 1314), not Edward III or Edward Balliol, who controlled most of the country.

One other factor which told heavily against Edward III and Balliol was the help David II's cause received from France under the treaty of Corbeil. French interests needed an independent Scotland, hostile to England. Therefore in 1334 David II and his entourage were given refuge, supplies of arms and food were sent to Scotland, and Philip VI of France began to exert diplomatic pressure on behalf of the Scots. At sea French and Scots together preyed on English supply ships for the forces in Scotland. Most importantly, Philip threatened to go beyond the terms of the treaty of Corbeil and either send French troops to Scotland (there was a plan to send 1,200 cavalry and 20,000 infantry) or attack southern England, which while immune from Scots attacks was vulnerable to the French. Thus while he was campaigning in Scotland Edward III continually had to be looking over his shoulder; troops and ships were diverted to the south coast in case the French invaded. Eventually in 1337 open war broke out between England and France – the 'Hundred Years War', which lasted on and off until 1453. While Anglo-French relations were deteriorating for other reasons, Edward III's aggressive reactions to the French help for David II were probably what sparked off the Hundred Years War. It meant Edward III's attention was increasingly focused on France, so that he could not repeat his efforts in Scotland of 1335 and 1336. Therefore, although Andrew Murray's death in 1338 slowed the speed of the Bruce recovery, it did continue – with Robert Stewart as guardian – against limited opposition. Between 1337 and 1342 the remaining strongholds (except Berwick) were recaptured, cross-border raiding resumed, and in summer 1341 the 17-year-old David II returned from France to begin his personal rule. The Bruce cause had triumphed again.

VIII

David II's return and the expulsion of Edward III and Balliol's forces did not quite end the Bruce–Balliol phase of the Anglo-Scottish conflict. Neither Edward III nor Balliol renounced their claims, and since they had repudiated the treaty of Edinburgh, the situation was the same as after Bannockburn. David II faced the same task as his father: to make the English crown recognize

Scotland's independence. He set about it in much the same way, by attacking northern England. Heavy raids were launched in 1342, 1345 and 1346. In 1346 there seemed an especially good chance of putting pressure on England, for Edward III and a large army were occupied in France at the siege of Calais. At the same time, Philip VI, who had recently been heavily defeated by Edward III at Crécy, was desperately seeking a Scottish diversion. David had to help the French, not only because of the treaty of Corbeil but also because if Edward III were victorious in France full English attention would once more revert to Scotland. He therefore invaded England in strength in October. But his army was too large for rapid manoeuvres, and he did not have his father's control over it. Moreover Edward III had left troops in the English border counties, and had improved the machinery for their defence. David's army was caught and forced to battle at Neville's Cross (outside Durham); English men-at-arms and archers fighting on the defensive again destroyed a Scottish army. Six earls and many great barons were killed or captured; even more seriously, King David himself was taken prisoner.

Neville's Cross was like Halidon in its immediate effect: the English overran much of southern Scotland, and in 1347 Edward Balliol led an expedition north in another attempt on the Scottish crown. But here the similarity ends. Balliol did not repeat his successes of 1333–5, and the English soon left him to fend for himself. While Edward III was keen to consolidate his grip on southern Scotland, he was no longer interested in making Balliol king. That is partly because it was obvious that the Balliol cause was at last dead in Scotland, but more because Edward himself was now deserting it. For Edward to exploit David II's capture fully, by making David accept English overlordship, he had to recognize David Bruce rather than Edward Balliol as king, or at least ruler, of Scotland. Balliol maintained his claim for some years, but received no more English cash, troops or supplies. He eventually accepted the changed political situation, and in 1356 resigned his claims to Edward III.

Paradoxically, therefore, it was not so much David II's triumphant return in 1341 as his disastrous defeat in 1346 that finally ended the Bruce–Balliol civil war. Neville's Cross and David II's capture transformed the military and diplomatic relationship between Scotland and England. The three-cornered contest between Bruce, Balliol and England was over, with the Balliol faction defeated and the English king recognizing the Bruce regime in Scotland, though not of course Scottish independence. A third phase of the Anglo-Scottish struggle was beginning.

IX

In the fifty years from 1296 strenuous English efforts to conquer Scotland had failed. With hindsight it is clear that the English faced insurmountable geographical, logistical and financial problems. The factors behind the Scottish military success are also straight-forward. Yet the English failure was not inevitable. Contemporary Scots enjoyed neither hindsight nor consistent military success. English power must often have appeared irresistible, making it seem sensible to give up. Many Scots did submit, but some - enough - continued to fight. This resistance in the face of apparently overwhelming strength guaranteed English failure in Scotland.

There is no simple explanation for this. In the early fourteenth century Scottish attitudes concerning national independence were as ambivalent as in 1707 and nowadays. With the notable excep-tion of the Douglases, the Murrays, and William Wallace, few Scots can be found steadily and consistently supporting the cause of independence. Inconsistency spread right down the social scale and right across the country. Some historians have identified particular groups - the lesser nobles and 'middling folk', the inhabitants of 'Celtic Scotland', and the Scottish Church - as the mainstay of the Scottish cause, but that is unlikely; detailed analysis shows that none of these, nor any other element of society, was significantly more patriotic.

The absence of consistent patriotism was due partly to self-interest and self-preservation. Local rivalries, and after 1306 the bitter Bruce–Balliol-Comyn feud, were also important. But, equally significantly, there were great moral problems. Although Scottish national consciousness had developed strongly in the thirteenth century, people focused on the king, not the kingdom. Kingdoms were considered the property of their kings; whoever inherited a kingdom had to be obeyed as king, irrespective of his nationality. And they were not necessarily independent; there were subordinate kingdoms with overlords, although the overlordship was usually nominal. Kings could, however, be disobeyed if they were usurpers or committed tyrannical acts – charges which his enemies levelled at Robert I after his seizure of the throne. The issue of Scottish independence was further obscured by the supra-national laws of the Church and of arms. The papacy would not recognize Robert I, and released all Scots from their allegiance to him in 1319. And in 1346 David II, following the law of arms, had the English keeper of Liddel tower executed for surrendering it to David and thus betraying David's fellow king, Edward III. Finally, there was the belief that God would favour the just cause – but if He judged for Scottish independence at Bannockburn, He judged against it at Falkirk, Dupplin and Halidon.

There were therefore no clear guidelines for early-fourteenth-century Scotsmen's behaviour. Their actions could only be determined by individual considerations, and were bound to be inconsistent. And since Scottish governments rarely condemned anyone for submitting to superior English force, there was a strong temptation to submit during crises and rejoin the patriotic cause later. Robert Bruce himself had been active on the English side before 1306. The point is illustrated by the career of Alexander Seton, a Lothian baron. He appears under English suspicion in 1306, and in 1308 or 1310 made a bond with two Bruce adherents, 'to defend the freedom of the kingdom and Robert lately crowned king against all mortals . . . to their last breath'. But he was in English service from 1309 to 1314. He then joined Robert I the night before Bannockburn, bringing an invaluable report of English dissension. After that he became an important and well-rewarded royal councillor. Two of his sons died fighting for David II in 1332–3. He himself defended Berwick in 1333, refusing to surrender even when another son, a hostage, was hanged by Edward III. But following Halidon he worked with the English administration in 1333–4, and attended Edward Balliol's parliament in February 1334. Finally with the eventual Scottish success he reverted to his allegiance to David II. Seton is perhaps an extreme case, but in his inconsistency he was little different from most of his contemporaries.

It must be remembered, however, that Scottish inconsistency worked two ways. In 1334–5 Edward Balliol's cause was also seriously affected by desertion and disloyalty. And while the Scots were not consistently patriotic, they were not consistently unpatriotic, either. At each stage in the struggle some (not always the same) were bound to continue the fight for independence for various reasons, including patriotism, natural rebelliousness, personal feuds, or simply because they had little more to lose. Simplistic as this argument is, it seems the only general explanation of why Scottish resistance never died out.

X

Individuals' inconsistent actions are, of course, a poor basis for an independence struggle. But Scottish attitudes and behaviour did gradually become increasingly nationalistic. Widespread sympathy for Scottish independence was well established, although in crises it was often overridden by other factors. One English chronicler wrote: 'But all or most of the Scots who were with the English were with them insincerely or to save their lands in England, for their hearts if not their bodies were always with their own people.' Under the Bruces, however, the practical and theoretical considerations eventually came to accord, not clash, with that emotional nationalism, making mid-fourteenth-century Scottish attitudes and behaviour more united and unambiguous than in the past. This was one of the major achievements of the Bruce regime.

It probably resulted from military, territorial and constitutional developments. First, the longer the war lasted, the more Scottish Anglophobia would have grown. More importantly, after 1307 the military success necessary to make the cautious and fainthearted support the independence cause was achieved – spectacularly at Bannockburn, more usually by the guerrilla strategy of Robert I and later Andrew Murray. Yet military success alone was a weak foundation for independence. To base the Bruce regime purely on that was to follow the maxim 'might is right' – highly dangerous if the military situation changed, as in the early 1330s, and indeed inviting attempts at reconquest. More than military success was required for the maintenance of the Bruce regime and the cause of Scottish independence.

Much of that requirement was provided by the creation of a strong vested interest in the Bruce regime within the Scottish nobility. Although Robert I's territorial policy was essentially conservative, aimed at conciliation and restoration, nevertheless a dozen leading magnates did suffer forfeiture. With their lands, plus his personal and crown estates, Robert had a huge amount of territory for redistribution. Most of it went to about 20 close followers. His chief lieutenants, Thomas Randolph and James Douglas, had the lions' shares: Randolph's included the great province of Moray, Annandale, and the Isle of Man; Douglas's the lordships of Lauderdale, Jedburgh, and Selkirk, and seven baronies in the south. Among Robert's family, his brother Edward (and later Edward's illegitimate son Alexander) received the earldom of Carrick; his own illegitimate son Robert was given the Soules lordship of Liddesdale. Cunningham and seven baronies were added to the Stewart estates, following the king's choice of Walter Stewart to marry his eldest daughter and the birth of their son (later Robert II). Marriage to sisters of the king was also accompanied by territorial rewards: Nairn and Cromarty to Hugh earl of Ross; the lordship of Garioch to Andrew Murray (the future guardian); and the earldom of Atholl to the son of Robert's third sister and Colin Campbell of Lochawe. Then, beyond this new Bruce family circle, there were the survivors of Robert's companions of 1306, and others who had joined him later and had risen in royal service. They included Malcolm earl of Lennox, John Stewart of Bunkle (created earl of Angus), Gilbert Hay (created constable of Scotland), Robert Keith (hereditary marischal of Scotland), John Menteith (who while in English service had captured William Wallace), Malcolm Fleming, Robert Boyd, David Lindsay, Archibald Douglas (brother of 'the good Sir James'), Alexander Seton, and Walter son of Gilbert (progenitor of the Hamiltons). All these lords received handsome grants from the king.

Such men would have enjoyed royal patronage in any reign. The effects of Robert I's patronage were greatly increased, however, because the post-1314 forfeitures gave Robert an abnormally large amount of land and left a partial vacuum within the nobility. As a result, the higher nobility was radically changed. In 1306 only three earls had sided with Robert I, but in 1328 all 13 appear strongly committed to the Bruce regime. Among the baronage the Stewarts, Bruces and Murrays became even more prominent than before, but beside them at the top, instead of families like Comyn, Balliol and Soules, there were only the Douglases, whom Robert I had raised from relative unimportance. At a lower level there were few baronial families in the 1320s to rival the Hays, Keiths, and the other recipients of Robert I's patronage. Thus the most powerful section of late-medieval Scottish society was transformed. Only a minority of the higher nobility followed Robert I in 1306; by the 1320s it was dominated by his close supporters.

Robert I's grants did not guarantee absolute loyalty; several of the beneficiaries, including even Alexander Bruce earl of Carrick, cooperated with Edward Balliol. By 1334, however, it had become clear that circumstances had altered since 1296 and 1304–5; changing sides was no longer relatively easy and painless. Robert's grants had been mostly at the expense of the 'disinherited' members of the Balliol-Comyn faction, who naturally wanted their inheritances back in 1332–3. But restoring them automatically disinherited those rewarded by Robert I, or their heirs (most of the original 'Bruce establishment' had died at Dupplin and Halidon). Those men – now the majority of the Scottish higher nobility – had much to lose and little to gain from a Balliol victory. Accordingly, once the stunning effects of Dupplin and Halidon had worn off, their interests dictated that they should continue supporting the Bruce, and independence, cause. That was one of the main reasons for its eventual triumph.

At the same time a constitutional theory justifying both the Bruce regime and Scottish independence was created, by redefining the relationship between the crown and 'the community of the realm'. The community of the realm was a concept first used in the 1280s to embody the politically conscious classes (the nobility and higher clergy), and with them the whole Scottish nation. In the absence of a king it provided a focus for loyalty, which helped maintain Scotland's separate (not necessarily independent) status, laws, and customs. Initially it was not a completely nationalist concept. In 1291 when Edward I demanded to be recognized as overlord of Scotland, the community's representatives said this was a question for the king of Scots, not for them; and when the would-be kings, the Competitors, accepted Edward's overlordship, the community followed suit (albeit reluctantly). Thus the community was considered subordinate to the king; if the king had to have a foreign overlord so did the community. The Scots presumably envisaged a repetition of the loose English overlordship exercised by Henry II between 1174 and 1189, which respected Scotland's separate status. Edward I, however, acted differently. His policy towards John Balliol broke the rules as the Scots understood them. That caused a limited revolution: twelve magnates representing the community took over the government and began to resist Edward. The Scottish crown's superiority over the community was being challenged, for nationalist reasons. But with the defeat of 1296 and King John's removal, such a challenge was no longer necessary;

after 1296 the Scots fought to restore King John, and the issue of the crown–community relationship was shelved. The nationalist struggle which followed was eventually unsuccessful, and in 1304 most members of the community submitted. The concept of the community of the realm then reverted to its former, less obviously nationalistic, meaning; 'on behalf of the community of the realm' its representatives accepted Edward's rule, although as in 1291 they did try to make him agree to maintain Scotland's laws and customs.

It is questionable, therefore, how far the idea of the community of the realm inspired Robert Bruce in 1306; his main inspiration was probably his claim to the throne. But, having seized the throne, he used the idea of the community of the realm to identify his own cause with the independence cause and give his actions a wider, less selfish justification. That created a new, nationalist, constitutional theory in Scotland.

There were two stages to this development. The first is well illustrated by the clergy's declaration at St Andrews in 1309. This presented a conservative view of kingship and the crown–community relationship, stressing the king rather than the community or kingdom. The Scots, it argued, had always supported the Bruce claim to the throne. Edward I, however, had made John Balliol king – and had subsequently deposed him. Balliol's rule, although calamitous, had been accepted, but after his deposition the Scots turned to the man with the best claim by inheritance. Robert I was king because of inheritance, popular choice, virtue, and military success, but inheritance appears the most important reason; the argument seems to be that because he was the rightful heir by blood he was a successful king deserving popular support, in contrast to King John who was neither. There was no direct rejection of English claims to overlordship; that was probably taken for granted, but there may have been an echo of the attitude of 1291, that this issue was a matter for the king, not the community.

Unfortunately this argument was bad history. Although it has been believed until recently that Bruce the Competitor had the best claim in 1291–2, that was not true, and was not widely believed at the time. Inheritance was in fact a poor basis for Robert I's kingship, giving him no defence against subsequent challenges by a Balliol heir. Therefore, later in the reign, a new theory was developed. Its best expression is in the Scottish barons' letter to the pope of 1320, the Declaration of Arbroath.

The Declaration's theme was that kingdoms were by nature independent, and it was the king's function to defend that independence. Scotland had always been independent until the illegal and tyrannical attacks of Edward I. Its independence was restored by Robert I, king through 'divine providence, the succession to his right according to our laws and customs . . ., and the due consent and assent of us all'. But it was because Robert was fulfilling his duty of maintaining Scottish independence that the Scots actually accepted him as king. If ever he failed in that duty and tried to introduce English overlordship, 'we would strive at once to drive him out as an enemy and a subverter of his own right and ours and we would make some other man who was able to defend us our king'. This argument by-passed the Bruce–Balliol issue, because irrespective of inheritance rights no king who submitted to the English was fit to rule; John Balliol was not even mentioned. In that way Robert I's seizure of the crown in 1306 could be entirely justified.

The logic was that the rights of the community and the nation came before the king's – hence the threat of deposition if Scottish independence was not upheld. The community of the realm was essentially an aristocratic concept, and ideas of modern democracy must not be read into this part of the Declaration. But its argument contrasts sharply with the clergy's declaration of 1309, and even more so with the community's statement to Edward I in 1291 that overlordship was a question for the king, not the community. The Declaration of Arbroath was in accordance with the limited revolution of 1295, but it went much further, justifying the far greater revolution of 1306 with a nationalist theory of popular sovereignty.

Because of the modernity of its argument, the Declaration of Arbroath is important in its own right. But what was its contemporary significance? Although its arguments derive from the academic political theory of the time, it is not restricted to that world. Questions about Scottish kingship had concerned many Scots since the 1280s – one instance is the bond involving Alexander Seton – and the Declaration's theory at least gave them clear nationalist guidelines. As Seton's career shows, these were not necessarily followed, particularly in the 1330s. Nevertheless by the early 1340s the nationalist and Bruce cause was successful again, and this repeated success probably confirmed the Declaration of Arbroath's arguments. Acceptance of English overlordship had now no excuse save timidity or selfish ambition. Attitudes towards collaboration with the English began to harden. And after Neville's Cross a strong nationalist stance was taken over the terms for David II's release. Any proposal that implied future English overlordship was emphatically rejected. In 1353 there seems to have been a Scottish threat not to ransom David II and to choose another king unless he resisted Edward III's demands – echoing the Declaration of Arbroath.

Clearly, therefore, the Bruce regime, and consequently Scottish independence, found a strong permanent moral backing in the Declaration's political theory, which neither the circumstances of Robert I's accession nor the contemporary non-nationalist considerations of loyalty and duty could undermine. At the same time, Robert I's military methods – remembered later as 'Good King Robert's Testament' – gave a blueprint for dealing with English invasions. And his patronage provided the regime with powerful long-term support within the higher nobility. On their own, none of these developments would have been sufficient to end the ambivalence of early-fourteenth-century Scotsmen over the issue of national independence. That was, however, their combined effect, especially after the initial establishment of the Bruce regime had been tested in the early 1330s. Slowly but surely Scottish attitudes and behaviour came to be firmly united in favour of an independent Scotland ruled by the descendants of Robert I. The result was, as we shall see, that Scotland's independence was not to be seriously endangered again for the rest of the Middle Ages.

2

'Auld Inemie' and 'Auld Alliance'

I

During the rest of the fourteenth and fifteenth centuries Scotland's foreign affairs were less dramatic. Yet, since foreign policy is an obvious indicator of independent nationhood, they are still an extremely important part of late-medieval Scottish history. In the long run, despite the occasional catastrophe, the successful trend of the earlier fourteenth century was maintained. The 1460s saw its culmination. In the south, Roxburgh and Berwick, the last strongholds in English hands, were gained in 1460 and 1461 (though Berwick was lost again, permanently, in 1482); in the north, Orkney and Shetland, the last remnants of Norse rule in what is now Scotland, were acquired from Denmark in 1468 and 1469.

The acquisition of the northern isles reminds us that Scotland's foreign affairs were not solely confined to relations with England. Nevertheless in the later fourteenth and fifteenth centuries the war with the 'auld inemie', as England was coming to be called, still smouldered on, and Anglo-Scottish relations probably remained the chief concern of Scottish governments. They cannot, however, be studied in isolation, for England was also at war with Scotland's ally France in the Hundred Years War (1337–1453), and from the 1340s onward France, not Scotland, was the main sphere of English activities. After the Bruce–Balliol civil war had ended this fact dominated the Anglo-Scottish conflict. Its third phase can therefore be called the 'Hundred Years War phase'; it was to last until 1424.

Throughout this period the English crown never took the military initiative against Scotland, it merely garrisoned occupied territory and mounted punitive campaigns after Scottish provocation. The Scots crown, likewise, was not inherently aggressive towards England. It had no ambitions of southwards expansion;

moreover Scotland was much weaker than England, and the south-east was vulnerable even to short English campaigns. At first sight there seems little reason why the two countries could not have lived at peace with one another – and indeed most of this phase of the conflict consisted of truces.

The truces did not become a permanent peace, however, because of the fundamental issue of Scottish independence. The English crown would not renounce its claims to overlordship, even when it was prepared to suspend hostilities or relinquish territory. English peace terms were therefore always unacceptable to the Scots. Furthermore there were considerable pressures in Scotland for war. It probably appeared that military pressure on England was the only way to gain a favourable peace; that was how Robert I had won the treaty of Edinburgh. English-occupied territory could hardly be recaptured without military activity. On several occasions the French needed help against the English. And, over the years, fighting the 'auld inemie' came to seem increasingly natural for many Scots; it could be profitable, too, for successful border raiding brought plunder and booty. These pressures balanced what was generally a strong desire for peace in Scotland, and at times outweighed it, resulting in outbursts of hostilities initiated by the Scots.

The issue of Scottish independence was a perennial factor, but at this time another issue was almost as important: Scotland's alliance with France, which eventually became known as the 'auld alliance'. The English felt it threatened them with encirclement, particularly since it was beyond their resources to wage full-scale warfare against both countries simultaneously. Thus breaking the alliance became a major aim of English diplomacy. Failing peace, the English usually tried to neutralize Scotland through truces, which helps explain why truce terms often favoured the Scots. To the Scots, conversely, the alliance's object was protection from isolation against England and its maintenance was vital. This was straightforward in periods of Anglo-French stalemate or when the English were doing well in France. But it could be more difficult, because Scotland could never influence Anglo-French negotiations. There were sometimes dangers that France would have to accept English terms, including the renunciation of the alliance. Paradoxically, at other times there were dangers of outright French victory, which would have meant the French no longer needed the alliance, and might even have viewed it as a renounceable bargaining counter in negotiations with England. Another problem was that when Franco-Scottish military cooperation actually took place, it generally ended in defeat for the Scots or in bitter disputes between the allies. Nevertheless the Franco-Scottish alliance did survive throughout the later Middle Ages, and successfully fulfilled its function for the Scots. While it lasted, they never had to face the military might of England in isolation.

Because of English involvement in France, the Anglo-Scottish conflict steadily became less intense. Diplomacy largely replaced campaigns, truces became longer and the outbreaks of hostilities shorter. Hostilities generally began with Scottish provocation, followed by English reprisals. Scotland would be invaded, and the south-east ravaged. But after 1347 English armies never stayed more than three weeks in Scotland; their campaigns were not aimed at military conquest, and their rapid withdrawal was always forced by the Scottish policy of avoiding battle and employing scorched-earth tactics. The Scots then usually regained the lands that had been overrun, and the fighting would peter out, generally ending in advantageous truces.

This pattern meant that Scotland did not need paid contract armies like those developed in late-medieval England and France. Scottish armies continued to be raised according to the age-old principle that able-bodied men had to serve under arms, at their own expense, for 40 days a year inside or outside Scotland when required, and in an emergency fight for an unlimited time to defend their country. They were never paid, and so might appear to have been less reliable or effective than English armies. But in the early parts of the Anglo-Scottish conflict, when national survival was at stake, the question of paid armies was irrelevant. Subsequently, the system proved adequate for dealing with the short English invasions. And when the Scots attacked England, it was always simply in quick raids across the border; the problem of payment after 40 days did not arise, because the Scots either returned home speedily with their booty, or were caught and defeated by the English. Using unpaid armies did make long sieges virtually impossible, but those were probably against Scottish policy anyway, because of the risk of their leading to pitched battles between besiegers and relieving armies.

Rudimentary as the military system was, therefore, it did not seriously hamper the Scottish war effort. Although Scottish defeats were not uncommon, they are attributable to bad leadership rather than lack of pay – as we can see from the disaster that befell the one Scottish army that did receive pay (from the French) at Verneuil in 1424 (below, section v). Robert I's career proves that the system's apparent deficiencies did not prevent military success. And in the later fourteenth and fifteenth centuries the deficiencies were far outweighed by the general pattern of warfare, the effectiveness of Scottish defensive strategy, and the maintenance of the Franco-Scottish alliance.

II

The 'Hundred Years War' phase of the Anglo-Scottish conflict, like the previous one, subdivides into various parts. First there was the period between 1346 and 1357, when the main issue was David II's release. By itself David's capture at Neville's Cross meant relatively little; if Edward III was to profit from his good fortune, he had to make the Scots buy their king back for the highest price possible. Initially Edward's hopes were very high. Between 1347 and 1350 his demands included English overlordship, succession by an English king if David died childless, the restoration of the disinherited, and custody of the major Scottish castles. But the Scottish response (echoing the Declaration of Arbroath) put national independence before royal freedom. The lead came from Robert Stewart, David's heir-presumptive and lieutenant, who had personal reasons for resisting any settlement which would disinherit him. Edward's demands were therefore rejected, and the Scots continued fighting. By the early 1350s they had regained much of the territory overrun after Neville's Cross.

After three years Edward realized that the Scots would not take David II back regardless of price. In late 1350 he reduced his terms, offering the restoration of the remaining occupied territory, an Anglo-Scottish alliance, and a ransom of £40,000, on condition that if David died childless one of Edward's younger sons would succeed. (Edward was gambling on David's infertility; in 1350 David was 27, but had no children.) These terms would give Edward financial profit, a secure northern border, and a good prospect of Plantagenet rule in Scotland; since they only involved a change in the succession he presumably thought they had a better chance of acceptance. David II either agreed (gambling on having children?) or pretended to agree. In 1352 he went on parole to Scotland to propose Edward's terms and even prepare to force them on the Scots. His mission was a failure. The Scots, a council-general stated, would ransom their own king but never accept an English one. The threat of force had been countered in 1351 by an agreement with France for 1,000 troops to be sent if David invaded Scotland on Edward's behalf. And when Edward pressed his demands again in 1353 the Scots, according to an English chronicler, made their attitude plain by threatening to depose David and choose another king.

Thus by 1354 Edward III had gained nothing from Scotland. His terms now improved dramatically: he asked for a higher ransom – £60,000 over nine years – but nothing else except a truce until the ransom was paid. The likeliest explanation for the change of policy is that Edward had decided he had better prospects in France. In April 1354 Anglo-French negotiations had brought a draft treaty giving him roughly half of western France. This had to be ratified by the end of the year. The offer to ransom David almost unconditionally was presumably intended to pressurize the French into ratifying the April treaty by neutralizing their Scots allies with a favourable settlement.

Initially the Scots accepted the new terms. But neither of the 1354 settlements was ratified – perhaps Edward's readiness to make peace was taken on reflection as indicating weakness. Also a firm Anglo-Scottish truce would have left the English occupying parts of southern Scotland, including Berwick and Roxburgh, whereas military action might win them back. The French stimulated Scottish belligerence with a £7,000 subsidy in autumn 1355. Then Edward III crossed to Calais, and that finally persuaded some of the Scottish magnates: in November 1355 they attacked and captured Berwick. Edward immediately returned to England and marched north with a large army. Berwick was abandoned – because of Scottish disputes, wrote Fordun, but more probably because the Scots remembered Halidon Hill. Edward then devastated Lothian in February 1356 – the 'Burnt Candlemas' – and re-established his grip on the Scottish border shires. The show of force, although only lasting a fortnight, demonstrated that the Scots would not win better terms. Moreover in 1356 the French were routed at Poitiers, and their king was captured. Therefore when Edward virtually repeated his 1354 offer, there was no reason for its rejection. By the treaty of Berwick (October 1357) David II was ransomed for 100,000 marks (£66,667), guaranteed by 23 noble hostages and payable over ten years during which there would be a truce. The question of Scottish independence was not mentioned. The Scots bought their king back without surrendering any freedom; Edward III gained financial profit and peace in the north which let him concentrate on France.

III

The treaty of Berwick brought 27 years of truce, until 1384. This period was marked by further problems concerning David's ransom, and also, as the war in France started to go against England, by growing Scottish confidence. The problems over the ransom were caused by David II, who had little intention of paying it. First he tried to persuade the French to clear it off, offering to attack England on France's behalf if they did so. Then, when Edward III's French campaign of 1359–60 made French finance unobtainable, he took no steps to help the French but simply stopped the ransom payments in June 1360.

David's unwillingness to pay the ransom was no doubt largely due to the fact that although taxation, especially on wool exports, provided sufficient money, he had little revenue left for normal crown expenses. But his action caused resentment in Scotland, because the taxation was not reduced and the hostages were abandoned; this helped lead to a rebellion in 1363. On the other hand Edward III did not react, although he had just made a peace with France which seemed to isolate Scotland. Edward had learnt that despite his victories neither Scotland nor France could be conquered. Now he wanted to end his reign peacefully, enjoying his hard-earned glory, and indulging in lavish personal expenditure financed by his vast war profits.

By autumn 1363, however, Edward's government was encountering fiscal problems, and his attitude over financial obligations hardened. In November he and David met, with their councils, in London. Edward resurrected his earlier demands, proposing the succession of either the king of England or one of Edward's younger sons if David died childless (as he still was); in return the ransom would be cancelled, the surviving hostages released, the English-occupied territories returned, and permanent peace made. Also, if the king of England was to succeed, Edward would restore the Scottish crown's former lands in England, compensate the disinherited, and provide safeguards for keeping Scotland independent of England.

These proposals are sometimes compared favourably with the unions of 1603 and 1707. A better comparison – made by contemporaries – is with the treaty of Birgham of 1290, whereby Alexander III's heiress the Maid of Norway was to marry Edward I's eldest son. Had the Maid lived, Edward I's grandson might have ruled both countries. The treaty's terms for safeguarding Scottish independence were similar to those of 1363. The main 1363 proposal really amounted to turning the clock back to 1290 if the direct Bruce line died out, to make a settlement like that of Birgham, which the community of the realm had then accepted.

Scottish attitudes, however, had radically changed. Edward III's proposals were rejected; parliament declared in March 1364 that the Scots would make any concessions short of accepting English rule, but if peace were unattainable would resist any attacks and pay any ransom. Envoys were sent to offer peace terms, and if these were unacceptable (as was the case) to renegotiate David's ransom. Eventually in May 1365 it was agreed to pay a new ransom of £100,000 sterling at £4,000 a year, but after five years the truce was to be terminable on six months notice. This time the Scots paid regularly. But within five years the French reopened the Hundred Years War. Edward III immediately extended the Anglo-Scottish truce for 14 years, reduced the ransom to the original 100,000 marks (of which 44,000 had been paid), and lowered the instalments to 4,000 marks (£2,667).

This settlement suited Edward III very well. He could not renounce his claims on Scotland without disinheriting his descendants, but since he never considered using force in the 1360s, his objective (as in 1354–7) must simply have been a truce and the ransom. During a truce, the ransom payments would provide for English garrisons on the borders. Thus the 1363 demands were probably a bluff, meant to frighten the Scots into paying the ransom. Similarly the limitation in 1365 of the guaranteed truce to five years would have been intended to keep them conciliatory. This diplomacy was successful. The Scots paid the ransom until 1377 (when Edward III died), and despite the reopening of the Hundred Years War kept the truce until its expiry in 1384.

David II's attitude is less clear. Did he unpatriotically acquiesce in Edward's demands, or did he just relay them counting on parliament's refusal? Recent historians prefer the second explanation;

and he was no doubt confident of fathering a child after his second marriage in 1363. Nevertheless at times he gave the impression of sympathy towards England. For example, to gain first his freedom and later the cancellation of the ransom, David did entertain the possibility of an English succession. Also, there was the threat of deposition in 1353; a contemporary recorded that in 1364 'many people asserted that our King David greatly favoured the cause of the king of England'; and 'Wyntoun' described him as 'rycht wa and angry' when Edward III's 1363 proposals were rejected.

Whatever David II's attitude, the 'three estates of the realm' (this phrase replaced 'community of the realm' in the 1350s) would not have agreed to any possibility of English rule. Although lengthy debates were needed, they consistently took the nationalist standpoint. But they were extremely cautious. Remembering Edward III's victories and the 'Burnt Candlemas', they had a healthy respect for English might, and in 1364 offered concessions and a heavy ransom to avoid facing it. Yet they did not fear Edward III as Edward I had been feared, and would not compromise over Scottish independence and the succession. That was not bravado; experience had shown that Scotland could not be conquered by military force alone, and they may have realized that Edward III would not attack without provocation. In 1364 it was argued in the Scots parliament that England had neither the resources nor the inclination to mount a full-scale invasion. The cautious Scottish confidence is also evident in the decision of 1368 that peace negotiations were pointless while English terms remained unacceptable – the promised six-month notice of a cancellation of the truce was sufficient security. Such calculations were correct. In the late 1360s it is clear that so long as the Scots were careful to do nothing rash, Edward III would leave them alone.

This situation was unaffected by David II's sudden death – still childless – in February 1371. His successor Robert II (1371–90), whose career went back to the aftermath of Dupplin, had no intention of provoking Edward III. He reaffirmed the French alliance, but the provision for mutual aid was only to apply when the Anglo-Scottish truce ended; a French offer to have the truce annulled by the papacy, pay the ransom, and provide 2,000 troops, was declined. And although David II was dead the ransom payments continued.

Nevertheless the confidence of David II's last years continued to increase. This is neatly reflected in the record of an embassy to

Charles V of France in 1375. Robert II personally instructed his envoys to complain about the way Charles had failed him over two minor issues: how therefore could Charles be trusted over important affairs? This was a very high-handed tone, which the French, not surprisingly, found 'hard and painful', although they did in fact reply politely.

The Scots grew bolder towards England in the mid 1370s, as Edward III's death approached. In 1376 they attacked English-occupied lands and raided across the border. In 1377, on the accession of the 10-year-old Richard II, they stopped the ransom: some £50,000 had been paid in all. Pressure on the occupied territory increased, but fell short of attacks on major strongholds or other serious provocation – in 1378 when some borderers surprised and seized Berwick, the English March warden was allowed to regain it. This policy was complemented by carefully conciliatory diplomacy, and was successful. Although the truce became increasingly ragged, it never disintegrated – yet by the early 1380s the English merely held Lochmaben in Annandale, Teviotdale (with Roxburgh and Jedburgh castles), and the burgh of Berwick.

IV

The third part of this phase of the conflict, from 1384 to 1402, saw much more action: two major battles, three invasions of Scotland and two of England, virtually continuous border raiding, and the first active Franco-Scottish military cooperation. For most of the time the Scots were successful, and their confidence reached peaks unknown since Robert I's reign – only to collapse when they suffered a crushing defeat in 1402 at Homildon Hill.

When the long truce expired in 1384, the Scots probably had little alternative to reopening hostilities. English foreign policy had changed radically in 1383, towards disengagement from France and concentration on the British Isles: in May 1383 the English government demanded the return of the lands gained by the Scots since 1376, and in January 1384 proposed to punish Scotland's 'rebellion' with invasion and devastation if the Scots refused the balance of David II's ransom and Robert II's homage to Richard II. The Scots were also under French pressure, and in August 1383 it was agreed that, if war broke out, French money and troops (which the Scots had refused earlier) would be sent before May

1384. They had their own incentives for war, too: the recapture of English footholds in Scotland and the conclusion of a satisfactory peace. Since England appeared exhausted after 14 years of unsuccessful warfare with France, the time must have seemed ripe for achieving both these objectives, especially if French help was provided.

Within a week the Scots captured Lochmaben castle, and they regained Teviotdale by the end of March. A retaliatory English invasion was brief and half-hearted. England now only held Berwick, Roxburgh and Jedburgh. But help never came from France; the French had made a short truce in January. Since fighting England unsupported was too risky, Robert II and his council decided to consolidate their gains. After some negotiations, the English agreed to let Scotland join the truce, which was to last until May 1385.

The French plan was to prepare a dual offensive in 1385, combining a large-scale invasion of the south coast of England and a Scottish attack on the north. To help the Scots, 1500 troops and an £8,000 subsidy were sent in May 1385. The English response, following their new policy, concentrated on Scotland. In July Richard II invaded with a massive army. It caused much damage, but failed to penetrate beyond Lothian or confront the Franco-Scottish force, and the usual Scottish scorched-earth strategy forced its retreat after a fortnight. The French and Scots then attacked England – one of only two French invasions of England during the Hundred Years War. But it too achieved little. Apparently there was disagreement over whether to attack strongholds in Scotland (perhaps what the Scots government really wanted from the French aid) or invade northern England. Furthermore, in the south the French armada did not sail, and so the Scots were again left vulnerable. A truce was needed, and was concluded in September; the French returned home amid bitter recriminations.

Not surprisingly, the Scots now stopped relying on French help. In 1386-7 they kept the truce during further French attempts to invade England. But in 1387 England suffered a *coup d'état* by a magnate clique – the Appellants – who wanted energetic war against France. In summer 1388 their efforts brought military fiasco and bankruptcy. The Scots exploited the English crisis by mounting a massive three-pronged campaign, reminiscent of Robert I's in 1327. After a diversion against Ireland, the main army invaded north-west England, while a secondary force attacked the north-east and won a great victory at Otterburn.

The campaign made the Appellants regime collapse, but power returned to Richard II's faction, which preferred peace with France and war with Scotland. In contrast to 1327, English retaliation was contemplated. Financial exhaustion prevented that, but it was clear that the English could not be made to agree to Scottish terms. Moreover in 1389 the French, also exhausted, made a new long truce with England, and insisted against English opposition that Scotland be given the opportunity to join (that was the best kind of French help for Scotland). Refusal would have left the Scots isolated, as the English hoped. There was little hesitation; Robert II agreed to join the long truce, and that ended the Anglo-Scottish warfare of the 1380s.

This warfare is usually seen as being the work of selfish, uncontrollable nobles. That derives chiefly from Jean Froissart's unreliable chronicle, but seems to be supported by border raiding during the truce in autumn 1384, and by Robert II's apparent statement in the summer negotiations of 1384 that he wanted peace but could not check his nobles. The border raids were small-scale, however, and do not indicate general noble belligerence. Robert II's statement was probably diplomatic pleading to facilitate Scotland's entry into the Anglo-French truce. This was only sought after the Scots had gained their immediate objectives and had realized French help was not forthcoming. During the negotiations Robert's ambassadors never offered to restore Scottish gains – a truer indication of Scottish policy.

During Robert II's reign war did not cause serious political divisions, as happened earlier in the century or in Richard II's England; external, not internal, pressures dictated foreign policy. English armies had been repulsed and defeated, Scotland's independence maintained through skilful diplomacy and warfare, and almost all southern Scotland regained. Although the ultimate aim of final peace was not achieved, as far as success in foreign affairs is concerned, Robert II's reign was second only to Robert I's in late-medieval Scottish history.

Initially Robert III's reign (1390–1406) appeared equally successful, but eventually it was disastrous. Early in the 1390s the English, taking advantage of the truce with France, appeared aggressive: they demanded overlordship and territory, and tried to exclude Scotland from the truce. But from 1393 their policy became more peaceful, aimed simply at maintaining a quiet frontier. The

English crown had become more sensitive to the effects of border raiding, perhaps following the erosion of the buffer zone established by Edward III. Moreover peace in the north gave the crown a chance to curb its northern magnates, especially the Percy earls of Northumberland, whose wartime responsibilities had made them extremely powerful. Richard II's own interests, meanwhile, had shifted towards Ireland. Accordingly the truce with Scotland was maintained, and in 1398 its adherence was sought to a new 28-year Anglo-French truce.

Richard II took Scottish agreement for granted, but things were not so simple. Demands by the Percies for lands in Scotland granted by Edward III upset the 1398 negotiations. The Scots too were surprisingly unenthusiastic about the 28-year truce, despite the Anglo-French treaty. They perhaps calculated that if Richard II no longer wanted war, he might be pressurized into recognizing Scottish independence. More immediately, joining the new truce would mean abandoning Berwick, Roxburgh and Jedburgh. Also various matters arising from the existing 1389 truce were still unsettled. The Scots therefore played hard-to-get, simply prolonging the existing truce from year to year – an excellent demonstration of how confident they had become in the later fourteenth century.

Their confidence continued after Richard II's deposition in 1399 – when there was also, predictably, a Scottish raid deep into England. But Henry IV, Richard II's supplanter, reversed English policy. He decided on a campaign in Scotland, both to recover the territory and glory lost under Richard II and to repay his northern supporters, especially the Percies. His war preparations were encouraged in spring 1400 by the defection of George Dunbar earl of March, after Robert III's eldest son had apparently married and then repudiated March's daughter. Another factor was a Scottish proposal for peace on the basis of the treaty of Edinburgh of 1328. That set Henry searching the English records; armed with suitable documents, including forgeries purporting to record Robert II's submission, he replied with the old demand for superiority over Scotland. Henry's campaign in August 1400 was, however, completely unsuccessful. Finding Edinburgh castle garrisoned against him and a Scottish army threatening his communications, he simply retreated within a fortnight, declaring himself satisfied with a Scottish promise to think about his claims!

That was the last time an English king campaigned personally in

Scotland. The fiasco taught Henry IV that Scottish expeditions were pointless; like his two predecessors he realized that a quiet border was in England's best interests. But there was no truce – presumably the Scots did not want it – and war broke out at sea. Attacks on the vital Scottish trade route to the Low Countries were intensified on Henry's instructions. The Scots retaliated with French help, despite the Anglo-French truce. In 1402 the admiral of Scotland returned from negotiations in France with a large escort of French ships, which under his command (thus not breaking the Anglo-French truce) spent several months attacking English shipping. The war at sea put heavy pressure on Henry IV: it reduced English exports and customs revenue, helping to cause severe financial and political difficulties. But its effects were probably even worse for Scotland: in the early fifteenth century Scottish exports and customs fell sharply (see Appendix B, Table I). Only the French – and the successful pirates – really benefited.

On land there had now been over 30 years of increasingly successful Scottish warfare and diplomacy. There was a natural desire to maintain the momentum, especially among a new generation of leaders who had not experienced earlier disasters. They saw Henry IV as an insecure usurper, and responded to English rumours of Richard II's escape to Scotland by producing a pseudo-Richard. Other stimuli included Owain Glyndŵr's revolt in Wales, French encouragement once again (although internal crises kept the French themselves at truce), and raids on Berwickshire by the Percies and the renegade earl of March. Also the Scots thought they had countered the dreaded English archers by building up their own archery force and by acquiring from the Continent suits of the newly developed plate armour which gave greatly improved protection against arrows.

Confidence and military developments, however, could not compensate for poor leadership. When the full-scale invasion of northern England was launched in September 1402, the Scots plundered aimlessly to Newcastle, and on their return were caught at Homildon Hill near Wooler by English forces under Henry Percy ('Hotspur') and the earl of March. March was the best Scottish general of the period, victorious in all his battles, including Otterburn and later Shrewsbury (1403), where he helped Henry IV against the Percies' rebellion. At Homildon he outmanoeuvred the Scots and heavily defeated them, despite their archers and new armour. At least 82 Scottish nobles were killed or captured; the prisoners included Murdoch Stewart of Fife (son of the duke of Albany, Robert III's brother and lieutenant), the fourth earl of Douglas, three other earls, and a dozen great barons.

Homildon was as serious a disaster as Dupplin, Halidon or Neville's Cross, and indeed had effects comparable to those of Flodden (1513). The Scots' confidence evaporated; in 1403 they even hesitated to oppose a minor incursion by Hotspur. Hopes of regaining Berwick, Roxburgh and Jedburgh remained, but thoughts of seriously invading England or challenging English forces disappeared. Homildon persuaded them of the futility of border warfare; there were no more full-scale battles in the borders until Flodden, over a century later. On the other hand, unlike after Halidon or Neville's Cross, there was no sustained English follow-up; Henry IV had realized the days of English conquests in Scotland were over. Homildon therefore, paradoxically, marks an important step towards eventual Anglo-Scottish disengagement.

V

Homildon's effect is apparent in the next part of the war, which ran until 1424. For instance in 1417 the duke of Albany and the earl of Douglas attacked Roxburgh and Berwick, but retreated ignominiously before English relief forces: the 'foul' (foolish) raid, it was called in Scotland. There was one success in 1409 with the capture of Jedburgh castle by some local countrymen, and its subsequent destruction. Otherwise, however, the border region was no longer the main focus of Anglo-Scottish relations. This shifted to the issues of Scottish prisoners in England and, after 1419, Scottish military help for France.

The Scottish prisoners included not only those captured at Homildon but also, from 1406, the new Scottish king. It had been decided that Robert III's third, but only surviving, son, the 12-year-old prince James, should spend his youth in France (presumably because Robert feared his brother, Albany; see chap 7:iv). Unfortunately, despite an Anglo-Scottish truce, English pirates captured James's ship (understandable Scottish indignation is, however, misplaced, because both sides had been encouraging piracy for several years). Robert III died soon afterwards, and the duke of Albany became governor for the new, absent king, James I.

Henry IV's policy towards the prisoners was made clear immediately after Homildon. There were to be no ransoms without his permission – which helped provoke the Percy rebellion of 1403. Henry obviously saw the Scottish captives as a means of keeping the borders quiet. Therefore, although most of them were eventually ransomed, he kept Albany's son Murdoch Stewart and the earl of Douglas in captivity – and after 1406 he naturally refused to release James I either. Douglas, by breaking parole in 1409, did get back to Scotland, where he followed his rival the earl of March (March had quarrelled with Henry IV and made peace with Albany). James I and Murdoch, however, were still in England when Henry died in 1413.

Scottish historians generally blame Albany for the length of James I's captivity, and suggest he wanted Murdoch's release but not James's. Yet although James (with English encouragement?) perhaps believed that, the records in fact show equal efforts to ransom both prisoners. The point is that their continued captivity (unlike David II's) was clearly in England's interests. Only once under Henry IV, in spring 1412, were ransoms contemplated, and then both prisoners were involved. That was part of a reversal of English foreign policy after political changes the previous winter, but Henry IV died before it was implemented.

After 1413 English policy was determined by Henry V's reopening of hostilities with France. This did lead to Murdoch's release. Henry V, wanting a secure north of England, decided to restore the head of the Percies, Hotspur's son and heir, who had been a fugitive in Scotland since 1405. Percy was therefore exchanged for Murdoch in 1416. Could Albany have procured James I's release instead? That is most unlikely, in view of the statement by Henry's contemporary biographer that in 1416 major negotiations failed 'because the Scottish council refused to assent to submission, homage and other prerogatives due from of old to the crown of England from the kings of Scots and their people'. But things changed in 1419 when the Scots sent military aid to France. By 1421 Henry was considering releasing James, in exchange for a heavy ransom, substantial hostages, and the withdrawal of Scottish troops from France. And after his death in 1422 the government of his infant son pursued these points. James I was eventually released in April 1424, in exchange for a ransom of 50,000 marks (£33,333), 27 hostages, an Anglo-Scottish truce, and his marriage to a cousin of Henry V, Joan Beaufort. The result, the English government hoped, would be better relations with Scotland, and especially the recall of the Scottish army in France (though that did not actually happen).

The Scottish army had been sent following desperate requests for help by the dauphin (later Charles VII). French records show it was a considerable force of about 6,000 men, mostly archers – the psychological effects of Homildon were apparently outweighed by the prospects of French pay and booty. But, although authorized by a council-general, it was not a national army. The only magnates in it were Albany's younger son the earl of Buchan, the earl of Douglas's eldest son, and briefly in 1424 the fourth earl of Douglas himself. Its other leaders were either lesser nobles or cadets of magnate families. That makes it like the 'free companies' and other mercenary bands which flourished in the Hundred Years War, and it was a forerunner of the many later Scottish mercenary forces. The Scots' activities, too, were not unlike those of other mercenaries: although they received French wages, they often indulged in indiscriminate plunders, and their eventual annihilation at the battle of Verneuil in August 1424 (where Douglas and Buchan were killed) was apparently welcomed by many Frenchmen.

These, however, like modern historians but unlike Henry V and Charles VII, misunderstood the significance of the Scottish army. In 1419, because of the effects of Agincourt (1415) and the Armagnac–Burgundian civil war, the French were neither able nor willing to oppose Henry V in the field. This allowed Henry to follow a strategy of piecemeal conquest by capturing unopposed all the strongholds in a region (the difference with Scotland, where refusal to give battle to the English was a more effective strategy, is that after Robert I's reign there were few strongholds that English armies could occupy). By 1419 Henry was master of Normandy. The next step was to move south through Anjou to the river Loire; if the English could cross the Loire, central France lay open. But that was never achieved, partly because the Scottish expeditionary force (the nucleus of the first effective French army since 1415) hampered English operations. In spring 1421, therefore, Henry V's brother the duke of Clarence attempted to locate and destroy it; but the Scots defeated and killed him at Baugé, just north of the Loire near Angers. Although the main English army escaped, Baugé is extremely important. Had Clarence been victorious, the English would have crossed the Loire and possibly conquered central France.

As it was, shortly afterwards Henry V advanced to Orléans (the key to the Loire), but could not risk a siege. The theatre of operations was pushed well back into Normandy; Verneuil (1424) is some hundred miles north of Baugé. And although at Verneuil quarrels among the Scottish leaders and the unreliability of their French allies led to another crushing English victory, nevertheless the earlier success at Baugé (followed by Henry V's death in 1422) so stimulated French resistance that the English were unable to advance again to the Loire until 1428–9 – when they were repulsed at Orléans through the intervention of Joan of Arc. That is usually regarded as a major turning-point in the Hundred Years War. But had the Scots lost Baugé, Orléans would probably have fallen, and the English grip on France would have been infinitely stronger. Thus despite its eventual defeat, this Scottish expedition richly repaid earlier French assistance to Scotland.

VI

Although the Hundred Years War lasted until 1453, the Scottish expedition of 1419–24 was the last time that the 'auld alliance' worked really effectively during the Middle Ages. It was formally renewed in 1428 and 1448, but military cooperation ceased and the diplomatic ties were loosened. After 1424 the basic pattern of Scottish diplomacy changed significantly. The near-automatic alignment with France against England was replaced by a more complex quadrille involving Scotland, England, France and Burgundy; foreign policy became more neutral; and diplomatic relations were greatly extended, so that a full account (which cannot be attempted here) would include dealings with the papacy, Denmark, Austria, Milan, Castile, Aragon and Naples. Clearly a new phase of Scottish foreign affairs was beginning after 1424. Its trends may be summed up as 'internationalism' and 'self-sufficiency'; they continued to the second half of the sixteenth century, when permanent Anglo-Scottish peace was finally established following the Reformations in the two countries. Since this covers the period of 'Renaissance diplomacy', when the European states, including Scotland, were entangled in a broad, rapidly changing web of international relations, it can be called the 'Renaissance phase'·of the Anglo-Scottish conflict.

The disengagement from the Hundred Years War was largely

James I's work. His release was designed to improve Anglo-Scottish relations, at a time (before Verneuil) when English arms and resources were severely stretched in France, and from then on English diplomacy was conciliatory. James mostly responded in kind. Admittedly he took a tough line in truce negotiations, excluding Scots in France from Anglo-Scottish truces; he stopped the ransom instalments in 1427 with only about £6,000 paid (leaving his hostages to their own devices); and in 1428 when Charles VII, once more in desperate straits, asked again for Scottish help he renewed the Franco-Scottish alliance, betrothed his eldest daughter to Charles's son (later Louis XI), and agreed to send 6,000 troops. But he broke these promises: both the princess and the troops stayed in Scotland. Charles VII's rescue came from 'neither king nor duke, nor daughter of the king of Scotland, . . . [but] from me', so Joan of Arc declared in 1429. Although some Scots fought with Joan, Scottish government support for France at this critical period was practically non-existent. If anything James helped the English cause, by maintaining the truce with England until 1436.

This reversal of traditional policy may perhaps be due to factors like James's experience of English might under Henry V, his wife's influence, and his financial difficulties. But there were more important considerations. First, since 1419 the English had been allied with the duke of Burgundy, whose dominions included the Low Countries, Scotland's main trading partners. War with England, or even a strong Scottish presence in France, could easily have caused tension with Burgundy, disrupting Scottish trade and customs revenues. That probably happened between 1419 and 1424, and would have been something James I must have wanted to avoid. Secondly, James was probably optimistic about negotiating a settlement with England. In return for renouncing the French alliance, the English apparently offered Henry VI's marriage to James's eldest daughter, the surrender of Roxburgh and Berwick, and even a final Anglo-Scottish peace – although nothing concrete could be agreed while Henry VI was a minor.

In 1436, however, James came off the fence. He at last sent his daughter to France and even offered troops (which Charles VII no longer wanted), he let the truce with England expire, and in August he besieged Roxburgh with a large, national army. Rising border tension may have stimulated James; in 1435 a sizeable English raid had been repulsed at Piperden (Berwickshire). But the likeliest explanation relates again to Burgundy, for in 1435 the Anglo-

Burgundian alliance had collapsed. That greatly weakened the English position in France and ended the Burgundian complication for Scotland. Yet James's basic policy of diplomatic independence had probably not changed. After the capture of Roxburgh he almost certainly hoped to be able to pressurize Henry VI, whose minority had just ended, into countering Burgundy's defection by buying Scotland out of the French alliance with Berwick's surrender and a peace settlement.

Unfortunately James's plans disintegrated when his army abandoned the siege after a fortnight. The one fifteenth-century Scottish explanation, in the *Book of Pluscarden*, blames 'a detestable split and most unworthy difference arising from jealousy'. That is conceivable of the leading figures, James I and Archibald fifth earl of Douglas, for they had been on opposite sides in France in 1421–2, James with Henry V, Douglas with the Scottish force; also James had imprisoned Douglas in 1431. But the main reason for the retreat is probably northern England's well-oiled defensive machinery; the contemporary English account states the Scots fled when an English relief force approached. This, a repetition of 1417, is also suggested by the fact that the Scots abandoned their artillery. Whatever caused it, the Roxburgh fiasco not only destroyed James's foreign policy but also seriously affected his domestic prestige; it probably led indirectly to his assassination the following year.

VII

Throughout James II's reign (1437–60) and beyond, Anglo-Scottish relations are characterized by continuing English weakness. In France the English position steadily deteriorated after the ending of the Burgundian alliance, until they were finally expelled from Normandy in 1450 and Aquitaine in 1453. Shortly afterwards Henry VI became insane; then in 1455 the civil wars known as the Wars of the Roses began. Stability did not return to England until the mid 1470s.

This succession of English misfortunes was crucial for Scotland. During the Hundred Years War England's interests dictated a truce with Scotland, but once it ended there was a danger that English ambitions of conquest within the British Isles might be resurrected, while the victorious French no longer needed the

Scottish alliance so much. A warning was given in 1448. Until then the long truce concluded in 1438 had suited both countries (James II's minority was a time of political disturbance), but by 1448 the English had negotiated an armistice with France, which apparently encouraged Henry VI to order the escalation of border friction into an extensive attack – probably, as in Richard II's reign, to divert attention from the peace policy with France. But Henry VI's forces were no more successful in Scotland than in France; the invaders were defeated at the battle of the Sark, in Annandale (October 1448). Anglo-French hostilities resumed in 1449, when the English stupidly broke the armistice – but that led to the final French victory. In the event, however, after 1453 England was even less able to wage aggressive war. Indeed in their effect on the Anglo-Scottish conflict, the Wars of the Roses are comparable to the Bruce–Balliol civil war or the outbreak of the Hundred Years War. Because of them, the threat to Scotland posed by the ending of the war in France disappeared; the strongholds of Roxburgh and Berwick were at last regained; and significant steps were taken towards the ultimate Scottish goal of peace with England.

Until 1455 the Scots kept the truce with England, partly for reasons of domestic politics and partly perhaps from apprehension about the end of the Hundred Years War. But James II's final triumph over the Douglases (ironically greatly helped by English dealings with the last earl) coincided with the start of the English civil wars. James was thus well placed to pursue the traditional policy of exploiting England's domestic troubles. He attacked Berwick in 1455 and 1457, raided Northumberland in 1456, and besieged Roxburgh in 1460. From 1455 to 1457 his efforts were unsuccessful; each campaign ended in withdrawal before English defence forces. But the humiliations of 1417 and 1436, not to mention the disasters of 1346 and 1402, were not repeated. Unlike many other Scottish leaders James was a good general who kept control of his campaigns. He probed and stretched the English defences without taking risks, and probably presented the results to good effect in Scotland – as the *Auchinleck Chronicle's* tone indicates: in 1456 James 'maid his first wayage in yngland with 600 thousand men [*sic*], and brynt and heriit 20 mylis within the land, and wan and distroyit 17 towris and fortaliceis, and remanit on the ground of yngland 6 days and 6 nychtis . . . and come hame with gret worschip and tynt [lost] nocht a man of valour'. The contrast with chroniclers' scorn for the fiascos of 1417 and 1436 is striking. And in 1460 the Wars of the Roses were so intense that English defence forces did not materialize when James besieged Roxburgh. Although James himself was killed when a cannon exploded, the Scots army continued the siege, and the garrison had to surrender. Roxburgh castle was then destroyed, following the principle established by Robert I.

The Wars of the Roses also brought about the capture of Berwick a year later: it was handed over by the defeated Lancastrians in return for political asylum in Scotland for Henry VI. Apart from the Isle of Man (on which James II had had designs), all the terri- tory lost during the fourteenth century was regained. Therefore, although during the next two years Scottish–Lancastrian forces raided England, and the Yorkist Edward IV retaliated by intrigu- ing with the Douglases and the lord of the Isles, there were no longer any practical Scottish arguments against peace with England. In Yorkist England the traditional claim to overlordship was still difficult to renounce, while there was also the Scots' shel- tering of Henry VI and their possession of Berwick (which Edward IV eventually found unacceptable). But in the 1460s the Wars of the Roses took precedence with Edward; Berwick and the overlord- ship were issues worth shelving if the Scots abandoned Henry VI. After some arguments, James III's minority government agreed; in 1464 Henry VI was despatched to his supporters in northern England, and a 15-year truce was made with Edward IV. The following year this truce was extended until 1519. While not a final peace treaty, this serious, if over-optimistic, agreement in 1465 to more than half a century without hostilities was the next best thing. Admittedly the truce did not hold; among events which took place before 1519 were the English recapture of Berwick in 1482 and their victory at Flodden in 1513. Nevertheless those were now abnormal outbreaks of temporary hostilities. What is more significant is that the 1465 truce was followed by treaties in, for instance, 1474 and 1502, making a series of agreements which together demonstrate a growing Anglo-Scottish rapprochement that did lead to peace between the two countries in the later sixteenth century.

Meanwhile, Scotland's alliance with France loosened. Franco- Scottish contacts were still frequent, the alliance was re-confirmed in 1448, and the 1440s saw negotiations for James II and his remaining sisters to marry partners of Charles VII's choice. But this marriage diplomacy, while widening Scotland's international relations, had little lasting effect, and in 1449 James II instead married Mary of Gueldres, the duke of Burgundy's great niece and nearest eligible female relative. Since Franco-Burgundian relations were then fairly good, Charles VII had no objections; nevertheless the marriage and accompanying alliance with Burgundy continued James I's policy of diplomatic independence. Moreover, like his father, James II gave no assistance when the French asked for it towards the end of the Hundred Years War. Conversely Charles VII, doubtless conscious of the Scottish prevarication since 1428, politely but consistently refused James II's requests for help against England after 1455. The French were probably irritated by James's demands for the province of Saintonge, promised in 1428 in return for the unfulfilled agreement to send troops. Another problem was a strong pro-Burgundian influence exerted in Scotland after 1460 by Mary of Gueldres, which coincided with fresh Franco-Burgundian hostility. To make matters worse, Charles VII's successor Louis XI had little time for Scotland since his disastrous first marriage to James I's daughter; in 1463 he apparently discussed helping Edward IV of England conquer Scotland! Although the diplomatic realignments did not actually go so far as that, by 1469 Scotland's ties with France had been seriously loosened; the 'auld alliance' survived, but only as one among several international relationships maintained by Scotland.

Strangely enough, the main, if indirect, consequence of the 'auld alliance' at this time was Scotland's acquisition of Orkney and Shetland. These islands, formerly under Norse rule, were then subject to the king of Denmark. Danish relations with Scotland were tense in the fifteenth century, not over Orkney and Shetland but because of mercantile rivalries exacerbated by the fact that the Scots crown rarely paid the annual sum of 100 marks promised in 1266 when the Hebrides had been surrendered to Scotland. James I's treaty with Denmark of 1426 brought no improvement; so when in 1456 Christian I of Denmark made an alliance with France, one clause was that Charles VII should persuade his other ally James II to settle Danish grievances, especially over the 'annual'. Charles, obsessed with diplomatic marriages, proposed that James II's son should marry Christian I's daughter, and that instead of a dowry the 'annual' would be cancelled. Until then Scots governments had shown little concern for Orkney and Shetland, despite considerable Scottish infiltration and the inheritance of the earldom of Orkney by the Scottish family of Sinclair. But the rounding-off of Scottish territory was James II's main aim in the late 1450s, and for a time his chancellor was William Sinclair earl of Orkney. Therefore once the Danish marriage was proposed, the Scots not surprisingly developed the idea of a more tangible dowry: Orkney and Shetland. Now Scottish pressure was put on Denmark. Initially the Scots' demands were rebuffed, but eventually, when Christian I's other concerns made good relations with Scotland essential, the islands were demanded again, this time successfully. In 1468 James III married Margaret of Denmark, the 'annual' was cancelled, and her dowry was fixed at 60,000 florins, for which Orkney and Shetland were mortgaged; Orkney was handed over immediately, Shetland in 1469. That was a face-saving formula for Christian I, and indeed he may have intended the alienation to be only temporary. But since he could never raise the money, Orkney and Shetland came permanently into Scotland's possession – bringing the kingdom of Scotland to its fullest extent, and (except for Berwick) to its modern boundaries.

The gaining of Orkney and Shetland, so soon after the recapture of Roxburgh and Berwick, symbolizes Scotland's triumphant recovery from the nadir of the early 1300s. The achievements of the 1460s also reflect the new Scottish self-confidence and even strength in foreign affairs. This is reflected too in the fact that the royal family now found its marriage partners among the houses of European potentates; in James II's offers to mediate in the quarrel between Charles VII and the dauphin; and in his overtures to Castile, Aragon and Milan, as well as France, inviting 'confederate princes to concur with us against the English, who are the principal disturbers of the peace of all Christendom'. That is very different from the essentially defensive Declaration of Arbroath and the £20,000 'payment for peace' agreed in 1328. But the Europe of the 1450s and 1460s was very different, too: the French crown's position had hardly been re-established after the Hundred Years War; England was beset by civil war, and so was Aragon; the German emperor and the king of Castile were both extremely weak; and Denmark was eventually to be outfaced over Orkney and Shetland. The most powerful figure of the time was Philip duke of Burgundy, but he was not a king. Thus James II, towards the end of his reign, could stand comparison with any of the contemporary European rulers – as he and his successors after 1460 were well aware. In fact both James III and James IV overestimated their international strength, ultimately with disastrous results. Nevertheless, in the European diplomatic world of the mid fifteenth century, it is clear that Scotland was a force to be reckoned with – probably more so than at any other time in Scottish history.

VIII

Although the war with England gradually became less intense, this did not affect nationalist feelings in Scotland; if anything they grew. Scottish hostility to England was commonplace in fifteenth-century Europe. Pope Martin V is said to have declared, 'Verily the Scots are the antidote to the English', when he heard the news of Baugé; 'nothing pleases the Scots more than abuse of the English', stated the Italian cleric Aeneas Sylvius (later Pope Pius II), who visited Scotland in 1435; Louis XI's councillor Philippe de Commines wrote that the Scots were the divinely appointed opponents of the English.

The point, however, is sometimes questioned for the upper classes. Scottish nobles, for instance, often visited England and occasionally served in English armies abroad. But such fraternization was limited to times of truce, and even then can be balanced by instances of piracy. Latent hostility was common, typified when James Douglas of Balvenie (brother of the fourth earl) referred in a letter to Henry IV of England to 'Berwick quhilk standis in Scotland the quhilk toun yhe call yhouris.' In a lighter vein, Bower recounts how Scots in London for a tournament in 1390 were taunted that they were not really Scottish, because their mothers and grandmothers had been sleeping with English lords during the many English invasions. The riposte was that at least they were noble; while the English lords were in Scotland, what had *their* wives been doing with the local peasants and priests? The tension, at first sight perhaps similar to that at football internationals nowadays, is greatly intensified in retrospect by the fact that several of these Scots subsequently fought at Homildon. John Swinton, although Edward III's retainer in the 1370s, was killed there. Similarly the fourth earl of Douglas, having obtained substantial retaining fees from Henry V and John duke of Burgundy, eventually perished at Verneuil fighting against the Anglo-Burgundian army. Individual Scots nobles, of course, usually fled to England when they quarrelled with their own government; but when they did (unlike the Balliol–Comyn faction in 1306) they invariably lost their Scottish support – as the fate of the Douglases in 1455 demonstrates. In general, a distinct sense of Scottishness can be seen among the upper classes, which contrasts with the ambivalence sometimes shown before 1296 and after 1603.

This must be because the factors which helped Scottish independence between 1306 and 1346 had even more force thereafter. To begin with there was the long-term military and diplomatic success of the Scots, aided by the Hundred Years War. Although the English threat could never be disregarded, and English invasions were unpleasant and undesirable, there was clearly no longer any likelihood of actual conquest, even after disasters like Neville's Cross and Homildon. In the later fourteenth and fifteenth centuries Scotland's independence was regarded as axiomatic by the Scots.

Secondly, vested interests in the Bruce–Stewart regime and hence in Scottish independence grew ever stronger as English chances of controlling Scotland receded. Scots hungry for power and patronage could only find it within Scotland, at the royal court or in their own localities. The attractions of Westminster, so potent after 1603 and magnetic after 1707, were virtually non-existent for Scotsmen in the later Middle Ages. Nor were there any Scots–English marriages or trans-border estates during this period – which perhaps more than anything else distinguishes the late-medieval Scottish nobility from their predecessors before 1296 and their successors after 1603.

Finally there was the ideology of Scottish nationhood. While the Declaration of Arbroath was not repeated – it did not need to be – its main principle of national independence was upheld in every act of Scottish government. Moreover its arguments were developed by a series of Scottish histories: *The Brus* (1375) by John Barbour, archdeacon of Aberdeen; *The Chronicle of the Scots' Nation* (1380s) by John Fordun, a priest in Aberdeen diocese; the *Orygynale Cronykil of Scotland* (1420s) by Andrew Wyntoun, prior of Lochleven;[1] and the *Scotichronicon* (*Scots' Chronicle*: 1440s) by Walter Bower, abbot of Inchcolm. Barbour's *Brus*, impressive both as history and poetry, is a glorification of Robert I, Sir James Douglas and other early-fourteenth-century heroes, focused on the theme of freedom and independence; the lines beginning 'A fredome is a noble thing!' are his most famous. The other three are general

---

[1]Dr R.J. Lyall has recently stressed that the sections covering David II's and Robert II's reigns were by an earlier, anonymous chronicler, whose work was incorporated by Wyntoun; quotations from this part of the *Orygynale Cronykil* are therefore attributed to 'Wyntoun'.

histories of Scotland, running from the earliest times (the origins, or Creation, in Wyntoun's case) down to the authors' own periods. Unfortunately they are brief and bland on contemporary events. But that is because they were intended to inform contemporaries about the past, not the present. Their purpose was to give Scotland a history which could stand comparison with any other country's – especially England's. This explains why they devoted so much space to the distant past and the mostly mythical details of the reigns of the 'one hundred and thirteen kings of their own royal stock', as the Declaration of Arbroath had put it. Throughout the emphasis is on patriotism, nationalism, and hostility to England; Bower's concluding flourish, 'He is not a Scot, O Christ, to whom this book is displeasing', sums up all three. They were so successful that their 'official' account of Scotland's ancient history still had credence in the mid eighteenth century, while their version of the Middle Ages formed the basis of standard Scottish histories practically to the present day.

If anything, indeed, they were too successful. Until relatively recently historians of medieval Scotland hardly ventured beyond their framework of events – to the detriment of Scottish historiography when compared with more sophisticated modern English products. Nearer their own time, their influence was such that the cooler, sceptical John Major's *History of Greater Britain* (1521), which dealt in a remarkably modern way with both Scotland and England, was ignored in favour of other sixteenth-century works based on the Fordun–Wyntoun–Bower tradition; Major's was the only comparative general study of medieval Scotland and England until G.W.S. Barrow's *Feudal Britain* (1956). But their anti-English stance perhaps clashed with Scottish moves towards rapprochement with England in the fifteenth century. Bower relates that he himself helped persuade a council-general against a pro-English policy in 1433. And his anti-Englishness was developed in the popular vernacular poem *The Wallace* of the mid 1470s, which, while treating William Wallace much as Barbour treated Robert Bruce, also argued vehemently against the Anglo-Scottish treaty of 1474: 'Till honour ennymyis is oure haile entent'. By the end of the late Middle Ages, therefore, the ideology of Scottish independence seems to have become excessively aggressive, out of step with the peace which was surely in Scotland's best interests. It was no doubt one factor behind the enthusiasm of 1513, which perished on the field of Flodden.

II

The People of Scotland

3

Economy and Society

I

Where and how did the people of late-medieval Scotland live? The quick answer is in the countryside and off the land. Towns were scarce and tiny; at least 90 per cent of the population would have lived in small scattered rural communities. Within these they culti-vated cereals – oats, barley and wheat – and some kail, peas and beans, and they raised livestock – poultry, pigs, goats, sheep and cattle. Their settlements are still mostly inhabited today, but apart from that, their crops and livestock, and the rent they paid their landlords, their life had little in common with that of modern farm-ing communities. Field patterns were very different from today's. So were the returns from agriculture: grain yields were probably around 1:3 or 1:4, compared with around 1:20 today; a fleece gave one to two pounds of wool, compared with six or more; and annual milk yields were around 100 gallons per cow, compared with over 700. But housing is the most obvious area of difference. Medieval houses were small and primitive. Better-off peasant families would have had low oblong dwellings some 20 to 30 feet long by 10 to 15 wide, probably consisting of two rooms, of which one might also have held livestock. The less fortunate would have inhabited even smaller huts. Stone buildings were rare; most houses were timber-framed, with walls and roofs of wattle, mud, turf, heather or thatch. They were flimsy and impermanent – though as Froissart (who visited Scotland in the 1360s) related, they did have one advantage: after Lothian was ravaged by the English in 1385, 'the people of the country made light of it, saying that with six or eight stakes they could soon have new houses'.

Although uninspiring to modern eyes, these aspects of late-medieval Scottish life were the same throughout Europe. But, looking beyond the basics, we find geographical factors made Scotland very different from what is often considered the typical area of medieval agriculture, southern England and northern France. Scotland is hilly, and much of its soil is sour and stony. Therefore, although its surface area is half that of England and Wales, its arable and meadow land nowadays is only a sixth; and there is three times as much rough moorland grazing as arable. In the Middle Ages the relative amount of arable and meadow may have been even lower, for the bottoms of river valleys were undrained marshes until the eighteenth century. Moreover Scottish agriculture was affected by the cold, wet climate, which told against cereal growing, especially the most valuable crop, wheat.

The result was described by Fordun.

> Scotia, also, has tracts of land bordering on the sea, pretty level and rich, with green meadows, and fertile and productive fields of corn and barley, and well adapted for growing beans, peas, and all other produce; destitute, however, of wine and oil, though by no means so of honey and wax. But in the upland districts, and along the highlands, the fields are less productive, except only in oats and barley. The country is, there, very hideous, interspersed with moors and marshy fields, muddy and dirty; it is, however, full of pasturage grass for cattle, and comely with verdure in the glens, along the water-courses. This region abounds in wool-bearing sheep, and in horses; and its soil is grassy, feeds cattle and wild beasts, is rich in milk and wool, and manifold in its wealth of fish, in sea, river, and lake.

That contrasted sharply with the cereal-intensive English and French plains. Beyond Lothian and the east coast, the hardier oats and bere (a form of barley) predominated. An act of 1426 stipulating that each husbandman should sow one firlot (about $1\frac{1}{2}$ bushels) of wheat, half a firlot of peas and forty beans annually suggests Fordun exaggerated the extent of other crops, for these minimun quantities are hardly high. Yet he was clearly accurate about the pastoral bias of Scottish farming, especially in sheep and cattle. The customs accounts show that at their peak in the early 1370s yearly Scottish exports included the clip of over 2,000,000 sheep, some 100,000 sheepskins, and over 50,000 hides. Much came from landlords' flocks and herds: Melrose abbey and the earl of Douglas both had some 15,000 sheep, putting them among the largest sheep-farmers in Europe. But they were exceptional; as a whole the landowners probably produced less than half the total exported. The majority of the wool – and of the sheep – would have belonged to the peasantry.

Oats, bere, sheep and cattle were thus the staple of Scotland's late-medieval agriculture. The balance among them would have varied according to period and area, but extreme specialization appears rare. The upland regions were not entirely pastoral, for oats and bere were grown wherever possible; and flocks and herds were also common in lowland regions. In 1424 a Lothian laird, Alexander Hume of Dunglass, listed his assets as 2,618 sheep, 248 cattle, 20 chalders (each roughly 100 bushels) of wheat, 45 chalders of oats, and 25 chalders of barley. The proportion of wheat is high, but otherwise this mixture of farming – in an excellent arable area – seems fairly typical of late-medieval Scottish practice, although the peasants would have operated on a smaller scale. The point is important, for historians argue that much of thirteenth-century England and France experienced excessive concentration on grain at the expense of animals and their vital manure. In Scotland, because conditions were less suitable for extensive grain production, agriculture possibly maintained a better balance.

The type of farming conditioned most people's diet. It would have been based on oatmeal (in porridge, gruel, oatcakes and bannocks) and bere (in ale, broth and barley-cakes) supplemented by kail (an important source of vitamin C), milk and cheese. But some meat, generally mutton, and fish, for which medieval Scotland was famous, would also have been eaten – especially offal, cooked perhaps with oatmeal as in haggis nowadays. Indeed after his 1435 visit, Aeneas Sylvius stated that 'the common people . . . eat flesh and fish to repletion, and bread only as a dainty'. To repletion must be an exaggeration, but he was clearly struck by the amount of animal products eaten and by the absence of wheaten bread. Since white bread was then the most fashionable food, Aeneas was probably turning up his nose. Nevertheless a diet based on oatmeal, with animal and fish protein, is actually very healthy (provided vitamin C is also found) – probably much healthier than that of most European peasants at this time.

II

The basic conditions for agriculture also determined Scotland's

settlement pattern. Nucleated villages and huge open fields characteristic of grain-producing areas were rare. The fundamental agricultural unit was the much smaller 'toun', or township, held either
by one husbandman or by several living in a small hamlet and
sharing the tenancy. The 1376–7 rental for part of the Douglas of
Dalkeith estates (in Peebles, Dumfries and Fife) lists 88 touns, of
which 46 were held jointly by two or three (sometimes up to 10)
tenants – and many of the single-tenancy touns probably supported subtenants too. Some touns would have been near or con-
tiguous to one another; others would have been isolated pockets
surrounded by moors, bogs and hills – as in Fordun's 'hideous'
upland countryside, and as in parts of the north-west today. Wherever it lay, the toun's arable was cultivated in rigs – long ridged
strips 10 to 20 yards wide – normally running downhill to facilitate
drainage. In joint tenancies each tenant had a share of the rigs,
usually scattered throughout the arable in the system known as
'runrig'. By the later fifteenth century, and probably much earlier,
the arable generally consisted of 'infield' and 'outfield'. The infield
was intensively cropped and regularly manured (it was sometimes
called the 'mukkitland'); the outfield was poorer, and only partially
cropped each season. When crops were not growing, the arable was
used for grazing, which helped manure it. Otherwise livestock fed
off the moors and marshes beyond the arable, and in hilly areas
were often taken to upland pastures, or shielings, during the summer. Winter feed, however, was a serious problem: cattle (and perhaps sheep) were regularly slaughtered in November.

The touns fitted into larger communities through the system of
lordship now described as 'multiple estates'. Although learned discussions of these are complex, the general concept is simple: the
landlord's estate was focused on a base – a castle or hall – where
the tenants of the surrounding touns paid tribute or rent. This
structure, though probably ancient, was common in medieval
Scotland and elsewhere; it is an obvious way to exploit the peasantry in regions of scattered settlement. The size of multiple estates
varied considerably, from the great earldoms and lordships like
Mar or Annandale which covered hundreds of square miles and
corresponded to regions of the country (though these were usually
subdivided), down to little estates comprising one or two touns. But
something in between is most typical: an estate capable of sustain-
ing a substantial landowner, containing some 10 to 20 touns, and
often known as a shire (not to be confused with a sheriffdom), a

thanage, or (most commonly by *c*.1300) a barony. Many corresponded to parishes – Scotland's parochial system was largely established on the basis of landowners' estates – and that is probably the best way to envisage them nowadays. They were fairly cohesive communities: in the typical barony the tenants organized themselves and were disciplined through the barony court, ground their meal at the barony's mill, and were served by the barony's parish church. The neatness of this pattern must not, however, be exaggerated. It applied less well in the earldoms and great lordships, while outside them the late-medieval trend was to split up existing baronies, amalgamate others, and create new ones; the territorial patterns of lordship were growing increasingly complex by the later fifteenth century.

Rent from the touns – in cash or kind – was the main source of seignorial income, but not the only one. Fines and forfeitures levied by courts and profits from mills were both significant. Also landlords usually had their own fields – demesnes, often called mains in Scotland – worked by their own labour forces, together with their own flocks and herds. In thirteenth and fourteenth-century England demesnes were extremely important. Many were extended as far as possible and were intensively cropped with grain which was sold at high profit; in their late-thirteenth-century heyday demesnes produced over half the revenues of many estates. In Scotland, however, although there is evidence for twelfth and thirteenth-century expansion of demesnes (especially on ecclesiastical estates), the trend is not so marked. Scottish demesnes were probably directed more towards supplying food for the landlords' own households – perhaps especially wheat – than growing for the market. One of the explanations for this is simply that so much of Scotland was unsuitable for large-scale grain production; instead Scottish landlords may have concentrated more on livestock. This is another example of the way Scottish geography conditioned the rural economy.

III

For the people of late-medieval Scotland, the main social division was between the small minority who were freeholders and the rest who were not. Freeholders held land from their lords with full security, generally in perpetuity, in return for fixed amounts of service or yearly payments. In Scotland free tenure can be equated with feudal tenure; the service was honourable, often that associated with a knight, and the payments-in-lieu were generally called 'feu farms' (modern feu duties), that is 'feudal leases'. Legally the free-holder with one toun was no different from the magnate: both held their lands from their overlords (the magnate from the king) in essentially the same way. The rest of the rural population, on the other hand, usually rented their lands for a year or so at a time. From 1305, when peasants on Scottish crown estates petitioned Edward I of England to change their 12-month leases to ones with the same security as in England, to the 1376–7 Douglas of Dalkeith rental, where 108 out of 119 leases were for one year, to 1521, when John Major criticized them in his *History of Greater Britain* – indeed throughout the medieval and early modern periods – short leases were one of the most significant features of Scottish rural society. That does not mean yearly evictions, but that rents were renegotiable annually – which must have put tenants under pressure when economic circumstances favoured landlords, and generally discouraged agricultural improvement.

Before the fourteenth century the division between freeholders and the rest probably coincided with that between freemen and serfs, or in Scotland 'neyfs'. In medieval Europe the main characteristic of serfdom was arbitrary exploitation of the serf; Scotland's annual leases, which let the lord cream off as much as possible from each harvest, were part of this. Scotland also experienced other features of serfdom: neyfs belonged to the seignorial property, and usually had to perform labour services on demesnes. However, in the thirteenth century population pressure probably made it unnecessary to tie peasants to estates, and also provided plenty of employable labour for the demesnes – which seem to have been less important in Scotland anyway. Thus these features of serfdom gradually became irrelevant in Scotland, a trend compounded after 1296 by the dislocations of the Wars of Independence. By the mid fourteenth century neyfs and serfs virtually disappear from Scottish records: the last references are the recovery of three 'runaways' by the bishop of Moray in 1364, and letters of David II freeing William son of John from Tannadice in 1370. But while personal servitude vanished, several aspects of serfdom continued. Lords could still exploit peasants through their jurisdictional powers (especially if they held baronies), through their mills, and through the system of short leases – unless other economic circumstances told against them.

With the disappearance of serfdom, it is tempting to lump the mass of rural society together as 'the peasantry'. But there were several gradations, and especially a basic stratification into husbandmen and cottars. Husbandmen were substantial peasants, holding touns individually or jointly, cultivating the arable with eight-ox plough teams, and keeping sheep and cattle on the communal grazing. In the 1376–7 Douglas of Dalkeith rental, 88 touns were held by 229 husbandmen for an average rent of just under £2. Only 36 had rent levels below £1; 122 paid between £1 and £2, 43 between £2 and £3; and there were 28 peasant aristocrats paying over £3, going up to sums like the £8 10s 6d and £6 6s 8d paid by Gilbert and Thomas Gilbertson for three touns and shares in four others in the barony of Buittle (Gilbert also had the mill), or the £16 rising to £18 13s 4d Patrick Paxton paid for a three-year lease of the estate of Mordington. Some entries show the rent for the standard southern Scottish unit of arable, the oxgang (notionally 13 acres) varied from 3s 6d to 12s. That suggests that most of the husbandmen had at least four oxgangs plus their share of the grazing. That was ample to support their families, giving a surplus in good years; and the 12 per cent who afforded the higher rents were presumably quite comfortably off. (The rental, however, dates from the post-plague period of lower population; pre-plague holdings were doubtless smaller.)

Things were different for the cottars, crofters, 'grassmen', and so on, in the lower stratum. They had much less: a hut, kailyard, and some acres of arable (probably cultivated with spades, not ploughs), or merely some grazing in the case of the grassmen. The few cottar lands mentioned in the Douglas of Dalkeith rental were held for between 2s and 6s 8d, indicating no more than one oxgang and probably less. Most cottars, however, were subtenants, holding a small piece of land and grazing from the husbandmen, in return for work in the latter's fields. That means that cottars rarely appear in estate records, although they presumably were the bulk of rural society. The small cottar holdings obviously gave a much more precarious living. Yet cottars could supplement their own produce by working for others, and also through rural crafts; they often seem to have been local weavers, tailors, shoemakers, wrights, and other artisans.

Late-medieval Scotland's rural society must also have contained many landless men. Some were the unemployed beggars legislated against repeatedly in the fifteenth century. But most probably did work, in return for board, lodging and some wages in cash or kind:

servants and labourers, shepherds, cowherds and the like. That was often the lot of young men who had not yet acquired holdings of their own, and in parts of fourteenth-century England they were around a third of the adult males. Unfortunately they are even harder to find in Scottish records than the cottars; there are just stray references, like the three *famuli* (estate workers) and five servants employed on the earl of Strathearn's demesne at Fowlis Wester in 1379–80. Although an isolated instance, that seems typical, because Scottish demesnes and tenancies hardly needed large paid workforces. And since much labour was obtained from the cottars and the husbandmen's own families, landless labourers were probably a smaller part of the population than in England. But that is conjecture; the lower down the social scale we look, the more elusive the people of Scotland become.

One further point should be made. Scotland is often described as a country of two halves, Lowlands and Highlands. With respect to late-medieval rural society, however, this was not a sharp division. The Highlands were more pastoral, but not exclusively so; the general agricultural balance was little different from the upland parts of the south. The toun – *baile* in the Highlands – was as common as in the south, and so, probably, was the organization into multiple estates. There were technical differences in the units of land measurement, but by the late Middle Ages that does not appear significant. Another difference is that often a unit of estate was leased ('tacked') to one individual, the tacksman, who then sublet the various farms. Yet this is found in the south – for instance Patrick Paxton at Mordington – and below the tacksmen lands were doubtless farmed in much the same way. There was not even a clear-cut linguistic division at the beginning of the period, for Gaelic was spoken as far south as the Forth and Clyde and also in Galloway (by the fifteenth century, however, it had retreated more into the Highlands). And among the peasantry kinship and clannishness were probably just as important in the Lowlands. Admittedly the concept of the Highland–Lowland split did develop in the late Middle Ages (see chapter 8), but this was probably not a matter of rural life. So far as that was concerned, late-medieval Scotland seems fairly unified; there were many local variations depending on particular circumstances, but no great regional differences.

IV

Although the rural communities would have been largely self-supporting, late-medieval Scotland's economy did not operate simply on a self-sufficiency basis, but was monetized and commercialized – a point reflected in legislation of 1425 forbidding price rises in places visited by the royal court! The main monetization occurred in the thirteenth century: by 1286 the Scottish coinage amounted to between £130,000 and £180,000 – 30 to 45 million silver pennies. In the thirteenth and fourteenth centuries, however, the coins actually used in Scotland were mostly English (England's money supply was then about £1,000,000), because until the 1370s the two currencies had equal values and circulated interchangeably.

Money circulated chiefly through the markets and fairs held in late-medieval Scotland's 70 or so burghs. Burghs were urban communities established with an eye to fiscal advantage by kings (royal burghs) or major landowners (ecclesiastical burghs and burghs of barony). In 1306 there were 38 royal burghs and 18 non-royal; over the next 200 years the number of royal burghs declined somewhat (as a few were granted to magnates), while the number of non-royal ones roughly trebled. No burgh was very large; most had populations of only a few hundreds, and the biggest, Edinburgh, was described by Froissart as having 400 houses. But Froissart compared it with an important provincial centre, Tournai; his point was perhaps that Edinburgh was like that rather than exceptional cities such as Paris, Ghent or London. In general the Scottish burghs were probably little smaller than most ordinary towns elsewhere.

Although physically just glorified villages, the burghs were distinct in three ways. They had a separate constitutional position, with their own laws, privileges and institutions. Their inhabitants had specialist occupations: in addition to trade, carried out by a range of figures from merchant princes to pedlars, burgh industries included cloth and clothing, leather, food and drink, construction, and metal-working (the 'hammermen'). Most importantly, they controlled the country's commerce; their merchants had monopoly rights (confirmed in 1364 by a general charter of David II) of buying and selling all merchandise within the kingdom.

Their commercial dominance gave the burghs an economic importance out of all proportion to their size. Most trade was essentially local. All burghs were focal points for the surrounding countryside; peasants came and sold their produce, obtained cash to pay the rent, and bought food (when necessary), clothing, pottery, perhaps some equipment and livestock, and even the occasional luxury. But there was also international trade, channelled through the royal burghs – principally Edinburgh, Aberdeen, Dundee, Perth, Linlithgow and Haddington. Late-medieval Scotland's trading partners included England and Ireland (clandestinely in wartime), France, Scandinavia, north Germany, and especially the Low Countries; for most of the period the staple, or chief, port for Scottish traders was the great Flemish entrepôt of Bruges, though the later fifteenth century saw moves towards Middelburg and Veere, in Zeeland.

Although Scottish trade was only a small fraction of the Low Country's commerce, these ports considered it well worth having – and Flemings, Dutch and Germans were all prepared to run English blockades. That was largely due to the two main products of Scotland's pastoral economy, wool and leather. Customs accounts provide export figures for 1327–32 and for most of the period after 1360 (see Appendix B, Table I). Both commodities followed similar patterns. In 1327–32 annual wool exports (including sheepskins) averaged over 5,700 sacks or 900 tons (at 360 lb. per sack), leather exports over 36,000 hides or 700 tons (at about four tons per 200 hides). Later fourteenth-century averages fluctuated around similar figures, but wool exports boomed between 1370 and 1375, peaking in 1372 at 9,252 sacks (1,486 tons), while leather exports were highest in the 1380s, peaking in 1381 at 72,312 hides (about 1,450 tons). By the later 1380s, however, a slump had started; fifteenth-century exports were mostly around 2,000–3,000 sacks (300–400 tons) and 20,000–25,000 hides (400–500 tons). The quantities were thus much the same, with slightly more leather being exported over the whole period. But wool was worth far more. Prices varied greatly, but, roughly, a hide cost about one shilling and sixpence and a sack of wool between £4 and £5. Therefore annual leather exports were usually worth £2,500–£4,000 a year in the fourteenth century (over £5,500 in 1381), and £1,500–£2,000 in the fifteenth; whereas wool exports were worth some £25,000 a year in the fourteenth century (nearer £40,000 in the 1370s), and £10,000 in the fifteenth. For the period, these were considerable amounts. Late-medieval Scotland was a major European producer of wool and leather; in wool, indeed, the second largest exporter after England (though English wool exports were generally about six times as much). In addition, Scotland was an important producer of cured fish (salmon and herring) and wild animal skins, and in the fifteenth century was annually exporting between about 25,000 and 75,000 yards of low-quality woollen cloth, worth roughly £1,000–£3,000.

Scottish imports were much more varied. They included wheat (for upper-class and urban consumption) from England and the Baltic, thousands of gallons of French and German wine, and from the Low Countries exotic foodstuffs, quality cloth and pottery, armour and military equipment, and many other kinds of manufactured goods. One shipload belonging to four Scottish merchants captured by English sailors in 1394 contained woollen and linen cloth, canvas, wax, pepper, saffron, ginger, brass pots and plates, dishes, basins, linen thread, dyes and dyestuffs, wine, salt, bitumen, iron, wool-carding combs, Flemish belts, white and black dyed wool, hose, caps, hoods, saddles, bridles, spurs, boots, chests, gloves, weavers' shuttles, paper, parchment, candelabra, a helmet, swords (some second-hand), red leather, keys, and locks. This was worth some £170 sterling – whereas the ship and its equipment were valued at only £13 6s 8d!

International trade made the merchant-burgesses very rich. Collectively the royal burghs made significant contributions to financing the ransoms of David II and James I, and their representatives came in the fourteenth century to sit in parliament. Individually, several burgesses amassed fortunes: an English chronicler said the great John Mercer of Perth (d.1380) had 'inestimable wealth', while Adam Forrester of Edinburgh (d.1405) could afford to acquire the substantial estates of Liberton and Corstorphine outside Edinburgh. Mercer, Forrester, and others like them were active in government circles as well as commerce, and founded landed families; the progression burgess–administrator–landowner was well established in late-medieval Scotland.

But what did the trade do for the rest of the Scottish people? The basic pattern – exporting raw materials, importing manufactured goods – is typical of an undeveloped economy, which considering the amount of luxuries imported presumably operated chiefly to the benefit of the upper classes, as in Third World countries today. Yet not all manufactured goods sold in Scotland would have been imported; probably simply quality articles, in which domestic manufacturers could hardly compete with long-established and relatively sophisticated industries on the Continent. They indeed had no incentive to compete when imports could easily be afforded. That is the main point about medieval Scottish trade. The thirteenth-century growth in money supply demonstrates there was then a substantial balance of payments surplus, obviously resulting from expanding wool exports. This probably continued, if less comfortably, for much of the fourteenth century. Only after 1390 did things change significantly; the slump in exports was accompanied by exchange-rate problems, indicating balance of payments difficulties during the general European recession. One consequence, however, may have been a stimulation of domestic industries.

The main item of Scottish trade, wool, was perhaps the medieval equivalent of North Sea oil. But one important difference was that much of it belonged to the ordinary people. Admittedly when peasants sold their wool, most of the cash probably went on rent – but selling wool made rent-paying easier, and gave more to spend on other things. The wool trade brought considerable wealth to the Scottish countryside, and part must have stayed in peasant hands. Also the imports were not exclusively upper-class luxuries; many may have gone to the better-off husbandmen, like the expensive coloured cloth which husbandmen were supposed not to wear, according to fifteenth-century sumptuary legislation. The benefits of Scotland's international trade were not restricted to the burghs and landowners; they would have percolated through rural society as well.

V

How many people lived in late-medieval Scotland? Population statistics, unfortunately, are non-existent. There is circumstantial evidence that Scotland experienced both the great European population growth of the twelfth and thirteenth centuries and the sharp decline after the onset of plague in 1347–9. Beyond that, however, we have to rely on reasonable guesswork. A starting-point is the figure of about 1,100,000 calculated for the Scottish population in 1707. Its significance is that Scottish agriculture was then little different from that of the Middle Ages. Therefore medieval Scotland could have supported around a million people too. And if Scottish population trends followed English, there probably were a million Scots in the early fourteenth century: nowadays historians argue convincingly that the English population at its medieval peak was between five and six million, which was the same as its level in 1700. The rough 1:6 ratio which that implies is supported in several ways.

Today Scottish arable is a sixth of England's, and although it was less in the Middle Ages the extra Scottish grazing makes up for that. Scottish wool exports between 1327 and 1332 averaged between a fifth and a sixth of English. And 1:6 is also close to the likely ratio of the two countries' money supplies in the late thirteenth century. That is particularly important. If the Scottish population was significantly below a million, Scotland would have had greater *per capita* wealth than England; but if the Scots were much poorer, then the Scottish population must have been well above a million. Both points are improbable. Therefore if we think of the Scottish population at its peak in the early fourteenth century as approaching the million mark, we are unlikely to be far wrong.

Eighteenth-century statistics also show over half the people of Scotland living north of a line from Tay to Clyde. This, very different from nowadays, was presumably closer to the medieval distribution; the national land assessment of 1366 valued Scotland north of the Forth higher than the south. Of course since the total population was much lower than today's, the overall density was much less. Medieval Scotland also seems less densely populated than other European countries; calculations for the seventeenth century, which are also applicable to the early fourteenth, give densities of 11 per square kilometre, compared with between 34 and 40 for England, France and the Low Countries. However the Scottish figure includes the mountainous areas; in the habitable regions the density must have been closer to those of other countries.

It can even be argued that because of today's urban preponderance, population densities in the modern Scottish *countryside* are little greater than in the Middle Ages. Today roughly $3\frac{3}{4}$ million people live in settlements of over 2,000, of which there were hardly any in medieval Scotland. Subtracting these from the present population of around five million leaves only about $1\frac{1}{4}$ million in the countryside. Therefore, despite the difference in total population figures, we should not imagine the late-medieval Scottish countryside as significantly emptier than today's. In the early fourteenth century, most rural areas would have had almost as much human habitation; indeed parts of the north and borders were more densely populated.

From the mid fourteenth century, however, bubonic and pneumonic plague greatly reduced Scotland's population. The late-medieval pandemic of plague started in the East in the 1330s, reached Europe in 1347, England in 1348, and Scotland in 1349. Its effects were devastating: in much of Europe, including England, between a quarter and a third of the population probably died. And while the initial outbreak soon subsided there were fresh attacks at frequent intervals. This is plague's most significant feature; immediate population losses might have been replaced, but the new generations were also decimated, which accentuated plague's initial impact and kept the population low for many years. The English population appears to have been $2\frac{1}{2}$-3 million in the 1370s, and $2\frac{1}{4}$-$2\frac{3}{4}$ million as late as the 1520s.

Plague in Scotland followed the general pattern. After 1349, outbreaks are recorded in 1361-2, 1379-80, 1392, 1401-3, 1430-2, 1439, and 1455. But Scotland may have escaped the full force of the disease. Admittedly, according to Bower, 24 - about two-thirds - of the canons of St Andrews cathedral died in 1349. But the chronicles devote little space to the plague; fowlpest epidemic in 1347 received almost as much attention, and estimates of the 1349 death-rate, at one-third, are lower than in English and French chronicles. Bubonic plague in particular was perhaps less severe: it is transmitted by rat fleas, which need warmer climates than Scotland's to thrive, and is most dangerous in towns and concentrated settlements. Cold was no impediment to pneumonic plague, but if that were widespread, a far higher death-toll might be expected, since it is extremely infectious and lethal. Localized outbreaks of pneumonic plague, with the victims dying before the disease spread far, are more likely. In 1361-2 David II travelled to Aberdeenshire to escape, which implies that only southern Scotland was hit; and later references are mostly to outbreaks in burghs. If, as some authorities state, resistance to plague is partly determined by general health, this may be another factor, because Scottish diets seem relatively healthy. And that possibly meant that the Scots suffered less from the more mundane diseases that ravaged late-medieval Europe - though they were certainly not immune from illnesses like 'le Quhew' (? whooping-cough) of 1420 or the 'wame ill' (? dysentery) of 1439.

Perhaps, therefore, Scotland's population fell less than England's, and its recovery was faster. Signs of growing rural population are evident in the later fifteenth century, while there were several famines in the period after 1435. If we can trust the poem called 'The Harp', probably written in the 1450s, Scotland was then 'fertile of folk, with grete scantness of fude'. The argument may be supported from the experience of Scottish nobles. One source for studying late-medieval English population is the landowners' inheritance records, which indicate negative replacement rates (10 fathers being survived by less than 10 sons) from 1348 until 1440. Now in Scotland a rough preliminary survey of important noble families shows negative replacement rates only until 1380, and an abundance of sons in the fifteenth century. Much work is still needed on this point, but it does correspond to the general hypothesis.

Nevertheless the Scottish population must have fallen significantly. Since the demographic trend may have differed from England's, it is impossible to suggest population figures for the period after 1349; but they can hardly have approached pre-plague levels again until well beyond 1500. Even if Scotland suffered only half as badly as England, that would still mean around one in six of the population dying initially, and a long-term fall of about a third. That is much worse than the seventeenth-century 'killing times' of famine, or the decimations of World War I. Although Scotland may have escaped relatively lightly, plague still appears to have been the worst disaster suffered by the people of Scotland in recorded history.

VI

Discussion of the population trend takes us beyond the static account of late-medieval Scottish society given in the first part of this chapter. Demographic changes obviously have social repercussions, both when population is growing – the background to most European history – and even more when it falls, as in the late Middle Ages. Plague, moreover, was not the sole cause of change in late-medieval society. Some historians argue that Europe's population was already contracting in the early fourteenth century. Others stress non-demographic factors like warfare, class relationships, climate, and money supply. Clearly, then, many forces were at work; late-medieval Europe's society was far from static.

In early-fourteenth-century Scotland, the war against England and the accompanying Scottish civil war would have caused the most obvious disruption of people's lives. By 1306 English policy was one of maximum destruction, while the Scots employed scorched-earth tactics and attacked English-controlled areas. Southern Scotland was naturally worst affected. One random example is a freeholding in Paxton-on-Tweed – a house, four acres of arable, five husband-lands of 15 acres each, two grassmen's holdings of pasture, and two cottages – worth £2 16s 8d 'in time of peace', but valueless in 1315. Yet the north did not escape either, for there was much fighting beyond the Forth: Fordun stated that in 1337 'Gowrie, Angus and Mearns was for the most part almost reduced to a hopeless wilderness, and to utter want'; and Robert I's 'herschip' (ravaging) of Buchan in 1307 also presumably caused severe devastation.

Nevertheless, although most early-fourteenth-century Scots would have experienced one or more campaigns in their neighbourhoods, the war's effects must not be exaggerated. There is no evidence of lasting depopulation of the combat zones, like that caused by the Hundred Years War in fifteenth-century France. Even in Lothian there is striking continuity of landownership among the local freeholders and probably the husbandmen too – perhaps because high population levels meant land could not be acquired elsewhere. And the fighting always stopped or moved on eventually; when it did crops could be sown and livestock replenished. Within a year of the expulsion of English forces in 1341–2, wool exports were nearing 4,000 sacks; arable farming probably recovered just as quickly. The war's only direct long-term consequences were in the borders: Berwick and Roxburgh, hitherto the leading burghs, were lost, and in the countryside cattle-rustling became almost a way of life. Indirectly, the dislocations of landlordship probably helped bring about the disappearance of serfdom – the most momentous but also the most obscure social change of the period. But otherwise, despite its miseries, the war seems only to have had short-term effects on Scotland's economy and society.

The other problem before the plague was the relatively high population level. Expansion of settlements was petering out, and pressure is also indicated by the extension of farming into hunting reserves. Oats were being grown 1,100 feet up on Lammermuir. And late-thirteenth-century records suggest that husbandmen had at most two oxgangs (notionally 26 acres) – enough to live on, but without much to spare. The rest of the peasantry, below that level, were therefore probably badly off. In such conditions short leases favoured landlords. The peasants would have to pay high rents and entry fines unless they moved elsewhere, which would have been difficult. But that also helps explain why serfdom disappeared: landlords would have had nothing to gain by enforcing actual servitude, and much to lose through peasant resentment.

Does this imply an overpopulation crisis, as some historians argue for England and France? The case rests partly on seignorial records which show falling grain yields and hence perhaps soil exhaustion, and partly on various indications of rural distress, especially a severe famine throughout northern Europe in 1315-16. The general argument however is inconclusive, and must remain not proven for Scotland, where the strong pastoral element in agriculture and the suitability of infield-outfield farming for marginal soils possibly cushioned the effects of population pressure. Admittedly population cannot increase indefinitely without dramatic increases in agricultural productivity, which did not happen in the fourteenth century. And in general life was no doubt becoming harder for most of the Scottish people. Fordun mentions famine in 1310 (possibly misdating the 1315-16 famine, which otherwise Scotland apparently escaped). Another difficult time came in the late 1330s, when in addition to war and population pressure Scotland probably suffered from monetary contraction, the indirect result of Edward III's efforts to finance a campaign against France (he disrupted English wool exports, causing chronic scarcity of coin in England, which probably drained currency from Scotland too). The region round Perth suffered particularly badly then; 'Wyntoun' recorded a case of cannibalism. Nevertheless – although the war complicates matters – none of this amounts to clear evidence of a significant, permanent turnaround in the rural economy. A crisis presumably was approaching, but we do not know whether it had already arrived in the early fourteenth century. And – the most important point – within a few years existing trends were obliterated, because the plague completely transformed the rural situation.

VII

Looking back from the 1440s, Bower remembered a 'great fertility of victuals' in Robert III's reign (1390-1406). That neatly sums up the general situation in post-plague Europe. Pressure on resources had ended; the population fall meant less demand for food and land but more for labour, pushing prices and rents down but wages up. Thus there was more to go round the surviving people.

There are various pieces of evidence about developments in Scotland. First, national land assessments (like rateable values nowadays) were revised in 1366; the figures (excluding Argyll, where the returns are incomplete) fell from the thirteenth-century level of £45,575 to £23,826. Secondly, major landowners, following the European trend, were relinquishing what demesnes they had: James Douglas of Dalkeith had done so in Kilbucho and Aberdour by 1376; in 1380 the earl of Strathearn had only a small demesne, at Fowlis Wester, and even that was rented out by 1445; while all Coupar Angus abbey's demesnes were leased over the same period. The Douglas of Dalkeith rental also indicates larger peasant holdings: each husbandman probably had at least four oxgangs (notionally 52 acres) compared with one to two on late-thirteenth-century estates. Next, the Exchequer Rolls contain price figures for the periods 1326–31 and 1358–84: after the plague, wheat and malt cost significantly more, oats and meal stayed about the same, but meat – cattle and sheep – became cheaper (see Appendix B, Table II). Finally, this was the period of high wool and leather exports – peaking in the 1370s and 1380s – before the eventual slump started.

The evidence shows that landlords faced severe problems. The 1366 reassessment indicates sharply falling rents, yet although grain prices were good it still made sense to lease the demesnes, which suggests labour costs were rising steeply (three-quarters of the £18 9s 2d spent on the Strathearn demesne at Fowlis Wester in 1380 was on labour). Probably only the less labour-intensive livestock farming remained profitable for landlords. But the peasantry's situation must have improved greatly. They were obviously able to get more land at lower rents per acre. What they did with it is indicated by the price and export data. Grain production, presumably now concentrated on the best land, must have contracted roughly in line with the population fall, while the rest would have been devoted to livestock farming, which probably expanded.

Contemporaries, who called the old assessments values 'in time of peace', perhaps blamed the war for the fall in rents. But that is unlikely, because the detailed figures show no correlation with the combat zones, and the north declined almost as much (44 per cent) as the south (52 per cent). A recent argument is that the main cause was deflation resulting from monetary contraction – as we shall see, Scotland's balance of payments had deteriorated. Yet while a shortage of money in the economy would depress rents, it would surely have made prices fall fairly evenly – which apparently did not happen. Thus population fall is the likeliest explanation, especially in view of the trend towards larger holdings. Population fall alone, however, would not necessarily have had such effects. If peasant mobility had still been restricted through serfdom, landlords could have maintained cheap labour and high rents. It was serfdom's disappearance that left the landlords vulnerable to the population fall; they could then only make tenants stay on their estates by agreeing to lower rents. The Douglas of Dalkeith rental provides glimpses of the process: tenants who did not come to negotiate their rents were put down at the old figure. In these circumstances the Scottish system of short leases benefited the peasantry, not the landlords.

The apparent trend towards livestock farming was common throughout Europe. As well as requiring less labour, it was stimulated in Scotland by two other factors. The fourteenth-century European climate was deteriorating, and oats would not ripen at such high altitudes as before; arable farming became impossible on Lammermuir, for example. Secondly, many people in Europe were better off after the plague, which increased demand for wool and leather goods. Since Scotland was a major exporter of wool and hides, production of these commodities would have boomed – between 1370 and 1375 yearly wool exports averaged 7,600 sacks. In 1372, however, when English wool exports were suffering government restrictions and foreign manufacturers were presumably desperate for Scottish wool, 9,252 sacks were exported (plus 1,875 of English wool smuggled through Scotland). Since wool production cannot be increased overnight, the regular Scottish wool clip must then have been around 9,000 sacks, from some $2\frac{1}{4}$ million sheep – well above the amount normally exported. The difference – some 2,000 sacks – must usually have been consumed in domestic cloth manufacture, which implies quite a respectable Scottish cloth industry. High wool and leather production would also have resulted in a relative abundance of meat – reflected in the price data, in Bower's comment on the plentiful victuals, and in Aeneas Sylvius' description of Scottish diets.

VIII

Unfortunately the boom was only short-lived. In the 1380s warfare in Flanders had permanently damaged the Flemish cloth industry. Then, by about 1400, as the general population fall continued, the expansion of demand stopped and Europe entered an economic recession. And things were made worse for Scotland by English piracy in the North Sea after 1400, by commercial conflicts with Holland from 1410 to 1423, and by the Anglo-Burgundian alliance of 1419. Had international trade been healthy these might not have mattered; as it was, they badly affected Scottish exports.

The customs accounts show what happened. In the late 1380s annual wool exports had declined to just over 3,100 sacks on average, and from 1400 to 1420 they were about 2,600, with some years' totals being much lower. Efforts by James I to stimulate wool exports brought some improvement, but only to around 4,000 sacks in 1425–30, and they soon slumped again, to just over 1,300 sacks in the 1450s. Leather exports were slower to fall, being high in the 1380s, but after 1390 they followed a similar trend (see Appendix B, Table I). The impact on producers is shown by the fact that even Melrose abbey's top-class wool did not always sell: in 1404 it exported only 30 sacks, as against 50 or more normally. And although the duke of Albany had a concession of 16 sacks duty-free, in the 1410s he was exporting less than a dozen.

The Scottish wool trade did not suffer alone, for the trend of English wool exports was worse. But in England this was countered by growth in cloth exports; England eventually became the leading European cloth producer. The Scottish cloth industry could not follow suit, however, largely because most Scottish wool tended to be fairly low quality – European manufacturers probably blended it – and cloth made entirely from it could not compete with superior products from elsewhere. Some Scottish cloth was exported – from 25,000 to 75,000 yards a year – but its value was at most around £3,000, whereas the lost wool exports were worth some £10–£15,000 or more. Therefore while England's balance of payments stayed in surplus throughout the fifteenth century, Scotland's did not.

Even before the slump, Scotland had been experiencing balance of payments problems. Both the £20,000 'payment for peace' of 1328 and David II's ransom, over £50,000 between 1357 and 1377, must have affected a money supply of £130,000–£180,000; and so must the English currency crisis of the late 1330s. During the first half of the fourteenth century the weight of Scottish coins fell by 20 per cent, and they were reduced by a further 15 per cent in 1367. Then, from 1390, there was a series of devaluations (see Appendix B, Table III). By 1470 the £ Scots was the equivalent of only 780 grains of silver, compared with 2,764 in 1390, 4,320 in 1357 and 5,400 in the thirteenth century; copper alloy had to be used in Scots pennies from the 1430s. Meanwhile the English currency, which until 1367 had weighed about the same as the Scots, fell by less than half. This meant that the centuries-old parity of English and Scottish coins was broken. In 1373 the English government imposed an exchange rate of 3:4; in 1390 it became 1:2, and in 1451, 1:3.

Scotland's monetary history suggests that the balance of payments fluctuated between surplus and deficit during the fourteenth century and eventually slid into long-term deficit. That corresponds with the export figures. But it must be added that the currencies of almost every European state declined by about the same amount, and sometimes more rapidly. While in France in 1423–4, Henry Douglas of Lugton lent his brother 1,800 French francs, at exchange-rates of three, six and ten francs to the gold noble (then worth 10 shillings Scots). Only England was different, and even there devaluations took place. The problem was a general shortage of European silver, caused by unfavourable trading balances with the Middle East, and by exhaustion of the main silver mines. All states reacted not only with devaluations but with unsuccessful efforts to conserve silver; the concern with the problem of the money shown in Scottish parliamentary records from the 1390s is common elsewhere, including even England. Scotland's currency difficulties are not simply a reflection of an undeveloped economy; they would have happened (if not on the same scale) even had the export trade not declined.

Initially, because the coins circulating in Scotland were mostly English, the devaluations probably had little effect. But this changed in the 1390s. A new term, 'usual money of Scotland', became common then, reflecting the realization that Scots coins were now worth only half as much as their English, sterling, equivalents. Thereafter Scottish prices, expressed in 'usual money', quickly rose. 'All things are dearer than they were in times past', lamented the abbot of Dunfermline in 1409. By the mid fifteenth century, food prices had doubled or trebled (see Appendix B, Table II), while manufactured goods, especially imports, perhaps went up even more. Wages no doubt followed suit. And estate records show that the 'true value' assessment of land was returning to thirteenth-century levels by the 1420s, implying a doubling in valuations since the national revision of 1366. Details of actual rent rises are harder to find, but in the early fifteenth century many rents in Douglas of Dalkeith baronies were between 10 per cent and 25 per cent higher than in 1376–7, while in Strathearn the gross rental rose by 40 per cent between 1380 and 1445. The fall in the value of money was therefore producing general inflation – or more accurately, since it was happening in a contracted economy, the modern disease of 'stagflation'.

IX

The inflation greatly increases the difficulty of elucidating the fifteenth century's economic trends, but some tentative points can be made. Food prices apparently rose in line with currency depreciation (see Appendix B, Table II), but oats and meal, fairly static in the fourteenth century, now seem to have caught up with wheat and malt. That suggests increasing demand for food, connected with the beginnings of demographic recovery. But although meat prices rose they were still low relative to the 1320s. Moreover, unless Scottish cloth production had expanded considerably, the export slump must have made livestock farming less profitable. Conditions may therefore eventually have encouraged a reversion towards arable. That seems to correspond with the recent demonstration that the term outfield was first appearing in the later fifteenth century. It is likely that after the plague arable farming contracted to a minimum, in the infields; but that from the mid fifteenth century it was expanding again, into lands which since about 1350 had been used solely for grazing. The profits which could be made when poor harvests drove grain prices up (as in 1434-5, 1438-9, 1453-4, and 1457) possibly stimulated that trend too.

Rents however behaved differently. Cash rents probably did not keep up with inflation, especially as the century went on. Inflation-proof rents in kind were not uncommon, but there is no evidence of any switch to them; if anything, the reverse. Also, after the middle of the century, crown rentals contain many references to deserted touns. And the early-fifteenth-century rental for the Douglas of Dalkeith estates shows some rents were actually lower than in 1376-7. All this indicates that the hard times continued for landlords, just as elsewhere in western Europe; keeping their lands tenanted would have remained their first priority. The corollary should be that circumstances favoured the peasantry. Yet if, as the export figures suggest, the market for animal products was depressed, then many peasants could have been badly hit. It may have become harder for cottars and the like to pay their rent – especially if their holdings had growing numbers to support. Rural impoverishment, exacerbated by currency problems, is one way of reconciling the rental evidence with the indications of rising population and with Bower's recollections of more plentiful victuals in his youth.

But that does not apply to all the peasantry. Consider Thomas Gilbertson, in the Douglas of Dalkeith barony of Buittle. He already had a large tenancy in 1376, and by the early fifteenth century had acquired extra lands at well below the 1376–7 rents. Obviously he had driven a hard bargain with his landlord, perhaps to take over land which might otherwise have been deserted. Gilbertson seems typical of many substantial husbandmen, who, having large but manageable tenancies, would have been well placed to take advantage of improving grain prices and cheap rents – possibly expanding their arable at the expense of poorer neighbours. Their workforces would have consisted of family, servants, and some cottars, probably working not so much for wages as for sublet smallholdings at low rents plus a quantity of oatmeal. The result, it may be suggested, was a trend towards increased stratification between rich and poor within peasant society.

This is not unlike what happened in late-medieval England, where rural society came to be roughly divided between yeomen farmers and agricultural labourers. It was not simply an economic division; the yeomen had much in common with the gentry, and together these classes dominated local society. That was probably true of Scotland too. John Major wrote that

> In both of the British kingdoms, the farmers rent their land from the lords, but cultivate it by means of their servants, and not with their own hands. They keep a horse and weapons of war, and are ready to take part in his quarrel . . . with any powerful lord. . . . Though they do not till their land themselves, they keep a diligent eye upon their servants and household, and in great part ride out with the neighbouring nobles.

This echoes Scottish legislation on weapons enacted in 1426. Gentlemen with net incomes of £10 had to be 'sufficiandly harnest and anarmyt', poorer gentlemen were to be armed 'at thare gudly power', 'honeste yeman [i.e. substantial husbandmen] hafande sufficiande powere that likis to be men of armys' were to be 'harnest sufficiandely', and other yeomen just had to have bows, swords, bucklers and knives.

For the landlords, substantial husbandmen were desirable tenants, being most able to pay their rents. So long as there was a danger of land being deserted, husbandmen would enjoy considerable security. Indeed after serfdom had disappeared, the concept of kindly tenure emerged: a peasant could expect to succeed to a tenancy if he was 'kindly' – kin – to the previous tenant. Another fifteenth-century development benefiting tenants was a trend towards longer leases. But that had disadvantages as well as advantages for landlords in a period of inflation. An act of 1467 stated that changes in the value of money 'gretly hurt and skathyt' landlords who agreed long leases; in future the original value of the rent was payable even if the currency depreciated. This presumably reflects landlords' worries about very long leases. Although some long leases can be found, church estate records show the mid-fifteenth-century norm was five to seven years, while three years were commonest on crown lands.

The same argument probably applies to the practice of 'feuing' land – letting it be held in perpetuity, in return for a substantial initial sum and higher annual payment. Feuing dates from the twelfth century, but became increasingly common after 1500. It gave well-off tenants a fixed rent, full security, and entry to the ranks of lesser landowners. But for landlords the benefit was short-term, and this is probably recognized in the so-called 'feu-farm act' of 1458: 'Item anentis feuferme the lordis thinkis speidfull that the king begyne and gif exempill to the laif [rest].' That was not an act encouraging feuing, but the cautious result of a parliamentary debate on its desirability. The landlords were probably resisting pressure to grant feus; because of inflation, short leases were more in their interests. If so, the pressure may have been two-fold: from the crown, possibly anticipating John Major's argument that short leases discouraged agricultural improvement; and from those who wanted feus, that is small freeholders, townsmen, and especially husbandmen, judging by the analysis of sixteenth-century feuing. This perhaps reflects, again, the rising position of the substantial husbandmen in this period.

X

What, meanwhile, was happening in the burghs? One theme is the growing power of the merchants. While trade was booming, their wealth and national prominence was such that in most royal burghs they came to be the only burgesses who mattered. In the fifteenth century their position was maintained and apparently strengthened. Well-organized merchant guilds took over burgh councils, courts and offices. And a sequence of acts of parliament, starting with one in 1469 stating that new councils were no longer to be elected but would simply be chosen by the old ones, gave them oligarchic strangleholds over most royal burghs' affairs.

This was apparently at the craftsmen's expense. There was some internal friction; in Aberdeen in 1398 the merchant-dominated court banned 'conspiracies' made by weavers against the community's interests. In 1427 parliament prohibited burgh craftsmen from electing 'deacons' to supervise their crafts, and even from 'holding their customary congregations which are presumed to savour of conspiracies'. Several acts stated that craftsmen could not engage in trade unless they renounced their craft, while only 'worthy' craftsmen, approved by the merchants on the burgh councils, could become burgesses. All this indicates a victory for the mercantile interest. Nevertheless, despite the 1427 act, craftsmen's 'conspiracies' did not disappear; indeed they were tacitly recognized in the 1469 act, which gave a voice in electing burgh officers to one person elected from each craft. Socio-religious craft associations were already well established in the mid fifteenth century, and after 1469 craftsmen in most burghs started to form individual guilds.

These developments are important for the burghs' institutional history, but in the fifteenth-century context they probably reflect more important economic changes. After the 1370s the merchants' profits must have suffered greatly from the decline in exports. Exchange-rate fluctuations and legislation like the requirement imposed in 1436 of importing three ounces of bullion for every sack of wool exported presumably increased their difficulties. And since Edinburgh gained the bulk of the declining export trade (it had 35 per cent of wool exports in the 1370s, 45 per cent between 1400 and 1435, and 62 per cent in the 1450s), things must have become even harder for the merchants of the other royal burghs.

Conversely the economic climate favoured the craftsmen. The export slump and international recession must have made imports gradually contract – at a time when growing wealth among at least part of rural society probably increased demand for manufactured goods. But the population fall would have reduced the amount of work they could do. With supply restricted and demand growing, craftsmen would have been well placed to increase their charges, probably beyond the rate of inflation – which is what their 'conspiracies' were about. The merchants' reaction is understandable: several acts empowered burgh councils to fix prices and wages. However, the forces of supply and demand would have been hard to resist, especially when craft guilds emerged. Thus the balance of economic power in the burghs may have been shifting. In that case the institutional developments appear as desperate efforts by the merchants to maintain the dominance achieved in earlier, more favourable circumstances. Given the economic forces, their victory may have been illusory.

The changing economic balance has a general importance. If conditions favoured domestic craftsmen more than international traders, did they perhaps stimulate growth in Scottish industry? Since domestic commerce left few records, it is impossible to say. Yet Scottish craftsmen would obviously have been more competitive in home markets in the fifteenth century. There is, at least, a clear trend towards Scottish manufacture of artillery and armour. Also, there was a considerable amount of fifteenth-century building work on churches and, especially, on castles. More mundane crafts have not left the same evidence, but possibly they followed the same trend – though whether in the main industry, cloth, sufficiently to compensate for the fall in wool exports is doubtful.

Another related development was the growth in burghs of barony. The later fifteenth century saw 13 new foundations between 1450 and 1469, and another 26 by 1500. Landlords may have seen them as status symbols, but would have expected profits too. Unfortunately, although some cloth was made outside the royal burghs, there is no evidence that any burghs of barony flourished through cloth in the way that fifteenth-century English villages like Leeds or Halifax did – except perhaps Paisley, founded by the local Benedictine abbot in 1488. Nevertheless their inhabitants were entitled to work at crafts, sell their goods, and hold markets and fairs, which indicates some increase in economic activity. This may be one slight aspect of a general late-medieval European trend away from single large regional economic units towards many smaller local ones. And if we ask who benefited from the creation of burghs of barony, apart from individual landowners, the best guess would be, once again, the wealthier husbandmen on the particular estates.

XI

There is one final issue. The late Middle Ages witnessed considerable rural unrest, which occasionally flared up into spectacular risings like the French *Jacquerie* of 1359 or the English Peasants' Revolt of 1381. Scotland, however, seems to have escaped it. Apart from an act of 1469, stating that annual rent-fixing and changing of tenancies 'makkis gret discensioune and causis oft tymes gret gaderings and discordis,' evidence for landlord-peasant tension is conspicuous by its absence.

To suggest why, we may start with the one record of peasant violence that is recorded, in Froissart's account of the 1385 French expedition to Scotland. 'Whenever [French] servants went out to forage, they were indeed permitted to load their horses with as much as they could pick up and carry, but they were waylaid on their return, and villainously beaten, robbed and sometimes slain.' The episode's significance is that living off the countryside was a common practice for French nobles – and it was also a major cause of the *Jacquerie*. Obviously, however, it was not a normal problem for the Scottish peasantry.

Similarly the immediate cause of the English Peasants' Revolt, sustained taxation culminating in a heavy poll tax, is also missing from Scotland. Scottish taxation was lighter and less frequent (see chap. 6:v). There is even perhaps a conscious decision to avoid anything like the ill-fated poll tax: in 1409 Robert duke of Albany, the governor, rejected a parliamentary proposal to pay for dismantling Jedburgh castle through a hearth tax, 'lest the poor folk should curse him'.

Furthermore Scotland did not experience the class tension which underlies the *Jacquerie*, Peasants' Revolt, and other peasant movements. One example is the seignorial efforts to freeze wages in England and France after the plague had made labour scarce, which antagonized peasant employers and employees alike. Another, in post-plague England, is a temporary reversal by landlords of the trend away from serfdom. And in France there was the practice of not taxing nobles because they performed military service in person –

something non-nobles bitterly resented at the time of French defeats in the 1350s. Such developments widened the gulf between nobles and peasants, and most importantly gave the wealthier peasantry a common cause with their poorer neighbours against the upper classes, at least in the later fourteenth century.

None of this happened in Scotland. By medieval standards Scottish society was relatively fluid; there was a much narrower gulf between nobles and non-nobles than in France and other Continental countries (see chap. 5:i), and no noble tax exemptions to cause bitterness. Moreover, in contrast to England, there was nothing that can be described as a seignorial reaction after the plague. The 1366 reassessment shows landlords apparently reconciled to the reduced value of their estates; among the reasons are no doubt the relative unimportance of demesne cultivation, the disappearance of serfdom, and the difficulty of keeping rents high in the system of short leases. Therefore Scottish landlords did not attempt to resist the inevitable economic changes – consequently avoiding social tension. And since the changes particularly favoured wealthier husbandmen, these – the most important members of peasant society – would have had little incentive to lead any general movements against the landlords, as they probably did in other countries.

Furthermore, if we consider late-medieval Switzerland, where peasant unrest was also absent, we find peasant consciousness focused on foreign rather than domestic enemies. That is probably true of Scotland, too. National awareness, greatly stimulated by the Anglo-Scottish wars, extended well beyond the upper classes to the ordinary people of Scotland. Barbour's *Brus* contains several stories of the exploits of individual peasants: William Bunnock's blocking the gates at Linlithgow with his hay waggon in 1313 is the most famous. In general, it must have been the husbandmen – required in the fourteenth century to have at least a spear, and if they had goods worth more than £10 a padded jacket, iron headpiece, and sword as well – who made up the bulk of the Scots armies. And perhaps most significantly, Barbour's best-known lines equated freedom from serfdom with freedom from foreign subjection. We can probably, therefore, find at least part of the explanation for the apparent absence of acute landlord-peasant tension in late-medieval Scotland in the general heightening of national consciousness that resulted from the Wars of Independence.

4

Church and Religion

I

The people of late-medieval Scotland all belonged, through the practice of infant baptism, to the international Catholic Church. Within it, their religious needs were catered for by 3,000–4,000 Scottish churchmen in holy orders. The churchmen's main functions were to administer sacraments and wage holy war on the devil and sin through divine worship, prayer, and especially the sacrifice of the mass. Thereby, in theory, they protected the rest of society from spiritual dangers. The churchmen were also the educated class, able to read and write – as the terms 'cleric' and 'clerk' demonstrate. In the earlier Middle Ages they virtually monopolized these skills; and although later that was no longer so, the close association between churchmen and education continued. Another distinguishing feature of the churchmen was that they could not marry, and were supposed to lead chaste lives – though in practice the rule of chastity was frequently broken.

Late-medieval Scotland's churchmen were part of the whole Church's supra-national organization – which for the fourteenth century has been described as 'the most impressive hierarchical imperialism that Europe has ever seen'.[1] This ecclesiastical 'empire' encompassed all western Europe, and was run by the greatest administrative machine of the period. At the centre was the huge bureaucratic Curia, which was located at Rome or, for a time, at Avignon. Beyond it, throughout western Europe, there were the local hierarchies, from archbishops down to parish priests, connected by a system of Church courts, councils and visitations. Ties

[1]G. Holmes, *Europe: Hierarchy and Revolt, 1320–1450* (London, 1975), p. 94.

with the Curia were maintained by a constant stream of letters, petitions, appeals, commands and personal visits.

Scotland had been integrated into this international system since the twelfth century. In the late Middle Ages the country had over 1,000 parishes, irregularly grouped into a dozen dioceses (Caithness, Ross, Moray, Aberdeen, Brechin, Dunkeld, Dunblane, St Andrews, Glasgow, Argyll, the Isles, and Galloway). Under the bishops, cathedrals had their deans and chapters, and dioceses were usually administered by archdeacons, 'officials' and 'deans of Christianity' (like English rural deans). These ran courts which had jurisdiction over the clergy as a whole, and, over the laity, with respect to promises, contracts, wills, debts, marriages and morals. Scotland also had its religious houses – by the early fourteenth century 30 abbeys, 27 priories, nine nunneries and some 20 friaries – plus the universities of St Andrews (founded 1412) and Glasgow (founded 1451). Institutionally, indeed, it was a typical part of the Catholic Church. But one anomaly was that there was no Scottish archbishopric until 1472. Galloway and the Isles were in the archbishoprics of York and Trondheim respectively (though in practice that connection had lapsed by *c.*1400), while the rest of the Scots bishoprics were directly subject to the pope; the Scottish Church was the papacy's 'special daughter'.

Among the higher clergy, the Scottish Church's integration was consolidated at the personal level. Before 1412 the bishops and their important subordinates were mostly graduates of foreign universities, and even after then it was customary to proceed from St Andrews or Glasgow to further study abroad. Thirteenth-century Scottish students generally went to Oxford and Cambridge, but after the Anglo-Scottish wars started Paris became their favourite university, while attendance at Orléans, Avignon, Louvain and Cologne was also common. Their education gives the Scottish higher clergy a cosmopolitan appearance – more so than their English counterparts.

Scottish relations with the head of the international Church, however, were not straightforward. A medieval churchman's allegiance to the papacy was generally balanced by commitments to his own and his country's interests, and in addition he was subject to his king's commands. In medieval Europe the interests of papacy, crowns, and national hierarchies frequently diverged, sometimes sharply. Although by 1306 the period of most dramatic conflict was ending, in the late Middle Ages there were still three main areas of tension. One concerned the papacy's interference in wars, either in the attempt to bring peace by exerting ecclesiastical pressure, or less worthily to further papal concerns in Italian politics. A second resulted from the Church's centralization: the papacy attracted countless appeals in ecclesiastical lawsuits, and steadily took over appointments (provisions) to bishoprics and other valuable benefices, requiring substantial payments from the appointees in return. The third was over the fundamental question of whether ultimate authority belonged to the papacy or to general Church councils: the question arose during the Great Schism (1378–1417), when the cardinals quarrelled with one pope and elected another, producing two, and eventually three, rival popes, a situation that was rectified only when the Council of Constance deposed them all. But subsequent popes rejected conciliar authority, and that, at the time of the Council of Basle, caused a second Schism (1439–49). Such issues provoked conflicts in most late-medieval European countries, including Scotland.

After 1306, for instance, most Scottish bishops supported Robert I, despite the fact that he was under papal excommunication for his sacrilegious murder of John Comyn. Moreover, from 1319 to 1328 they refused to apply an interdict on formal religious activities, imposed because the Scots had ignored papal efforts to end the Anglo-Scottish war, because these favoured England. Another interdict was threatened when Queen Margaret Drummond appealed against her divorce by David II in 1369, but the deaths of both parties forestalled the crisis. In 1363 the bishop of Glasgow complained that 'the multitude' of people obtaining benefices directly from the pope meant he could not provide for his own dependants. Under James I, parliament prohibited churchmen from going abroad (presumably to get papal provisions to benefices) without permission, and from buying (from the papacy) pensions out of the revenues of benefices – a practice known as 'barratry'. Such 'purchessing of pensionyss ande dismembring of benficis' was declared illegal, and 'rycht inconuenient to be tholit in the kynrik'; but Pope Martin V condemned the legislation, and threatened the bishop of Glasgow (who, as chancellor of Scotland, was held responsible) with deprivation from his bishopric.

The doctrine that Church councils were superior to popes also caused contention. During the Great Schism Scotland, like France, Castile and Aragon, acknowledged the Avignon popes; but it remained loyal to the last, Benedict XIII, longer than any other country, and had little to do with the Council of Constance. That was probably because leading figures of the early-fifteenth-century Scots Church, especially the 'inquisitor of heretical pravity', Laurence of Lindores, were strongly committed to Benedict, and denounced as heretical the conciliar proposal to depose him. A younger generation of Scottish churchmen, however, apparently followed conciliar ideas, and in 1418 their arguments made the Governor Albany and the three estates follow the rest of Europe and recognize Martin V, the pope elected at Constance. Their influence lasted to the 1430s, for over 60 Scottish churchmen attended the Council of Basle, some prominently; Thomas Livingston, abbot of Dundrennan, was closely involved in the election of the Council's anti-pope in 1439. But while James I had been sympathetic to the Council, during James II's minority conciliarism was associated with the Livingstons (the abbot's kinsmen) and the seventh earl of Douglas, and was rejected by their opponents, especially the bishops of St Andrews and Glasgow. The political struggles to the 1440s were mirrored by ecclesiastical ones in which the conciliarists were eventually defeated.

The level of conflict, however, must not be exaggerated. During the 1319–28 interdict Pope John XXII dealt with appointments in the usual way; and when Edward II demanded that Englishmen should have Scottish bishoprics, he replied that since they could not enter Scotland the Scots would therefore have no bishops, which would be intolerable. After 1337 papal diplomacy concentrated on the Hundred Years War; that was resented in England, where the papacy was seen as biased towards France, but did nòt upset the Scots. Similarly Scotland witnessed nothing like the English hostility to papal provisions. The English objection (apart from the fear that the money levied was going to France) was that provisions often went to absentee foreigners. That rarely happened in Scotland, presumably because Scottish benefices, being poorer, were less desirable to foreigners; thus the Scottishness of the Church in Scotland was not affected. The success of Scottish 'benefice hunters' at the papal court may have been irritating, but was not a major problem; despite the bishop of Glasgow's complaint, episcopal patronage remained effective so long as nominees also applied to the Curia. Since the universities were particularly adept at obtaining provisions, the system enhanced the career prospects for graduates. And it meant that disagreements over conciliarism were normally subordinated to the need to gain approval for appointments from whichever pope was officially recognized in Scotland.

In general, therefore, conflicts were more apparent than real; usually collaboration and working the system characterized Scotto-papal relations. That was particularly so after 1378, when the popes desperately needed support during the Schism and the subsequent conciliarist period. The popes of this era generally regarded the European monarchs as their most vital supporters – and, to keep that support, allowed them increasing power over the national Churches, especially by agreeing to appoint crown nominees to benefices. Through the Schism and the conciliar movement, there-fore, the medieval papacy's ecclesiastical empire was seriously undermined. The trend is clear in fifteenth-century Scotland, where almost all the bishops were chosen by the kings; the practice was tacitly confirmed by the papal 'Indult' of 1487.

This use of papal provisions to the crown's advantage greatly outweighs the confrontation caused in James I's reign by the anti-barratry legislation. That was not a major clash, for both king and pope realized the value of cooperation and soon reached a compro-mise; the original initiative probably came from the Scots clergy, not the king. But the legislation is significant because it was passed by parliament, not by a Scottish Church council. This confirms the constitutional principle of parliamentary supremacy already evi-dent in 1418 when the decision to abandon Benedict XIII was taken in a council-general. Thus the Great Schism also stimulated parlia-mentary authority over the Scottish Church – which was taken to its logical conclusion in 1560. The circumstances of the Reforma-tion, however, were very different from those of the late Middle Ages. Late-medieval Scotland is in fact remarkable for the absence of serious anti-papal feeling. In the papacy's own metaphor, the Scottish Church was still its 'special daughter' – but by the 1460s the relationship was that of married daughter and aged parent.

II

One of the major points about the internal history of late-medieval Europe's national Churches is that the dynamic, expansionist age of the great ecclesiastical institutions had ended. This is as true of Scotland as elsewhere. It was during the twelfth and thirteenth centuries, not the fourteenth and fifteenth, that Scotland's episcopal sees and almost all its monasteries were established, organized and endowed with the bulk of their possessions. After 1300 the only significant monastic foundation was James I's Carthusian priory at Perth in 1429. And while James patronized this austere order, he vehemently denounced the other Scottish monasteries for 'somnolence and sloth', which had brought monastic religion to the verge of destruction. James was greatly exaggerating; yet his attack reflects the fact that by then Scotland's great ecclesiastical institutions were long past their hey-day.

The change was not so much a matter of declining religious zeal as the effect of new religious and economic circumstances. The cathedrals' and monasteries' main religious function was the offering by canons and monks of continuous prayers and masses on behalf of the Christian faithful, particularly their own benefactors. These, the kings and major landowners, had provided for the canons' and monks' upkeep by granting land to the cathedrals and monasteries, and by making them the nominal rectors of parishes, with the right to the teinds (English tithes) from the parishes' inhabitants (the practice known as 'appropriation'). By the early fourteenth century, however, supplies of land and parishes for ecclesiastical endowment were becoming exhausted (by 1300 about half Scotland's parishes were already appropriated). Some late-medieval landowners may have considered their predecessors over-generous with gifts to the Church; the sentiment attributed to James I, that his ancestor David I was 'ane sair sanct to the croun', was perhaps not uncommon. At any rate, the pattern of endowment changed: grants of land were increasingly replaced by annual payments of money to maintain one or more priests (paralleling the simultaneous trend away from traditional feudal grants by lords to their followers. The priests, normally known as chaplains, were employed to celebrate regular masses, often daily, for the souls specified by the donor: normally himself, his family, friends and benefactors.

Many chaplainries (equivalent to English chantries) were established in cathedrals, where private masses were celebrated in side chapels, and they can also be found in monasteries; but, since the endowments were to maintain individual priests, they did not increase the cathedrals' and monasteries' general resources. Most, moreover, were founded elsewhere: in parish churches, especially in burghs; in private chapels attached or near to castles; in the friaries of the Dominicans and Franciscans, the new religious orders which appeared in the thirteenth century; and in collegiate churches, where several chaplainries were combined in corporate foundations. Chaplainries in private chapels – John Major stated in 1521 that every little laird had one – and parish churches were particularly common; they provided a very attractive form of pious foundation for the moderately rich.

The collegiate churches, however, are the most striking examples of the trend. By 1469 24 had been established: one in the thirteenth century, five in the fourteenth, and 18 after 1400. All but four were erected by magnates like the ninth earl of March (Dunbar, 1342), Archibald 'the Grim', earl of Douglas (Lincluden, 1389; Bothwell, 1398), James Douglas of Dalkeith (Dalkeith, 1406), and William Cunningham (Kilmaurs, 1413). Leading figures in James II's minority (1437–49), including Lords Crichton and Hamilton, founded seven; collegiate churches had perhaps become status symbols. They were also the late-medieval equivalent of the earlier cathedrals and monasteries; and although smaller institutions, usually with between five and 10 priests as opposed to the 15 to 30 canons or monks normally found in cathedrals or monasteries, they would have provided a greater number of masses to suit their patrons' wishes at considerably less cost (chaplains in collegiate churches generally received between £5 and £10 a year). Founding chaplainries and collegiate churches was thus more cost-effective than granting lands to cathedrals and monasteries. That was doubtless particularly relevant in the period of economic contraction after 1350.

In that period, the new pattern of endowment must have hurt cathedral and monastic finances badly. Extra possessions were acquired, especially through appropriations; the proportion of appropriated parishes rose to about 85 per cent by 1560 (though some went to chaplainries and collegiate churches). But that was insufficient to offset falls in rents and teinds – in the 1366 revision of land values the Church's total assessment was reduced by 37 per cent – and also, after about 1400, in incomes from wool. Payments required for papal provisions made matters worse. Prelates would still have had large revenues at their disposal; yet Bower's comment that Bishop Wardlaw of St Andrews (1403–40) 'entertained daily with a lavishness beyond his means', and the temporary excommunication of Wardlaw's successor Bishop Kennedy for slowness in paying papal dues, presumably indicate financial pressure in even the richest Scottish see.

One response was to manage existing possessions as efficiently as possible. That was a moral as well as a financial imperative, for Church lands were regarded as being held in trust for God and the saints, and maintaining their profitability was a divine obligation; this helps explain why medieval churchmen were sometimes seen as grasping. In fact their estate management could be sensible and enlightened, as Coupar Angus abbey's records demonstrate. In the adverse economic circumstances, however, even the most efficient management would not have maintained revenues from land at thirteenth-century levels.

But for the cathedral clergy, if not for the monks, a second response was possible: the acquisition (with papal dispensation) of extra benefices and appointments. This pluralism – comparable to the expansion of lay estates through marriage and inheritance – became common for archdeacons, deans and canons. Even bishops followed suit in the fifteenth century, receiving monasteries '*in commendam*'; that is they looked after monasteries (and the revenues) in the place of abbots or priors. Bishop Kennedy of St Andrews (who before becoming a bishop was simultaneously sub-dean of Glasgow and rector of Tannadice) held Scone abbey *in commendam*, while Paisley abbey was held by his successor Bishop Graham. In this way the institution of the commendatorship, which was so abused in the sixteenth century, was established within the Scottish Church.

III

The men who staffed the great ecclesiastical institutions were still, of course, the Scottish Church's élite; they often had noble birth and university education, they had excellent career prospects, and – despite the economic difficulties – they were wealthy, sometimes outstandingly so, by contemporary standards. The parish priests were very different. These came from the peasantry and ordinary freeholders, had rarely been to university, had little chance of promotion, and were badly-off financially by comparison with those above them. The same points apply to priests employed in chaplainries, collegiate churches and cathedrals (where they often deputized for higher dignitaries). This priestly proletariat accounted for most of the late-medieval Scottish Church's manpower, but received only a relatively small proportion of its revenues.

The financial imbalance is largely due to the fact that the rectors of parishes, who received the bulk of the teinds, hardly ever acted as parish priests. That was impossible in appropriated parishes, where the rectors were ecclesiastical corporations. And in unappropriated parishes the rectorships were usually secured by members of the ecclesiastical élite, such as cathedral dignitaries, royal clerks and magnates' secretaries, who treated their parishes simply as sources of revenue; often, moreover, promising students were given parochial benefices to finance them at university. Rectors therefore had their parishes looked after by vicars, who were maintained either by a share (roughly a quarter) of the teinds, or more commonly by a yearly pension. Vicars, in turn, could employ curates. Thus the norm in late-medieval Scottish parishes was for the priests to be stipendiary vicars or curates, who rarely received more (sometimes less) than the £10 minimum stipulated by the Scottish Church from the early fourteenth century.

The diversion of parochial revenues from the priests is easily seen as a serious abuse. The result can be shown to be a situation where the 'fat' (John Major's epithet) upper clergy enjoyed wealthy worldliness, whilst a poverty-stricken priesthood was driven to make heavy demands on its parishioners for offerings and fees, especially at funerals; later reformers accused priests of charging for the eucharist. Other material is also available to demonstrate that the late-medieval Scottish Church was in a sorry state. Breaches of the rule of clerical chastity were common. There were several cases of clerical violence, as in *c*.1447, when the vicar of Tranent killed a sailor in a brawl at Leith. And the late-fourteenth-century diocesan statutes from St Andrews include references to the following problems: churchmen carrying weapons (forbidden except on journeys, when long knives were allowed); dances, wrestling-matches and unseemly sports held in churches and churchyards, causing bloodshed and immorality there; churchmen having concubines; and priests celebrating several masses a day for financial gain.

Such evidence must, however, be treated cautiously. Clerical concubinage usually involved unofficial wives, about which contemporary attitudes, despite the official rules, were fairly relaxed. More scandalous behaviour, whether sexual, violent or whatever, was much less common. Church statutes are a poor guide, for they never indicate the extent of abuses. Similarly, attacks by later satirists and zealous reformers (Catholic and Protestant) are generally misleading. While ecclesiastical standards in late-medieval Scotland, as throughout Europe, were far from perfect (were they ever, anywhere?) judging them on this evidence is as absurd as judging the modern medical profession by popular newspaper accounts of occasional scandals and the official rules against unethical behaviour. Respectable, conscientious churchmen would not have featured as such in the records that survive for the late-medieval Scots Church; but that is no reason for supposing they did not form the great majority of the priesthood.

Also, the financial imbalance may not have seemed so bad at the time. When status was measured by display and worldly success was seen as reflecting God's favour, the leading churchmen would have been expected to radiate magnificence. And it is anachronistic to suppose that parochial teinds should simply have gone to the parish clergy. The principle was that a tenth of the laity's produce went to the Church as a whole, to enable it to achieve its main function of combating sin. Although priests were responsible for mitigating the consequences of individuals' sins, the upper ranks of the clergy can be said to have striven to reduce sin altogether. Monks and canons offered continuous prayers and masses; theologians maintained and defended the faith; lawyers worked to check offences and settle disputes; and administrators tried to ensure that society ran smoothly. Even purely secular activities, like the prominent role of bishops in royal government, theoretically had a religious purpose: the better a country was governed, the less sins were likely to be committed. In the medieval Church these activities were probably considered more important than those of the ordinary parish priests. Also they required far more ability, training, and (in the case of monks) holiness than parish priests needed. Therefore perhaps it was not unreasonable to contemporaries that the élite who performed these functions received most of the Church's revenues. This conclusion is possibly supported by the fact that the first surviving Scottish church court records, for early-sixteenth-century Lothian, do not indicate widespread popular antipathy to teinds.

Moreover, the ordinary priest may not have been so badly-off educationally and financially as is sometimes claimed. They did not need university degrees; they could gain sufficient education either in schools or by assisting other priests, in a form of apprenticeship. There were probably 'refresher courses'; the St Andrews statutes proposed annual assemblies for instructing priests about the sacraments and other matters concerning the salvation of souls. And of course common sense, not educational excellence, is the chief requirement in parish clergy – something that cannot be taught academically. As for their incomes, during most of the period a Scottish priest would not have been poor, by his parishioners' standards, with a £10 stipend plus a manse and some arable (the glebe); late-medieval military legislation, indeed, required laymen with £10 incomes to be horsed and armed as gentry. Economically, the parish priests would have been on a par with the ordinary freeholders and substantial husbandmen – probably the classes from which most priests were drawn.

This argument, however, applies chiefly to the fourteenth century. In the fifteenth, while the husbandmen's economic fortunes improved, those of the parish priests declined. Priests must have been badly affected by inflation, because their rectors (themselves under economic pressure) generally kept stipends down to the minimum, which was not raised until 1549. Although the case of the vicar of Berwick – who after the Scots regained the burgh in 1461 suddenly found his stipend changed from £20 sterling to £20 Scots, worth only a third as much – is exceptional in the suddenness with which the value of his income fell, it neatly illustrates the deterioration in the Scottish priests' economic position between the 1390s and 1460s. And, while their plight may still not have been desperate, it continued to worsen steadily for almost another century.

IV

Whatever the financial situation of the late-medieval Scottish priesthood, the parish churches rarely had much money spent on them, presumably because priests and parishioners had insufficient funds, while rectors used their revenues for other purposes. Medieval Scottish churches were generally small, undistinguished buildings, with a simple rectangular plan rather than the cruciform shape commonly found in England (the main exceptions were in major burghs and where cathedral, monastery or collegiate churches served parishes). During the late Middle Ages they seem not to have been enlarged or embellished as so many English parish churches were; at best they were probably merely kept in an adequate state of repair.

The ordinary parish churches must therefore have contrasted sharply with the cathedrals, abbeys and priories – vividly illustrating the financial imbalance within the Church. Yet the great ecclesiastical institutions were also suffering financial pressure in the late Middle Ages, and this is reflected in their buildings too. The greatest age of Scottish ecclesiastical architecture, when the cathedral and monastic churches were planned and mostly built, was in the twelfth and thirteenth centuries; its end is symbolized by the consecration in 1318 of St Andrews cathedral, at 392 feet one of the longest churches in all Britain. Admittedly much building still went on; some thirteenth-century projects were being completed, while damage from warfare, fires, storms and age necessitated near-continuous repairs. Nevertheless the scale and tone of Scottish ecclesiastical architecture are not so impressive as before. Late-medieval Scottish prelates, unlike their English counterparts, rarely embarked on extensive alterations; probably the only building operations comparable to the projects of the earlier centuries were at Melrose abbey, Aberdeen cathedral and St Giles church in Edinburgh.

One aspect of this is that the new English perpendicular style is not found in Scotland, except in the uniquely ambitious reconstruction of Melrose abbey, where York masons worked (perhaps because it had Richard II's patronage after his army burned it in 1385). Most late-medieval Scottish church building – not only in the cathedrals but also in the large new churches constructed in leading burghs – was in a fairly traditional gothic style. Sometimes, moreover, features apparently derived from twelfth-century churches and from contemporary tower-houses, such as simple cylindrical columns, round-arched windows, and barrel-vaults, can be found: for instance at Aberdeen and Dunkeld cathedrals, and on a smaller scale in most of the collegiate churches, including the fantastically carved Roslin (founded *c*.1450).

Part of the explanation for this conservatism may be French influence (at Melrose, where French as well as English features appear, a Parisian master-mason left an inscription stating that he 'had in keeping all mason work' of St Andrews, Glasgow, Melrose, Paisley, Nithsdale and Galloway); the later fourteenth and fifteenth centuries did not see great architectural innovation in France. But cost was no doubt the main factor. Elaborate ecclesiastical architecture was very expensive. David II spent over £600 between 1362 and 1370 on remodelling the church of St Monans in Fife, where he founded several chaplainries; that is almost as much as the cost of the great tower at Edinburgh castle. Yet when David died St Monans church was still unfinished. Similarly, with the collegiate churches, the funds made available by their founders were generally insufficient to complete the planned buildings. And although the new burgh churches were finished, the work was usually extremely slow, over a century at Stirling and Linlithgow, for instance; only in Edinburgh was there enough money to build its church, St Giles, at a significantly faster rate. In the cathedrals and monasteries the same pattern can be seen; even relatively conservative rebuilding dragged on for decades and sometimes for over a century. Therefore it is hardly surprising that radical – more expensive – reconstructions were rarely attempted, or that when they were, as at Aberdeen cathedral and Melrose abbey, the work was still incomplete in 1560.

Yet it must be remembered that the great architectural achievements of the earlier period continued to grace the kingdom after 1300. The beautiful cathedral at Elgin deserved its description, 'the ornament of the realm, the glory of the kingdom, the delight of foreigners' in the fifteenth century as much as in the later thirteenth (it was, contrary to what is often stated, repaired after the attack by the 'Wolf of Badenoch' in 1390: see chap. 7:ii). And the late-medieval Scottish building styles, while hardly rivalling English perpendicular, are not unattractive. Moreover the interiors would have been embellished with rich wood and stone carvings, pictures and (probably a late-medieval innovation in Scotland) stained glass; excellent examples of fifteenth-century carving can be seen at Glasgow cathedral and at Roslin and Fowlis Easter (Angus) collegiate churches, while at Fowlis Easter vivid wall paintings also survive. Whatever their architectural history, the cathedral and monastery churches were clearly the most splendid edifices in the country. Regardless of the financial pressures, the impression given by these buildings would always have been one of magnificence directed to the glory of God.

V

The Church's main contribution to late-medieval Scottish culture was not, however, in the visual arts but in the field of literature. The establishment of a national history by Barbour, Fordun,

Wyntoun and Bower has already been discussed. Scotland also produced some notable philosophers, including Laurence of Lindores (whose reputation reached Prague and Cracow) in the early fifteenth century, and later John Ireland and John Major (both prominent in Paris university). But the greatest Scottish philosopher, John Duns Scotus (died 1308), who was presumably from Duns in Berwickshire, spent his entire career outside Scotland and was a figure of the international, not the Scottish, Church.

Most importantly, there were the vernacular poets. The late fifteenth and early sixteenth centuries were a golden age for Scottish poetry, in which three churchmen, Robert Henryson, William Dunbar and Gavin Douglas, were the leading figures. While Dunbar and Douglas are outside the scope of this book, the Dunfermline schoolmaster Henryson (*c.*1420–90), just falls within it. Henryson has been described as the greatest of all Scottish poets, and certainly his technical mastery, his skill with language, his depth in serious poems, his lightness in humorous ones – his sheer poetic brilliance – make him a major figure in Europe's, let alone Scotland's, cultural history. He is perhaps second only to Chaucer among the medieval vernacular poets of the British Isles.

Henryson was partly inspired by Chaucer; poetry transcended the Anglo-Scottish frontier. But he also belonged to a long Scottish tradition. Among the best-known of earlier Scottish poems are Barbour's *Brus*, Wyntoun's *Orygynale Cronykil*, and *The Buke of the Howlat*, a long allegory celebrating the Douglases composed in about 1450 by Richard Holland, chaplain to Archibald Douglas earl of Moray. James I's remarkable *Kingis Quair*, although more typical of English poetry than Scottish, must also be included. Then there are other fourteenth- and early-fifteenth-century poems by shadowy or anonymous authors; and the list of 20 dead Scottish poets in Dunbar's 'Timor Mortis Conturbat Me' of *c.*1505 names many whose works are partly or entirely lost. In reality, therefore, late-medieval Scottish poetry must have been far 'richer than any reconstruction now open to scholarship and criticism'.[2]

Apart from James I, all the authors named above were churchmen. So were most of these listed by Dunbar. Some, however, were not: 'the good Sir Hugh of Eglinton' was almost certainly the magnate of that name, Robert II's brother-in-law; four others were

[2]J. MacQueen, 'The Literature of fifteenth-century Scotland', in J.M. Brown, ed., *Scottish Society in the Fifteenth Century* (London, 1977), p. 208.

probably late-fifteenth-century lairds; and a sixth was a townsman. The Church did not quite have a monopoly over late-medieval Scottish poetry. From this, and the use of Scots rather than Latin, wider questions are raised about the extent of lay literacy and the appearance of vernacular writing.

The second issue is straightforward. The chronology of the vernacular in Scottish documents roughly coincides with that of the poetry. Until the later fourteenth century, Latin was virtually universal (with occasional French exceptions). But in 1397 the 'statute of Stirling', an important enactment on law and order, was written in Scots, probably to ensure accurate proclamation and wide understanding. By James I's reign Scots was the norm in parliamentary records. Similarly it appears in landowners' documents in the 1370s, and by the mid fifteenth century was being used for almost everything except formal title deeds. Literary Scots prose, however, was slower to emerge; the first examples are translations of French books on chivalry and romance made in the 1450s, while the earliest surviving original prose work in Scots is John Ireland's religious treatise *The Meroure of Wyssdome* of 1490 (apart, that is, from the short, unfinished *Auchinleck Chronicle*, written in the 1450s and 1460s, and another brief chronicle from the 1480s).

The spread of lay literacy is a more complex issue, best approached through the medieval Church's educational system. This had a three-tier structure, the forerunner of today's. At the top, universities provided intensive education, especially in arts (chiefly rhetoric, logic and philosophy), law and theology. Until about 1410 Scottish students went abroad, but then, in the general late-medieval proliferation of national universities, St Andrews was founded in 1412, followed by Glasgow in 1451 and Aberdeen in 1495. Secondly there were grammar, or 'high' schools, which gave a thorough grounding in Latin grammar. Little is known about medieval Scotland's grammar schools, but scattered references suggest that, as elsewhere, they were originally closely associated with cathedrals, but soon spread to most other urban centres – a conclusion supported by the wide provenance of Scottish university students. The same arguments apply to the bottom, elementary tier, which is even more obscure in Scotland. Its formal manifestation was in 'little' or 'song' schools – teaching choirboys and potential priests to sing the liturgy as well as read it – found at the cathedrals and monasteries, and in most burghs. But elementary education, unlike grammar, was not predominantly urban. In the countryside, song schools were attached to collegiate churches. Usually, however, rudimentary schooling in 'the ABC' would have been provided informally by chaplains in noble households, and by ordinary parish priests, who whatever their own academic standards must at least have been able to read.

Although the system's main purpose was to produce new generations of churchmen, that does not mean it taught religion. Theology was only studied specifically at universities, and there it was a minority, specialist subject. Most university students studied arts or law. That prepared them for careers as ecclesiastical or lay administrators (bishops were commonly law graduates), lawyers, and schoolteachers (Henryson perhaps taught law at Glasgow before becoming a schoolmaster); but it was a technical, not religious, education. Similarly, elementary and grammar education taught the technical skills of reading and writing Latin accurately. These were necessary professional qualifications for churchmen, but there was no ecclesiastical exclusiveness about them. Strictly speaking, because of the rule of clerical celibacy, the medieval Church could gain recruits only by educating the children of laymen; although the rule was often broken, it meant education never became the preserve of a closed hereditary caste, as happened in some other societies. The reverse happened; medieval church law actually encouraged priests to teach village children. Thus it is clear that, in principle, the medieval Church's educational system was open to all who wanted and could afford to take advantage of it, regardless of whether they intended an ecclesiastical career.

Who took advantage of the opportunity? Obviously the merchant class must have done. Medieval merchants could hardly have run their businesses, which often involved large-scale international trade, without being able to read, count, and usually write. Although there is little direct evidence of this among late-medieval Scots merchants, the point applies to them as to others; the fact that many of them were administrators (especially of the customs), the existence of an early-fifteenth-century merchant's ready-reckoner, useless to someone who could not read, and the normal location of grammar schools in the burghs, all support that conclusion.

Secondly, as the instances of lay poets suggest, many of the nobility were also literate. That is not so axiomatic as with the merchants. Yet it has been shown that literacy had become common among English landowners in the thirteenth century; and since many important Scottish nobles then held land in England, this was presumably true of them, too. Robert Bruce apparently read French romances to his followers while they were fugitives in 1306. Later in the fourteenth century enough examples can be found of literacy among Scottish magnates (including the poet Hugh Eglinton, James Douglas of Dalkeith, who possessed books of grammar, romance and law, and John Lyon of Glamis, who was David II's secretary), to imply that it was fairly general at that social level. In the fifteenth century, William Lord Crichton began a sequence of highly literate nobles who held the office of chancellor. Some handwriting by the fourth earl of Douglas survives; later in the fifteenth century it became usual for landowners to sign documents; and by the end of the century the literate laird appears to have been reasonably common.

Thus literacy percolated downwards through the Scottish land-owning classes, just as it did in England. But whether the process was as quick as in England is doubtful. By the thirteenth century England's precocious administrative development appears to have made not only the great nobles but also the gentry and many peasants appreciate the value of the written word – the vital precondition for the spread of lay literacy. Also the growth of the English common law created a demand for lay lawyers, who in the late Middle Ages were trained at the Inns of Court, outside the ecclesiastical educational system. Neither factor applied to Scotland; Scottish administration would not have stimulated so much awareness of literacy, and late-medieval Scottish lawyers were all churchmen. In Scotland, therefore, the spread of literacy to the lesser nobility, and beyond them to the peasantry, was probably considerably slower, later and less comprehensive than in England.

The numbers of Scottish university students give some idea of the trend. About five per year matriculated throughout the fourteenth century, about 10 in the first half of the fifteenth century, and about 30 in the second half; by the mid sixteenth century possibly as many as 100 were doing so. This reflects a build-up in the number of those qualified to go to university, and so suggests a general expansion of education. But the most significant period was clearly the later fifteenth and sixteenth centuries. And while in the sixteenth century the number of Scottish students compares reasonably with those in England, that is not so earlier; this again indicates a slower spread of education in Scotland. The figures also, of course, demonstrate the small numbers involved in late-medieval

Scottish education: only a handful each year went to university, and presumably too only a handful went to each of the grammar schools.

Finally, the Scots literature is worth considering again. In its metres and use of alliteration, fifteenth-century Scottish poetry was strongly influenced by traditional oral verse – more so than in contemporary England (which perhaps helps explain the higher quality of the best Scottish poetry of the period). This may indicate that Scottish poetry was designed to be read aloud to an audience rather more than English was. Similarly, the Scots verse histories by Barbour and Wyntoun were presumably meant to be read publicly, while Fordun's and Bower's Latin prose ones were for more private reading. And significantly, vernacular prose works for private reading occur much later in Scotland than in England. These points all support the conclusion that Scotland, unlike England, did not experience a widespread expansion of lay literacy beyond the mercantile and upper landowning classes until the second half of the fifteenth century – and that therefore the Church's identification with education and literacy, while no longer absolute, remained extremely close in late-medieval Scotland.

VI

Education and literacy were only a by-product of the Church's major, religious, function. It is now time to turn to that, and discuss the kind of religion presented to the people of late-medieval Scotland. The first point is that, in Scotland as elsewhere, there was no organized system of preaching and formal religious instruction. Most of what preaching there was would have been done by Dominican and Franciscan friars, for it was one of their main duties; some of the new 'Observant' Franciscans were brought to Scotland specifically as preachers in the 1460s. Bishops apparently employed friars as diocesan preachers; the rambling late-fifteenth-century poem 'The Contemplacioun of Synnaris', by a Franciscan (probably Observant) friar, looks like the versification of a series of sermons. But there were probably never more than 150 friars in late medieval Scotland, from some 12 Dominican and six Franciscan friaries (before the Observants arrived); what impact they had outside their bases in the burghs is unclear. Apart from the friars, it can be noted that St Salvator's College, St Andrews (founded by

Bishop Kennedy in 1450) was partly for training preaching parish clergy - but only six 'poor clerks' at a time. And although a century later sermons by priests were apparently more common, a Scottish church council referred in 1559 to elderly clergymen who were unaccustomed to preach; widespread preaching must have been a recent phenomenon in the mid sixteenth century.

The shortage of formal preaching and religious instruction by the parish clergy was a common feature of Christianity throughout rural Europe (though England was perhaps an exception). It has led some historians to doubt whether the country areas of medieval Europe can be considered Christian at all. They are perhaps correct, according to the sixteenth-century criterion of detailed religious knowledge. But basic religious instruction can be imparted through less formal means than sermons and catechisms, and can be given by parents as well as priests; thirteenth-century ecclesiastical statutes show the Church attached great importance to the parental role. Accordingly the opinion followed here is that 'without succumbing to the "legend of the Christian Middle Ages", . . . it is possible to believe that the rural Church of medieval Europe did, in its own mode, transmit a respectable view of Christianity to the average rustic'[3] - even if to sixteenth-century reformers (Catholic as well as Protestant) it was an inadequate view.

In the medieval Church, the priest's essential task was not preaching, but administering the sacraments and rituals deemed necessary for his parishioners' salvation. The main sacraments were baptism, marking an infant's entry into the Christian community; absolution, after confession and penance (generally in the late Middle Ages the recitation of prayers) signifying the true repentance essential for divine forgiveness; communion, at mass, which was seen as a re-enactment of Christ's passion, from which all hopes of salvation derived; and extreme unction, following the rites of confession, communion and absolution at the time of death. It was believed that those who went through these rituals and truly repented of their sins would avoid eternal damnation; but, since it was thought that God, while forgiving sins, also required the expiation of guilt, a period of punishment after death would usually have to be spent in purgatory.

[3] J. Bossy, introduction to J. Delumeau, *Catholicism between Luther and Voltaire* (English translation, London, 1977), p. xviii. I have relied heavily on Professor Bossy's work in the later sections of this chapter.

What was the people's response? There is no evidence to suggest that baptism, the *sine qua non* for salvation, was anything but universal in late-medieval Scotland. The last rites were probably nearly as common; when, at Bannockburn, the Scots knelt in prayer before attacking, this was no doubt part of a collective ritual of confession and absolution in anticipation of death in battle. Dying unconfessed was a major fear in the Middle Ages, especially after the onset of plague, which struck people down before they could prepare for death: to 'de [die] as beistis without confessioun' is how Henryson's 'Ane Prayer for the Pest' described that dreadful fate.

Beyond that statements about religious observance are more difficult. As everywhere, the Scottish Church required attendance at mass on Sundays and holy days, and confession followed by communion at least yearly, at Easter. But moralists warned strongly against postponing confession and repentance until old age. They did not inveigh against ignoring it altogether, and so the widespread existence of complete religious indifference can probably be discounted. Moreover, they also criticized the practice of only confessing yearly, since a sinner who did so, 'Fra Pasche to Pasche rycht mony a thing forgettis' (Dunbar, 'The Maner of Passyng to Confessioun'). That indicates that annual confession at Easter, followed presumably by communion, was the norm. Scottish church statutes also give that impression. At other times, however, church attendance was clearly much lower – although the case of Strogeith (Strathearn), where in 1419 the parishioners were offered indulgences if they came to church, appears exceptional.

The purpose of re-enacting Christ's passion in the mass was to assuage God's wrath at human sins and re-establish peace between him and mankind: 'O king most he [high], now pacife thy feid [feud]', as 'Ane Prayer for the Pest' put it. So holy was the main ritual that the priest was usually screened from any congregation by a rood screen (a magnificent example can be seen at Fowlis Easter church). Participation in it each Easter, by consuming what was taught to be the body of Christ, was no doubt an extremely awe-inspiring experience – especially since St Paul's doctrine that to do so unworthily deserved damnation was emphasized strongly. Unworthily was taken to mean not being in a state of true repentance; hence the emphasis on the preparatory rituals of confession, penance and absolution, which were probably undertaken towards the end of Lent.

At other times only the priests normally took communion. Yet those who attended Sunday and holy day masses were not completely passive. They were expected to recite prayers (the wealthy may have had books of prayers) and contemplate the crucifixion and last judgement vividly depicted on church walls (such paintings survive from the Angus churches of Fowlis Easter and Guthrie). They made their offerings, symbolizing Christ's offering of himself. And, as in other countries, they took part in two important rituals. First, after the *Agnus Dei* ('Lamb of God, . . . grant us thy peace'), a small object called the 'pax' or paxboard (commonly recorded among Scottish church furnishings) was kissed by everyone, representing a collective kiss of peace. Secondly, after the priest's communion, they received the 'kirk loaf', blessed but not consecrated bread, as a substitute eucharist. The latter practice apparently emerged in Europe in response to popular demand, and presumably indicates increasing religious devotion.

VII

It was probably believed that Easter masses chiefly benefited the communicants themselves. But the countless masses performed daily during the rest of the year were understood differently. For instance the remarkable chapter on 'The merits of the Mass' in Abbot Bower's *Scotichronicon* called it 'the salvation of the living and the redemption of the dead'. For the living, wrote Bower, it surpassed all other prayers; hearing it devoutly built up credit against the dangers of dying unconfessed, reduced the devil's power, temporarily suspended the ageing process, protected against sudden death or blindness, improved digestion, and facilitated childbirth. These are typical late-medieval beliefs. They can be dismissed as superstitions, but really relate to the medieval concept of divine and diabolical agency in this world's affairs; 'salvation' and 'deliverance from evil' (as in the Lord's Prayer) were applied to this life as well as to the next. Viewed like that, Bower's statements appear less fantastic – and are echoed in the belief in divine aid for the righteous in battle, which survived into the twentieth century.

As for the unredeemed dead, Bower repeated in various ways that 'a soul suffering in purgatory will find mitigation or at least its punishment will be more bearable so long as a priest is celebrating mass for it'. The problem about purgatory was that no one knew how long would have to be spent there, except that it was not for *ever*, and that it was related to earthly sins. Moreover, although purgatory led to heaven, its punishments were described as remarkably like hell's. Thus, while *eternal* damnation could be avoided, long, horrendous sufferings could be expected after death. But through the mass, especially the increasingly common masses for the dead, it was believed that divine mercy could be directed towards souls in purgatory, and be focused on specific souls. Innumerable masses were therefore said to reduce the purgatorial pains of people's own souls and those of their families, friends and benefactors, both alive and dead – their entire kinship groups. Wealthy Scots followed the normal late-medieval practice of ensuring regular masses by endowing chaplainries, most spectacularly in the collegiate churches. And for many ordinary people, occasional special masses and the dedication of normal Sunday ones to their kin were quite easy to arrange. But through this practice the living carried a huge burden of responsibility for their dead kin – a burden which perhaps weighed particularly heavily in late-medieval Scotland, given the general importance of kinship there.

Other ways of improving prospects in purgatory included prayer: not only to God and Christ but also to the Virgin Mary and the saints, who were expected to intercede with God (there are parallels with secular patronage and 'good lordship'). As was the case everywhere, the Virgin Mary was particularly important; her presence permeated Scottish religious poetry, and her shrines – such as Our Lady of Paisley – were major pilgrimage centres. Nevertheless devotion to Mary and the saints complemented rather than replaced devotion to Christ. The chief religious festivals were those of Christ – Easter, Christmas and Corpus Christi, when Scottish burghs followed the late-medieval urban practice of mounting passion plays. And Christ is the main focus of the religious poetry. If one particularly Scottish devotion can be identified, it is to the Cross of Christ (perhaps because of the traditional link between St Andrew and the Cross?); the early-sixteenth-century collection of Scots religious poetry which includes 'The Contemplacioun of Synnaris' is 'the most substantial collection of vernacular verse devoted to the Passion now extant'.[4]

Then there were pilgrimages. These counted as heavy earthly penances, which could reduce the expiation required in purgatory. Short, local ones were perhaps most popular, such as to the chapel of

[4]See J.A.W. Bennett, *Poetry of the Passion* (Oxford, 1982), chapter V, 'The Scottish Testimony' (quotation from p. 120).

the Holy Cross near Montrose or St Catherine's well at Liberton. But there were also national pilgrimages to cathedrals, monasteries, and shrines like St Duthac's at Tain; and many intrepid Scots, especially those with a strong sense of guilt, embarked on the great European routes to the Holy Land, Rome and Compostella.

Pilgrimages were closely associated with indulgences, which were certificates showing that a certain penance had been performed, and so, because of 'the abundant superfluity of Christ's sacrifice', time in purgatory would be remitted if repentance was sincere. 'Plenary indulgences' assuring full remission – direct entry into heaven for those dying truly repentant – could even be obtained from the pope. The practice started for Crusaders, and was gradually extended. In the fourteenth and fifteenth centuries people could petition for the privilege of receiving a plenary indulgence from their confessors at the time of death; 16 Scots, ranging from Robert earl of Fife down to a certain Simon Laverok of Dunkeld diocese, did so in 1379. Also, all who went to Rome during the periodic papal jubilees initiated in 1300 received plenary indulgences – including in 1450 the eighth earl of Douglas, Bishop Kennedy of St Andrews and their entourages. They could also be given for lesser pilgrimages associated with jubilees; the 1450 indulgence was offered to all (probably many thousands) who visited Glasgow cathedral during a four-month period.

But most indulgences were partial, remitting the time in purgatory deserved by a certain sin or equivalent to a certain length of earthly penance. These were issued, with papal licence, by all kinds of ecclesiastical authorities, who wished to encourage pilgrimages in order to gain offerings, generally for building work on churches, bridges and hospitals – hence the idea that indulgences were sold. These indulgences, while perhaps less common in Scotland than elsewhere, were nevertheless widely available. The Avignon pope Clement VII (1378–94), for instance, authorized them for three Scottish cathedrals, one collegiate church, two parish churches, two chapels, a hospital and a bridge. By the mid fifteenth century they were probably obtainable at most cathedrals, monasteries, collegiate and burgh churches, and at many parish churches too.

VIII

Masses for the dead, repeated prayers, pilgrimages and indulgences became so popular in the late Middle Ages that they swamped late-medieval religion. Part of the explanation for this was developments in theological fashions. To the early-medieval Church, God was a very harsh judge, but in the twelfth century He began to be seen as more loving and humane – and approachable through human reason. Was it therefore possible to deduce what He wanted, and so earn salvation? Thirteenth-century theologians – especially Duns Scotus – came close to answering yes. Their academic safeguards, moreover, probably disappeared as their views filtered down to the parochial level. Then in the fourteenth century there was a reaction. Increasingly it was argued that God was beyond fallible human reason and could only be approached through non-rational faith; it was this theology that Laurence of Lindores imposed on St Andrews University. The result was to emphasize God's incomprehensibility and awesomeness. This – particularly in the oversimplified forms which reached the people – encouraged devotions to more approachable figures like Christ, the Virgin Mary and the saints; it strengthened belief in supernatural agency in human affairs; and, especially, it added great uncertainty to the idea that salvation could be earned – God wanted something from humans, but what? The consequence must have been to stimulate greatly the mechanical, often neurotic, repetition of prayers and masses, and the acquisition of indulgences.

The growth of theological uncertainty coincided with the devastations of plague, which seemed inexplicable except as divine punishments. Plague intensified anxiety about death and the afterlife; the 'dance of death' (carved at Roslin church) became a common European motif. Moreover, the new theology blurred the dividing-line between orthodox religion and magic. The Church was aware of the danger; there were fears that the phrases of the mass would be used as spells. Also, Scottish church statutes required fonts to be covered, to preserve holy water from blasphemous use. Yet it was impossible to deny that holy water had supernatural powers – that if applied with appropriate prayers, like those in the preface to an early-fifteenth-century Scots merchant's handbook, it would, for example, calm storms at sea. Nor, as Bower's case demonstrates, could what were probably popular rather than theological ideas about the power of the mass be rejected. The trends in orthodox belief encouraged the supernatural, magical side of religion.

But the main point is probably that, for the first time in the Middle Ages, the opportunity of significantly improving prospects after death had been brought within ordinary people's reach. Arranging masses for the dead and undertaking pilgrimages were not difficult, hearing masses and repeating prayers were extremely easy. Indulgences were readily obtainable; in the fourteenth century the papal fee for a plenary indulgence was about ten shillings sterling, and the offerings required for partial ones were presumably considerably less. The idea of paying for an indulgence has, of course, been roundly condemned since the sixteenth century – yet nowadays the principle of paying money fines for secular offences is common, while churches often have building funds. Also, whatever the theological objections, the late-medieval system was a great improvement on previous requirements of impossibly long harsh earthly penances before there was any likelihood even of avoiding damnation. Furthermore, whereas the effects of ordinary late-medieval people to improve their lot after death through financial offerings linked to indulgences are criticized, the efforts of earlier kings and magnates to do the same by founding monasteries and making spectacular grants of land are often praised as evidence of conspicuous piety; there is a curious snobbery here. At any rate, the circumstances make it hardly surprising that the apparatus associated with purgatory expanded so much in the late Middle Ages. It doubtless brought much spiritual comfort – evident, perhaps, in one of the *Auchinleck Chronicle's* references to the 1450 jubilee indulgence at Glasgow: in 1456 'thair decesit in glasqw master willam turnbull bischope of glascow That brocht haim the pardoun of it'.

If understood in these ways, late-medieval religion does not seem as bad as the reformers' attacks imply. And the grossest abuses, like the hawking of indulgences and spurious relics by 'pardoners', do not seem common in Scotland. Nevertheless, in Scotland as elsewhere, the mechanical attitude to religion which the system stimulated was clearly excessive. Furthermore, theological niceties like the distinction between offering and indulgence were presumably not widely appreciated; most people would have seen nothing wrong with 'buying indulgences'. Thus the spiritual comfort brought by the religious system may generally have been for the wrong reasons.

The sixteenth-century reformers' attacks are therefore understandable. But they were not, initially, part of any widespread opposition; it was the popularity of indulgences that provoked Martin Luther. Demands for reform were, however, symptomatic of a movement among the minority who took their religion especially seriously. Such people would have suffered agonies from the principle that the religious apparatus only worked effectively if sins were *truly* repented; was their repentance sincere enough? Similarly, purgatory could only be alleviated for souls which were not already damned; would their souls escape that dreadful fate? Difficulties raised by awkward consciences could not be solved by repeating mechanistic observances *ad infinitum*. Instead, the late Middle Ages saw a growth of conscientious introspective lay devotion, especially among landowners and the urban bourgeoisie, which tended to by-pass much of the Church's formal apparatus. In Scotland this is best exemplified by the religious poetry; 'The Contemplacioun of Synnaris', for instance, hardly mentions purgatory, and emphasizes hell and individual consciences. Because of this trend it has been argued that 'the Reformation came not so much because Europe was irreligious as because it was religious'.[5] What happened to the late-medieval Church was that, while catering for the majority who were probably perfunctory about religion, it stimulated the evolution of a devout minority with which it fell out of step.

Yet was that characteristic of the entire late-medieval period in Scotland? There were no doubt many tender consciences. One early-fifteenth-century example is Thomas of Pethearn, a layman from Brechin diocese. Having unsuccessfully attempted a pilgrimage to Jerusalem, in 1417 he was absolved from his vow to go there. But, 'having a scrupulous conscience', he tried again in 1431, and again failed. Therefore he petitioned the pope for a confessor to absolve him from further fulfilment of the vow. We may doubt whether his conscience was satisfied – but the main point is his use of the orthodox religious system of the time.

In general, indeed, there is little evidence of any Scottish reaction against that system – certainly not on the scale of English Lollardy, which rejected most of the ecclesiastical machinery. Admittedly Lollardy reached early-fifteenth-century Scotland. Bower wrote that an English Lollard, James Resby, gained 'great fame by preaching to the simple folk', and 'his conclusions are still held by some Lollards in Scotland' (in the 1440s). Also, the threat of heresy was taken seriously. On becoming lieutenant of Scotland

[5] O. Chadwick, *The Reformation* (London, 1964), p. 22; applied to Scotland by J. Wormald, *Court, Kirk and Community* (London, 1981), p. 86.

in 1399, the duke of Rothesay swore to 'restregne' heretics; the duke of Albany 'All lollard hatyt . . . and heretike' (Wyntoun); and in 1425 parliament ordered the bishops to conduct inquisitions and punish 'heretikis and lollardis', with secular help if necessary. Nevertheless, although the inquisitor of heretical pravity, Laurence of Lindores, 'never gave rest to heretics' (Bower), there was no wave of persecutions. Resby was burned in 1407 and a Bohemian who preached the Hussite version suffered the same fate in 1433, but those are the only certain executions. Perhaps Scottish Lollards recanted when challenged; the fact that the two burnings were of foreign 'missionaries' suggests that, and implies that Lollardy was given little chance to spread. John Knox's *History*, 150 years later, also shows that Scottish Lollardy was not extensive; after 1433, he stated, 'we find small question of religion moved within this realm', until 1494, when some 30 Ayrshire Lollards were accused by the bishop of Glasgow. It is unclear whether that indicates the survival of Lollardy or a fresh outbreak. In either case, the point is that the only example of an important group of Scottish Lollards comes from very late in the fifteenth century.

One major feature of Lollardy was its emphasis on reading the Bible in English. Another reason for its lack of impact in Scotland, therefore, might be the relatively slow spread of lay literacy suggested above. This has a wider significance, because the new introspective lay devotion of the late Middle Ages (which did not challenge the Church's authority, although it attached little importance to much of the apparatus) also involved reading and meditating on religious texts. Now in Scottish literature, evidence of this introspective devotional trend appears only towards the end of the fifteenth century; before then, religious passages, by for instance Wyntoun and Bower, are extremely conventional. That contrasts strongly with England, where the new devotional approach is found in fourteenth-century writing, and with the Continent, where a steady expansion of introspective lay piety occurred throughout the fifteenth century, in conjunction with a spread of literacy which in the mid-century stimulated the invention of the printing press. In Scotland, where there was little demand for printing until the sixteenth century, the implication is that the new devotional attitudes were a later phenomenon. Probably, therefore, any serious reaction against the conventional late-medieval religion presented by the Scots Church should not be looked for until the end of the fifteenth century at the earliest.

IX

'Love the Lord your God with all your heart, . . . and your neighbour as yourself'. If the late-medieval Church made God difficult to love, it had greater success with the second part of the Christian message. The suggestion has, indeed, been made that during the Middle Ages there was a general belief that 'sinful' actions were condemned by God not because they were morally wrong but because they damaged good neighbourliness within a community. Adultery, for instance, was perhaps a sin not so much for sexual reasons but because it might cause a feud between husband and lover.

The hypothesis is persuasive. The Church emphasized that restitution had to be made to the victim of a sinful act before divine forgiveness could be hoped for; without restitution repentance was not sincere. Also, arbitrating in disputes or feuds within the parish community was widely understood as one of the priest's main tasks. This function was ritualized by the introduction into the mass of the congregation's collective kiss of peace, represented from the thirteenth century by the symbolic kissing of the paxboard. As with penance, this combined social and religious aspects: the mass could hardly establish peace with God if the members of the congregation were not at peace with one another. Kissing the paxboard was apparently a vital part of the weekly church services and an essential prerequisite for participation in the Easter communion – which in this context can be described as a solemn religious affirmation of community togetherness.

Do these points apply to late-medieval Scotland? As we shall see (chap. 6:iv), restitution was a particularly prominent feature of the Scottish judicial system, and so its religious significance was presumably widely appreciated too. Similarly, the early-sixteenth-century Lothian court records indicate that the church courts' main function was settling disputes (over debts, contracts and wills) rather than ecclesiastical censure; they met a popular demand, for ordinary people initiated most of the cases. Outside the courts, the Church's integration into Scotland's 'formalized bloodfeud' system of community justice is demonstrated in items like the papal authority granted to the chancellor of Dunblane cathedral in 1380 for dispensing 20 men and women from the rules concerning consanguinity, 'so that by arranging marriages between the contesting families an end may be put to the feuds, murders and factions existing in those parts'. There is a case in 1438 of the Church helping end a feud through an arrangement for the killer's son to marry the victim's daughter!

Moreover, the idea of settling feud between God and man through the mass must have been apposite in Scotland, where ritualized secular feud was common. Henryson's imagery – 'O king most high, now pacify thy feud' – is striking. The concept that all who took communion, or even attended masses, should be in a state of peace with each other, would also have been powerful. The existence of paxboards in Scottish churches shows the collective kiss of peace was practised. Evidence of its importance comes from the island of Eigg, in 1625: a Franciscan missionary was trying to reintroduce Catholic worship there, and an old woman who remembered pre-Reformation practices objected that he had not let her have the kiss of peace by circulating the paxboard. Also, diocesan statutes forbade the kiss of peace to priests' concubines, who were to be ostracized symbolically from the local Christian community and disqualified from receiving God's peace through the mass. The implication is that other members of parish communities who were not at peace would be similarly excluded from God's peace. This added a powerful religious element to the mechanisms upholding community justice.

Thus the social side of medieval Christianity must surely have been very important in Scotland. The argument can, tentatively, be taken further. The sense of collective Christianity was perhaps especially strong in medieval Scotland, because of the importance there of kinship, the frequent correspondence of parish, community and unit of lordship, and the ways in which the religious and secular machineries for settling disputes fitted together. And if at the parochial level the late-medieval Scots Church was very close to the local communities, that possibly helps explain why refusal to pay teinds does not seem very common, why Lollardy did not spread significantly, and why the newer, individualistic devotional trend was slow to appear in Scotland.

Moreover, despite the sweeping changes of the mid sixteenth century, the post-Reformation Scottish Church strengthened its social integration within the local communities. This can be seen in the parishes' 'kirk sessions' and in the parochial organization of the new poor law and education system. Continuity is visible, too, in the Reformed communion service. Although that differed from the mass in many ways, it retained the traditional sense of collectiveness in the communal singing of psalms, in the liturgy's portrayal of the service as a communal feast, and in the sharing of the consecrated bread and wine (especially when taken from a common cup, which perhaps compensated for the reformers' abolition of the paxboard). Also, most significantly, the pre-Reformation practice of taking communion very infrequently, after solemn preparation, continued. As a social ritual, therefore, the yearly or at most six-monthly 'Lord's Supper' was probably not very different from the Easter Mass which preceded it.

This is particularly significant in view of developments elsewhere. In Catholic worship, the trend towards individualistic religion diluted the sense of community togetherness; the kiss of peace was discontinued, the private confessional box was invented, and individuals were encouraged to take communion as frequently as they wished, making it more a personal than a community practice. Much the same happened in Protestant Churches, apparently against the initial intentions of the reformers. Lutheran and Anglican communions became individualized and frequent, while in most Calvinist Churches they were simply periodic extensions to the preaching of God's word.

Thus the Reformed Scottish Church appears exceptional in the degree to which it maintained the collective social ritual of the medieval Easter mass. It did so because its communion service was special, infrequent, and used a dramatic liturgy[6] – factors making it an extremely solemn occasion for the whole parish community. The reasons for this could lie simply with the leading Scots reformers. But they, in other respects, did not exhibit the traditional Scottish sense of community. As was common in sixteenth-century Europe, they saw sin as a moral rather than an anti-social offence, and they demanded punishment rather than compensation for crimes. Also, most significantly, they intended communion services to be more frequent: monthly in the burghs and at least quarterly in the countryside. Their failure to achieve this frequency seems to indicate that the local communities insisted, so far as they could, on retaining their traditional practices. The implication is, therefore, that the collective spirit of the Reformed Scots communion service really derived from the strength of local community consciousness in late-medieval Scotland.

[6] Y. Brilioth, *Eucharistic Faith and Practice, Evangelical and Catholic* (London, 1930), pp. 187–9.

The argument, as has been said, is tentative; whether it could be fully proved is doubtful. But if it is valid, its relevance extends beyond the fifteenth and sixteenth centuries. The Reformed Scots communion service has survived, with modifications but without fundamental change, until the present day. In 1917 the similarity between the medieval Church's annual communion and the contemporary Church of Scotland's 'Sacrament Sunday' was stressed in the seminal study of late-medieval English popular religion.[7] In rural Scotland, especially the north, the comparison still applied in the middle of this century. And, although modern congregations cannot be said to correspond to their local communities, nevertheless an intense feeling of collective togetherness is still evoked by the Church of Scotland's communion ritual. In this, it may be suggested, we have an echo of the world of medieval Scotland – an echo of that powerful sense of local community within the national framework that was such a prominent feature of late-medieval Scottish history.

[7]B.L. Manning, *The People's Faith in the Time of Wyclif* (Cambridge, 1917), p. 63.

5

The Nobility

Medieval society's other special group was of course the nobility. That, however, is a surprisingly elusive concept, and despite the obvious prominence of 'the nobles' in Scottish history, the late-medieval Scottish nobility is much harder to define than the churchmen. The first thing to stress is that our modern British concept, equating nobles with parliamentary peerage, does not apply. There was no Scottish peerage until the mid fifteenth century, and even after then the Scottish nobility clearly contained many individuals who were not peers of parliament. The Scottish concept of nobility, therefore, was probably akin to the Continental one, which included those who in England would be called gentry and in Scotland lairds.

What was the Scottish dividing-line between nobles and non-nobles? Contemporaries probably thought in terms of noble birth – as in the anti-English joke related by Bower (see chap. 2:viii) – and the right to bear coats-of-arms, but in practice these ideas were too vague to be helpful in defining the nobility. Nor is the distinctive feature of Continental nobility, exemption from war taxation (because nobles were expected to fight personally) applicable here, for war taxation never developed in Scotland. Indeed the only clear-cut division between ordinary people and their social betters is the tenurial one between the mass of the peasantry who rented land from year to year, and the freeholders, who had security of tenure and generally held their land in perpetuity. Now since, in this context, free means privileged or honourable, and since all obvious nobles were freeholders, there is at least a case for equating the late-medieval Scottish nobility with the freeholders, at least at its widest. This issue requires further research, but certainly no better cut-off point is evident higher up the Scottish social scale.

The difficulty of definition is itself significant. The absence of such a clear division within the landowning class as in England (where the parliamentary peerage developed earlier and took over the concept of nobility) probably helped inhibit the growth among the lairds of the strong, even aggressive, self-consciousness visible among the English gentry, both nationally in the House of Commons and locally in the shire communities. Scots lairds could be just as assertive individually as English gentlemen, but did not exhibit the same collective sense of identity. Similarly because there was not the same division between nobles and non-nobles as in France (where tax-exemption privileges meant entrance to the nobility became more strictly regulated), Scottish nobles' sense of social supremacy was less institutionalized – especially the idea of their status as the exclusive military élite, an important cause of social tension in France. Although late-medieval Scottish society was not totally fluid, class-consciousness was probably relatively slight, while upward social mobility, depending on the acquisition of freeholdings and open to anyone with sufficient wealth, would have been fairly straightforward. The only real social barriers seem to have been economic ones.

Even with this extremely wide definition, the Scottish nobility was still only a small proportion of the population. Countless surviving charters give the impression that most of Scotland's thousand or so parishes contained at least one and often several families of freeholders. Therefore we can probably think in terms of around 2,000 heads of families, or some 10,000 nobles: probably little more than 1 per cent of the pre-plague population. This very rough estimate corresponds with figures for early-fourteenth-century France, where the nobility appears to have been between 1 and $1\frac{1}{2}$ per cent of the population. It also fits well with the fact that in August 1296 Edward I's officials recorded homages from some 1,500 Scottish landowners. Their list is not exhaustive – its most famous omission is William Wallace – but it probably gives a reasonable idea of the Scottish 'upper class' at that time. Thereafter the Scottish nobility presumably shrank and grew again following the general demographic trends; but unfortunately there is no data for estimating its size satisfactorily until the later sixteenth century.

Of this noble body, the vast majority were insignificant as individuals. The laymen who mattered in national affairs – the magnates or higher nobility – usually numbered around 50: for instance 48 are named in the Declaration of Arbroath,[1] 56 are listed as doing personal homage at Robert II's coronation in 1371, and 44 belonged to the peerage at the end of James II's reign. Beyond these, it is likely that there were only a few hundred substantial lairds with any great local importance. The rest of the Scottish nobility would simply have consisted of petty country gentry – 'bonnet lairds' is an apt later term – who often had no more land than wealthy peasants. These were the poorer gentlemen who just had to be armed 'at thare gudly power', according to 1426 legislation. Little wonder that well-off husbandmen probably had more in common with these small lairds than with cottars and rural labourers. Collectively, however, the small lairds, like the husbandmen, made a great contribution to the cause of Scottish independence – as the long English lists of forfeited freeholdings demonstrate. And despite their individual insignificance, they also provided the core of the followings essential to magnate power. The great nobles, on whom so much Scottish history focuses, could never have had the importance they had without the lesser nobility behind them.

II

At the top of noble society, one striking feature was the survival into the late Middle Ages of the earldoms and 'provincial lordships' of earlier medieval Scotland. There were 29 of these in Robert I's reign, ranging from Caithness in the north to Annandale in the south, and from Mar in the east to the Isles in the west (see map, p. vii); 14 carried the special status of earldom. In the late 1320s they belonged to 13 earls and five 'provincial lords' (the greatest magnates, Thomas Randolph, James Douglas and Robert Stewart each had several, while three were in crown hands). They all covered huge stretches of territory, containing hundreds of square miles and (as their names indicate) corresponding to provinces of the country; within them their earls and lords virtually acted as provincial rulers. Generally they dated back to the eleventh and twelfth centuries, and in some cases beyond, but perhaps the most typical

[1] Thirty-nine in the text, another nine on seals or seal-tags; see A.A.M. Duncan, *The Nation of Scots and the Declaration of Arbroath* (Historical Association pamphlet, 1970), p. 34.

was the earldom of Moray, created in 1312 for Thomas Randolph out of the shires of Moray, Nairn and Inverness, and held with full vice-regal powers. That creation, and the fact that nearly every earldom and lordship that came into the king's possession was granted out again, demonstrate that the continuation (and perhaps reinvigoration) of this centuries-old territorial pattern was the deliberate, conservative policy of Robert I – himself formerly earl of Carrick, lord of Annandale and part of Garioch.

The pattern of earldoms and lordships lasted throughout the fourteenth century, although there was considerable turnover in ownership. Well before 1400, however, the beginnings of change can be seen. In an increasing number of earldoms the association between the provinces and the lands actually held or supervised by the earl was dissolving. An act of 1401 institutionalized this by stating that whenever earldoms or lordships came into crown hands, any baronies within them must in future be held directly of the crown. And when two new earldoms were created – Douglas for William lord of Douglas in 1358 and Crawford for David Lindsay of Glenesk in 1398 – each was merely a personal promotion in rank, with no 'provincial' connotations (except that Douglas possessed several 'provincial lordships'). The same is true of the dukedoms of Rothesay and Albany, also created in 1398 for Robert III's son and brother. Honorific dignities – as the rank of earl had been in England for centuries – had appeared in Scotland.

There was also a trend towards the accumulation of territory. The Stewart possessions grew most, especially after Robert II became king. In the 1390s 12 earldoms and lordships were held by members of the royal family. This build-up of territory was unequalled, but the Douglases and Dunbars were also following suit. The result was the concentration of earldoms and lordships in the hands of fewer magnate families: 31 were now shared among 15 magnates from 10 different families – with the Stewarts, Douglases and Dunbars having 22 of them. Moreover, only three provincial lordships were held independently of earldoms.

Fifty years later the top of noble society appears radically different. The families which had accumulated most fell foul of either James I or James II, and their lands were forfeited. Several other earldoms and lordships reverted to the crown through natural causes. In a reversal of fourteenth-century royal policy, James I and James II mostly kept possession of territory which came into the crown's hands (doubtless for fiscal reasons, following the fall in customs revenues). So by 1455 – after the great Douglas forfeiture – the crown held no fewer than nine of the old 'provincial' earldoms and eight of the lordships.

Thereafter, although James II granted some out again, especially to his young sons, the former pattern was never recreated. In the 1460s there were only five 'provincial' earls or lords of the old type: the earl of Angus (who had part of Angus plus Liddesdale and Jedburgh lordships), the lord of the Isles (also earl of Ross), the earl of Sutherland, the earl of Atholl (James II's half-brother, given the earldom in *c*.1452), and the earl of Huntly (who although a new – 1445 – honorific creation, had the lordships of Strathbogie and Badenoch). Moreover five new personal earldoms had been created by James II: Errol for Lord Hay, Morton for Lord Douglas of Dalkeith, Rothes for Lord Leslie, Argyll for Lord Campbell, and Marischal for Lord Keith. All, like Crawford, were honorific dignities – especially Marischal, where the title derived from an office. The top of late-medieval Scottish society had been completely restructured.

III

The dukes, earls and 'provincial lords' were not the only nobles prominent in Scotland's national affairs. Throughout the period, some 20 or 30 others were also always important enough to count within the higher nobility. When the Scottish peerage emerged in the 1440s, these were the lords of parliament – the peerage's bottom rank. Like English parliamentary barons, whom they copied, lords of parliament had special titles (William Lord Hay rather than William Hay lord of Errol) and the right to personal summonses to parliament. Thereafter the Scottish higher nobility is an institutionalized, easily identifiable group: the 'lords' as opposed to the 'lairds'.

Earlier, however, it is much harder to identify this part of the higher nobility. The problem arises over the term 'baron'. In the earlier Middle Ages it meant an important lord, and 'the baronage' could be equated with the higher nobility – as remained so in England. But in Scotland 'baron' evolved differently. In the twelfth and thirteenth centuries, important lords possessed many 'multiple estates' – the basic units of Scottish landlordship above the individual toun, roughly equivalent to parishes (see chap. 3:ii) –

and these apparently came to be called baronies. Moreover barons had special powers; being important lords, close to the king, they were trusted to have criminals caught and dealt with on their estates. This jurisdiction, over theft, assault, and accidental homicide, became known as 'baronial jurisdiction', and probably spread to most baronies. Robert I developed the concept further, restricting baronial jurisdiction to estates which the crown permitted to be held 'in free (privileged) barony'. That reduced the number of baronies, but there were over 200 at the end of his reign, and subsequent grants of baronial privileges – a useful form of crown patronage, giving status and a significant boost to seignorial revenues – increased their number to over 350 in the later fourteenth century and over 1,000 (more fragmented ones) in the sixteenth. These baronies were shared among many nobles – more than 100 in the fourteenth century – who, since they held free baronies with baronial powers, were known as barons.

By the fourteenth century, therefore, baron was a tenurial, not a personal, concept, extending far beyond the higher nobility. Most barons were local lairds. Some, however, who possessed several baronies or were prominent in other ways, were important nationally and must be counted within the higher nobility. But there is no obvious dividing-line between these – whom we can call 'greater barons' – and the rest. As with the nobility as a whole, this in itself is significant. Ambitious nobles could easily enter at least the 'second division' of the higher nobility – as John Lyon (ancestor of Queen Elizabeth the queen-mother) did spectacularly, rising from king's clerk in the late 1360s to be chamberlain of Scotland, lord of five baronies, and husband of one of Robert II's daughters, before being murdered, perhaps by a jealous rival, in 1382. Conversely, once-prominent families could sink out of the second division – as happened with the descendants of Robert Lauder of the Bass or William Dishington of Ardross, close councillors of Robert I and David II respectively.

Compared with the earls and 'provincial lords', the territory held by 'greater barons' was not impressive; John Lyon probably had more than most. The Setons and Hays (both prominent throughout the period) appear more typical. The Setons' ancestral lands were the baronies of Seton in East and Winchburgh in West Lothian. Robert I granted Alexander Seton (whose career is outlined in chapter 1:ix) several territories, including Tranent, Elphinstone and 'the Barns' beside Haddington as baronies; but

Seton, Tranent and Elphinstone were all in Seton parish, and at most his lands seem the equivalent of two or three parishes. His descendants made no more substantial acquisitions during the late Middle Ages. The chief estates of Gilbert Hay, Robert I's constable, were his ancestral barony of Errol in Perthshire and the Aberdeenshire barony of Slains, granted by Robert I; Errol probably covered two parishes, Slains one. His descendants added the barony of Caputh, near Dunkeld, and in 1415 bought the former thanage of Cowie in Kincardineshire; even so, these four baronies were not a huge estate.

The only 'greater barons' to acquire significantly more were David Lindsay of Glenesk and James Douglas of Dalkeith, who in the later fourteenth century amassed complexes of a dozen or so baronies through inheritances and personal acquisition; these, though scattered over the country, probably did approach the earldoms in area, and Lindsay became earl of Crawford in 1398. But they were exceptional. In the early fourteenth century many of those who can reasonably be counted as 'greater barons' only had one or two baronies. At the end of the century, three or four baronies seem the norm, although some important men had less. This remains much the same in the mid fifteenth century, when the 'greater barons' became lords of parliament: James Hamilton's main estates, erected into the 'lordship of parliament of Hamilton' in 1445, consisted of the baronies of Cadzow and Machan in Lanarkshire, and Kinneil in West Lothian.

Lord Hamilton's three baronies had been granted to his forefather Walter, son of Gilbert (who had changed sides advantageously after Bannockburn), by Robert I. That is typical of the 20 or so early lords of parliament. Most headed long-established families, like Douglas of Dalkeith, Lyon, and Erskine, whose prominence went back to the mid fourteenth century; at least a dozen were descendants of leading barons in Robert I's reign; and five – Lords Hay, Keith, Graham, Seton, and Somerville – were from families important even in the twelfth century.

Why, then, did the new rank emerge? In the highly status-conscious fifteenth century, barons who were the greatest nobles below the dukes and earls, who were accustomed to having a voice in parliaments, and who doubtless equated themselves with the English parliamentary barons, presumably wanted some means of distinguishing themselves from the lesser landowners who were barons too. The English usage of baron was unsuitable, so the term lord of parliament was employed instead. The pressure went back to the 1410s, when peerage-type titles occur, but intensified after 1437, because by then the disappearance of so many earls had left both a political and a social vacuum. In the 1440s the greater barons included all but a handful of the most important nobles. Hardly surprisingly, their virtual takeover of the higher nobility was followed by the establishment of the new rank.

Thus the lords of parliament did not so much rise into the peerage as remain within the higher nobility while those above them disappeared. They were not a new nobility. But these developments made the top of Scottish noble society look very different. Compared with the old earls and provincial lords, most mid-fifteenth-century magnates were not such great landowners. And when James II promoted some lords of parliament to the rank of earl without giving them much extra land, the higher nobility's transformation was complete. Thenceforward it was a relatively homogeneous body, containing few really large landowners. The earls were no longer significantly different from the others; in early-modern Scotland, indeed, there were several with less power and influence than neighbouring lords of parliament.

IV

Late-medieval noble estates were normally heritable. With luck, they would pass to their owners' sons; but sons can never be guaranteed. Among the late-medieval French and English nobilities father son succession was remarkably precarious, with noble families dying out in the direct male line on average once every three or four generations, and few surviving much beyond a century. Failing sons the estates might go to daughters – generally being partitioned when a father left two or more – and thence to their husbands, usually themselves landowners. Or if the increasingly common entails to male heirs applied, brothers, cousins or more distant collaterals would inherit; again they would often be landowners already. Sometimes, when there were no heirs, estates reverted to the overlord or the crown. Over several generations, therefore, family territory was likely to be either dispersed, or (if it survived) to be enlarged by inheritance through entails or through marriages to heiresses. This is obviously important for the history of noble societies; inheritance patterns, indeed, were as influential as royal policies.

The most spectacular Scottish example of the process is the complicated build-up of the vast Douglas territories. The duke of Albany's earldoms of Fife and Menteith also came from heiresses; and both entails and heiresses helped. produce the estates of the Lindsays, earls of Crawford. Among the earls as a whole, the French and English pattern of extinction is repeated almost exactly. In 1300 there were 13 families of earls; 43 more appeared between then and 1469;[2] but in 1469 there were only 19, mostly James II's creations. In this period, every 25-year generation except one saw at least a quarter of the families fail in the direct male line; the failure rate was as high as 47 per cent in 1350–74.

The difficulty of definition makes the other magnates harder to analyse. But for the 1320s, the names in the Declaration of Arbroath plus those of other obviously important nobles give a list of 42 families: by 1350 14 had died out in the direct male line. And for the 1350s and 1360s 47 important families (those surviving from the 1320s, their successors, and others which were prominent then) can be examined: 13 had died out by 1400. Although more detailed study is needed, in the fourteenth century the rest of the Scottish higher nobility apparently conforms to the general pattern too.

Conversely, 16 – over a third – of the important baronial families of the 1320s survived beyond 1469 in direct father–son succession. Such survival is much less common elsewhere. And even more remarkably, out of the leading 40 baronial families of early-fifteenth-century Scotland (those which had peerages by 1450, plus others which were prominent earlier in the century), no fewer than 28 survived the entire fifteenth century in the direct male line, while 18 survived past 1600. That completely contradicts the experience of the English and French late-medieval nobilities.

One reason might be that the chances of untimely death were smaller for Scotland's fifteenth-century nobles. There was little civil war after 1340, and the wars with England slackened off, whereas in England and France civil and international war intensified; plague perhaps receded more quickly in Scotland too. The longer a noble lived, the more sons he could beget (though his wife's age obviously mattered too). Certainly longevity is another marked feature of the late-medieval Scottish nobility. The earls (for whom

[2]Following the guidelines in K.B. McFarlane, *The Nobility of Late Medieval England* (Oxford, 1973), p. 172, inheritance through an entail (as with the 3rd earl of Douglas) is counted as the appearance of a new family.

there is most evidence) lived on average to around 50; many nobles passed 70, and over a dozen reached 80 – including three successive earls of March. Also, since Scotland was less urbanized, nobles would have spent little time in the unhealthy conditions of large towns. Yet why did the barons' demographic pattern differ so much from the earls'? It is not simply a question of the latter's political vulnerability; for instance Duncan earl of Lennox was over 80 when he was executed in 1425, but only left two daughters. The explanation for the striking demographic resilience of the greater barons' families remains unclear; but it is an extremely important aspect of late-medieval Scottish noble society.

It meant that, despite the nobility's general fluidity, there was an increasingly large core of families who were continuously prominent. These, of course, have been encountered several times already: the Lindsays, Hays, Keiths, Setons, Hamiltons, Erskines, and so on. They were a major part of the 'Bruce establishment' of the 1320s, they made up the bulk of the greater barons of the fourteenth and early fifteenth centuries, they dominated the new peerage, and for hundreds of years after the 1450s their names reverberated through Scotland's history.

These remarkably durable families, moreover, produced not only heirs but a multiplicity of sons. Many greater barons of the later part of the period had several each, and many of their younger sons established lasting families of their own. But that is not true of the entire period. It seems that in the mid fourteenth century the greater barons were not, collectively, producing enough sons to replace themselves; only in the 1380s did male replacement rates apparently become positive. That suggests that the numerous cadet branches of the leading families of late-fifteenth-century Scotland were a relatively new phenomenon; certainly it is difficult to find anything similar in earlier centuries. This doubtless helps to explain the prominence of magnates' surname or kinship groups in the later fifteenth century.

The important families also had daughters. But because so many sons were produced, heiresses – very important in other medieval societies – are rare at this level of the Scottish nobility, especially in the fifteenth century. And since the greater barons generally intermarried, they rarely married heiresses; among the top 40 baronial families of the early fifteenth century, there are only six instances of marriages to significant heiresses during the entire century. Similarly, although most Scottish magnate families established entails to male heirs, these seldom needed to come into operation. Therefore among the greater barons, particularly after about 1400, accumulation and dispersal of territory were much less striking than among their English counterparts, or indeed among their Scottish predecessors. Also there was less occasion for property disputes (frequent in England) arising out of such indirect inheritances. These can be found – for instance over the Douglas inheritance in 1388, or in 1369 when James Douglas of Dalkeith and Thomas Erskine fought a judicial duel – but they seem at least relatively uncommon in late-medieval Scotland.

V

What happened to noble finances in late-medieval Scotland? This question is particularly hard to answer, since the available sources are scantier than for other aspects of noble society. Scottish medieval landlords did not preserve old estate records, perhaps because of the system of short, variable leases. In general, however, we have already seen that late-medieval trends were unfavourable to landlords; the most striking evidence is the near halving of national land valuations in 1366. Thereafter, although rents and valuations rose, they probably lagged behind inflation, especially in the fifteenth century. The brief boom in wool and leather exports would only have given temporary compensation from landlords' flocks and herds. Only in seignorial dues, particularly those involved in baronies, may there have been growth: the amount of land held in free barony expanded steadily during the period, and also several magnates received grants of regality, giving them jurisdiction over major crimes, and thus the fines and forfeitures from the criminals.

It has however been demonstrated for England that similar financial pressures were countered in various ways: through accumulating larger estates, as more territory came into fewer hands; through obtaining a share of royal revenues in annuities or other forms of patronage; and through war profits, in wages, ransoms, booty, and conquered lands. All these points applied in Scotland, but to a lesser extent. First, the Scottish inheritance patterns meant that large-scale accumulations of territory were less common, especially in the fifteenth century. Secondly, the Scottish crown could not provide great subsidies. Annuities were granted, particularly by Robert II and Robert III, but the peak of £1,300 paid to the nobility in the early 1400s hardly compares with the £30,000 then being paid by Henry IV of England. Little more than a quarter of the higher nobility enjoyed annuities; these varied from £13 to £340 (a brief, exceptional case), but generally were around £40–£50 – useful, but not huge, amounts. And many annuities were cancelled in the fifteenth century. The only other significant diversion of royal revenue was in the 1410s, when the earl of Douglas and his followers took large sums from the customs. Thirdly, Scots nobles had no opportunities for embezzlement, because Scots armies were unpaid; they suffered as much as gained from cross-border raiding; the balance of ransoms probably went against them; and there was no territory to be conquered.

The late-medieval economic contraction ought therefore to have affected Scottish nobles relatively badly. This is supported by evidence that they did not have large amounts of cash at their disposal; big payments were made by instalments, and occasionally magnates had to sell land to meet demands such as their reliefs (death, or inheritance, duties). On the other hand, only one or two magnates ever sold out altogether; sales of land were invariably to other magnates; and contemporary mortgages show greater nobles lending money to lesser ones. At the top of noble society examples of impoverishment are balanced by examples of wealth.

Moreover between about 1380 and 1500 – just the period of apparent financial pressure – there was a building boom. Almost every family of any importance had money to spend on their residences. Mostly they built tower-houses. These generally appear stark, even primitive, nowadays, and are sometimes taken to indicate their builders' poverty. But the starkest is probably Threave in Galloway, built by Archibald 'the Grim', third earl of Douglas; since he was rich enough to build what he liked, Threave's style was obviously not dictated by cost. The same is also true of the tower-houses constructed by David II at Edinburgh and Robert II at Dundonald in Ayrshire. The style was perhaps influenced by the realization that large curtain-wall castles were undesirable during Anglo-Scottish wars; they tended to be taken over by English forces, and were usually slighted on their recapture. Tower-houses were also relatively comfortable – certainly warmer, for the lord's apartments were above the main hall and fireplace. And most were splendid when inhabited, as those which have survived in something close to their original states, like Neidpath near Peebles or the highly sophisticated Borthwick near Dalkeith, demonstrate. No figures are available for the cost of noble tower-houses, but 'David's Tower' at Edinburgh castle cost £758 between 1367 and 1383 – under £50 a year – which was probably reasonably typical, and also quite within the means of many nobles.

What the nobility wanted from castles was prestige, comfort, and somewhere 'for the safe-keeping of his people and his goods', as William Keith the marischal stated in 1394 when building Dunnottar, near Stonehaven: functions the tower-houses fulfilled well. The possessions kept in them certainly needed safe-keeping. The will of James Douglas of Dalkeith, dated 1392, shows what a leading noble would have had. The bequests included: four sets of armour (the rest were to stay in the new Dalkeith castle), three jewelled gold clasps, two gold circlets, a gold collar, four gilt belts, several brooches and other jewels, eight rings, a cross made from the True Cross, a gilt reliquary containing St Mary Magdalene's hair, many silver and gilt utensils, including his best gilt cup weighing 18 lb. troy, a large quantity of cloth-of-gold, silk and fur clothing, and his books of the statutes of Scotland, romances, grammar and logic. The total was worth £1,559. Whatever the economic trends, James Douglas clearly lived in considerable splendour.

James Douglas of Dalkeith is also one of two magnates for whom financial details have survived: the value of the 1376–7 rental (see chap. 3:iii), which covered roughly half his estates, was £483, suggesting a total income from rents of over £900. David earl of Strathearn, Robert II's fourth son, is the other: in 1380 Strathearn's rents came to £273. It also appears that the earldom of Mar and lordship of Garioch were together worth between £1,000 and £1,300. To put the figures in perspective, an earl's minimum yearly income in fourteenth-century England was reckoned at 1,000 marks, or £667, sterling. While the Strathearn rents were much less (though Earl David had other income), the revenues of the lord of Dalkeith and the earl of Mar were both above that minimum.

There is one other set of figures, for James I's hostages. The 1423–4 negotiations give incomes for 35 nobles: six earls, 14 from families which had peerages by 1450, and 15 others. The earls' incomes average around 850 marks, the future peers' 770, and the others' 400. Unfortunately, some assessments are much less plausible than others. Moreover, are they in sterling (they come from English documents, and the ransom was in sterling) or Scots money, worth only half sterling? Either currency causes problems. And do they denote rents, Scottish 'extents' or valuations, or total incomes? If they are taken at face-value and assumed to be in sterling, they correspond quite well with the 1436 income-tax returns for 51 English peers, which average £768: the Scottish magnates have about a third less, which seems reasonable. But whether that is a safe conclusion remains unclear.

Since, however, the assessments for Douglas of Dalkeith and Strathearn are 1,500 marks and 500 marks, both close to those from the 1376–80 rentals, perhaps the 1423–4 figures give a rough guide to incomes in the later fourteenth century, before currency debasement complicated matters. At that period £10 a year appears a comfortable income for ordinary people: so we can probably multiply the figures by 1,000 or more to gain some idea of modern equivalents. Most magnates can be seen as having, in modern terms, over £500,000 (tax-free) a year, while the greatest men like the Albanies and Douglases (not assessed in 1423–4) had many times more. The exercise is crude, but it helps demonstrate how very well off the Scottish magnates were compared with the rest of the population. And they continued to enjoy great wealth, irrespective of the economic trends, throughout the late Middle Ages.

VI

Whatever happened to incomes, one point remains constant: noble estates were generally held from landlords 'in feu and heredity and in perpetuity', for honourable obligations. This kind of landownership is nowadays described as 'feudal'. The king was the ultimate landlord. Those holding directly of him were 'tenants-in-chief'; their estates were divided into parts providing them with steady revenue (peasant holdings and demesnes) and parts held of them by other landowners as feudal sub-tenants. The latter's land might be similarly divided, and so on. Feudal tenants, in return, had to be faithful to their lord, give him good counsel, and warn him of dangers. In addition they owed either personal service, mostly military, or a sum of money (sometimes substantial, sometimes nominal: called 'feu-farm' and 'blench-farm') in lieu. Feudal tenure was thus not merely a system of landownership, but involved reciprocal relationships between lords and followers within the nobility. It helped provide local government, too: feudal landowners were entitled to hold courts for settling disputes between inhabitants of their lands, while the barons (almost always tenants-in-chief) had baronial powers of criminal jurisdiction and sometimes the vice-regal powers of regality.

Feudalism – as this form of social organization is usually called – was never a static system. It was merely one stage in a process of social evolution beginning long before and ending long after the 'classic' feudal period of the eleventh and twelfth centuries. The evolution differed greatly from country to country, depending on particular circumstances. For instance the administrative-jurisdictional side of feudal society survived much longer in Scotland – where baronies and 'regalities flourished – than in England. That is partly because Scottish kings and administrators (mostly barons themselves) did not feel threatened by seignorial jurisdiction, and so did not try to undermine it. But the main reason is probably medieval Scotland's relatively neat territorial pattern. Since most disputes were between neighbours and most crime was local, the common, if rough, equation of local community with parish and with barony meant that barony courts were able to deal with the majority of cases. The point applies particularly strongly to the provincial earldoms and lordships. In England, where the territorial pattern was infinitely more fragmented, seignorial jurisdiction could not operate so well, and gradually withered away.

The tenurial side of feudal society also evolved differently in Scotland. There was no equivalent to the English statute of *Quia Emptores* ('Whereas buyers . . .') of 1290, which severely restricted the creation of feudal subtenancies. By then English land grants were generally commercial transactions, maintaining the feudal form chiefly to give the vendor the right to the 'incidents' of feudal tenure like relief (inheritance duty) and wardship (when the lord took over the holding during the minority of an under-age heir). But when a tenant sold most of a holding, the overlord often could not assert *his* rights. Therefore after 1290 the purchaser of land had to replace the vendor as the overlord's tenant. Although to the magnates' economic advantage, that stopped them making typical feudal grants for service. In late-medieval Scotland, in contrast, the magnates had the best of both worlds. Scottish overlords were always entitled to vet their tenants' grants, and in the late Middle Ages they mostly insisted on the purchaser replacing the vendor. Yet they themselves continued to grant land in straightforward feudal tenure. Feudal subtenancies thus continued, but normally only at one level below the tenant-in-chief; this again may be linked to the survival of the fairly neat early-medieval territorial pattern.

Few late-medieval Scottish land grants, however, were specifically for knight-service and incidents; the majority merely stipulate 'service used and wont', which may or may not indicate knight-service. And many were for money renders, either feu-farm (common since the twelfth century) or more usually its variant blench-farm, in which a penny or a token (such as a pair of spurs) was rendered to denote superiority, while the knight-service and incidents were waived. Monetary feudal tenure eventually replaced tenure by military service altogether in Scotland, and proved so convenient that it remained until recently the standard way of holding land: subject-superiors and feu duties (modern equivalents of tenants-in-chief and feu-farms) were only abolished in 1976. Until then, strictly speaking, Scotland was a feudal country! Modern Scottish 'feudalism', of course, was merely a legal fiction within which a purely commercial conveyancing system operated. And that was largely true of the late Middle Ages too: most property transactions were probably sales, especially grants in blench-farm. In that respect Scotland was like England, although their conveyancing practices developed differently.

On the other hand, straightforward grants of land in return for service were still being made. Moreover several blench-farm grants were made to men described as the donor's knight or esquire; the specific knight-service and incidents were being waived, presumably as a favour, but the basic, imprecise obligations of general fidelity, service and counsel were still expected. One of the most 'feudal' grants of all in Scottish history was made in the late 1380s, when the second earl of Douglas gave his illegitimate son Drumlanrig, in feu and heredity and 'in blench-farm [*sic*], . . . by performing the service of one knight in [the earl's] army in place of all other obligations'. The fiscal part of feudal tenure is set aside; Douglas simply wanted personal service. This remarkable charter shows the flexibility of late-medieval Scottish tenurial practice – and also the difficulty of generalizing about it.

VII

Feudal tenure probably explains why earls' incomes seem little higher than greater barons' (above, section v). In Strathearn, for instance, the five Highland parishes west of Crieff produced as much rent as the 12 easterly, more Lowland ones; but the latter supported at least 15 feudal tenancies and land held by Dunblane cathedral and Inchaffray abbey. The other provincial earldoms and lordships had similar patterns. This originated in Scotland's early feudal period, when power and prestige were measured more through knightly followers than wealth. Nobles had always kept sufficient land to finance their splendid life-styles, but had used the surplus to endow their followings. Earls and provincial lords had naturally been able to create most sub-tenancies, either from scratch or by converting pre-feudal arrangements. That reduced their revenues to much the same level as the more important barons', but their regional power would not have been significantly affected, for feudal tenants had always had to acknowledge their overlords' superiority and jurisdiction. And while in the fourteenth century not all the landowners in earldoms and lordships counted as the straightforward followers of the earls and lords (two of the Strathearn tenants were the earl of Douglas and James Douglas of Dalkeith), that probably would still apply to the local lairds whose main estates lay within those earldoms or lordships.

The relationship, however, was not simply feudal. Past endowment of younger sons meant that earls and provincial lords often had kinship ties with local lairds. Intermarriage among local lairds often led to the construction of large kinship groups focused on the earls and lords. These may have been reinforced by concepts stemming from pre-feudal, kin-based, Gaelic society: the office of earl derives from Gaelic provincial governors and ultimately from tribal leaders. That is seen in the 'law of Clan MacDuff', by which the kindred of 'Macduff' (the family of the original earls of Fife) could claim that only the earl of Fife had jurisdiction over them; it still operated even when Fife belonged to the Stewarts. Another consequence of the earls' pre-feudal origins was the 'army of the earldom'; until the late fourteenth century the earl was the automatic military leader of all the earldom's inhabitants. Also, in the twelfth century, earldom courts seem to have been held in gatherings of the armies presided over by the earls; these later presumably developed into the earls' barony and regality courts, through which the earldoms were formally run. There were of course similar barony or regality courts in the provincial lordships.

None of the ties of lordship, kinship and jurisdiction was

necessarily very cohesive. The complexity of inheritance patterns and the land market often weakened purely feudal relationships. Kinship ties which included cognatic relationships through females (as in fourteenth-century Scotland) could easily become over-extended and diffuse. And the mere possession of a seignorial court did not guarantee effective jurisdiction. But in medieval Scotland the simple yet extremely potent geographical connections between the earls and lords, the earldoms and lordships, and the local land-owning communities pulled the various ties together. The forces of lordship, kinship and jurisdiction became complementary, direct-ing the general loyalty of the local communities towards the earls and provincial lords, and making these extremely powerful.

Their power, moreover, probably extended beyond the bounds of their earldoms and lordships. Although those did not cover medieval Scotland entirely – there were many gaps between them, containing lands held by barons and lesser tenants-in-chief – nevertheless in the fourteenth century they lay at the centre of all the major regions, except the Edinburgh–Stirling–Perth triangle where the crown was the regional lord. Within most regions an earl or lord would naturally be the leading magnate, easily able to out-face other regional tenants-in-chief. Earls and lords can thus be seen as maintaining clear-cut spheres of influence, based on the earldoms and lordships but stretching beyond them. Admittedly the situation was never quite so neat in practice. Nevertheless it does appear that the provincial earldoms and lordships gave medieval Scotland extremely regionalized power-structures – much more so than in England – which, after their reconstruction by Robert I, survived at least until the end of the fourteenth century.

VIII

The mechanisms of lord–man relations within Scottish noble society were never static. The classic feudal tie was bound to evolve, because (except in the special circumstances of the provin-cial earldoms and lordships) it could not satisfy the inherently con-tradictory forces of hereditary landownership and personal service. We have seen part of the Scottish evolution in the fourteenth-century tendency for land to be granted simply for general, unspeci-fied service, with the fiscal elements of feudal tenure being waived. These grants, although feudal, emphasize general, personal service.

At the same time there are many instances of lords giving their followers money, usually annuities, instead of lands in return for service; such grants were attractive when rents were stagnating (at least until inflation started), but were easily withheld if the service was unsatisfactory. The follower might be appointed to an office, such as steward of part of the lord's estates, and given a fee. Sometimes, too, grants of land or money were accompanied by bonds of retinue recording the reciprocal obligations of lord and man. Although few survive, these were probably quite common in the later fourteenth century; in 1399 it was enacted that everyone had to obey the king's lieutenant, 'nocht agaynstandande ony condiciounis of retenewis'. They are like the indentures of retinue, the standard institution of lord–man relationships in late-medieval England. But in Scotland – where there was no restriction on granting land, and where ready cash was probably comparatively scarce – money grants never really replaced land grants; the earls of Douglas, for example, generally gave their followers land. Similarly bonds of retinue never completely replaced formal charters. For most of the late Middle Ages there was absolutely no standardization to Scottish lord–man relationships.

Then in the mid fifteenth century the institution of the 'bond of manrent' appeared. This was a written, witnessed contract given by the follower to the lord, in which he promised to accompany his lord when required, support him in all actions and disputes, give counsel and warning of danger, and help protect him from harm – all on the understanding (though a reverse contract was not automatically given) that the lord would maintain the follower's interests. The earliest known example dates from 1442, and thereafter bonds of manrent became common. Etymologically 'manrent' means the same as 'homage', and the reciprocal lord–man obligations are the same as the primary ones of the feudal relationship. But bonds of manrent concentrate on intangible human ties; it is unusual for them to be accompanied by grants of land or money. Thus they are the final Scottish stage of the general trend dissolving the 'classic' feudal connection between personal service and land tenure.

The other main tie, kinship, also changed significantly in late-medieval Scotland. Kinship ties, in which a magnate's family was expected to show special loyalty to him, were commonplace in medieval Europe. They are similar to lordship ties – indeed lordship is nowadays seen as a kinship substitute, with the symbolism of even the typically feudal act of homage being interpreted as creating an artificial father–son relationship. In practice the two kinds of tie were often combined, as when the fourth earl of Douglas granted Herbert Maxwell of Caerlaverock 40 marks a year in 1407, and obliged himself 'to suppowelle and defende the forsayde Syr Harbarte in all hiis ryghtwys cause, als we awe to do to our man and our kosyn'. But – as in this example – for much of the Middle Ages the concept of kinship in Scotland as elsewhere was mostly cognatic, including relationships through females. That produced very large kinship groups, with several potential heads – resulting in inherently weak ties (unless the special geographical conditions of the Scottish earldoms and lordships applied). And this was probably exacerbated in late-medieval Scotland by the fact that magnates married each others' daughters or the kings' daughters (between them Robert II and Robert III had 11 daughters, who had 16 husbands), and so were all interrelated. In those circumstances cognatic kinship was hardly an effective form of social organization.

By the later fifteenth century, however, typical Scottish kinship ties were no longer cognatic. They were male – agnatic – relationships, which linked all who had the same surname to the head of the family, producing a much more effective kinship group. The change is one reason why kinship remained a major force in Scottish noble society much longer than in other countries. Since agnatic kinship was predominant in Celtic societies, this was perhaps a legacy from Scotland's Gaelic past. But that cannot fully explain its re-emergence during the fifteenth century. There is probably a connection with the establishment in this period of the male entail, by which magnates stipulated that their estates should go to sons, brothers and other male heirs in preference to heiresses. This demonstrates growing awareness of agnatic relationships ·· and once entails had existed for a few generations they in effect created agnatic kinship groups linked by the prospect (however remote) of inheriting the family estates. Yet male entails were common elsewhere. In Scotland, however, the consciousness of male relationships shown in entails must have been accentuated by the fact that the main families creating them were also those which were so abnormally successful at producing sons and durable cadet branches. They were the families who dominated Scottish noble society from the mid fifteenth century, and it was their kindreds who became so prominent. The sheer demographic vitality of these families is almost certainly the major factor behind the flourishing of agnatic kinship within the late-medieval Scottish nobility.

IX

One striking feature of these new social relationships is that they usually operated within limited geographical areas. While later-fifteenth-century magnates often had scattered estates, their interests tended to focus on particular parts of the country – north-east Aberdeenshire with the Hays (despite their title earl of Errol), central Lanarkshire with the Hamiltons, and so on. These were their spheres of influence, within which local lairds gave them bonds of manrent, and where many of their cadet branches were established. Geographical proximity strengthened both the agnatic kinship ties and the bonds of manrent – just as it strengthened the provincial earldoms and lordships. Indeed the new power structures of the later fifteenth century were probably as highly region-alized as the old ones had been, even if the actual areas of power were not the same.

In a way continuity was inevitable. The provincial earldoms and lordships disappeared haphazardly, leaving a separate power vacuum in each region, which tended to be filled separately by one or more magnates within the general pattern of regionalized local power. But, again, the demography of fifteenth-century noble families is also very important. Usually in late-medieval Europe marriage to heiresses was the common means of acquiring lands, and so family estates and interests varied considerably from generation to generation.[3] In Scotland, however, heiresses were extremely rare among major fifteenth-century families. Therefore successive generations of magnates possessed much the same lands, and were concerned with the same spheres of influence. Also, they could not endow younger sons from their wives' lands (a common practice elsewhere); they either had to use their own estates, or marry them into the families of local lairds. As a result, the stability and durability of the new regional power structures were greatly enhanced.

[3]Landowners generally tried to stop lands going to heiresses by establish-ing male entails; but the difficulty of producing sons in the fourteenth and fifteenth centuries meant that, in England and France at any rate, succes-sion by heiresses was usually merely postponed, not eliminated.

Another striking feature is that the new social relationships were almost always exclusive. A later-fifteenth-century magnate's followers were associated with him and no one else. That was axiomatic with the kinship ties, because agnatic family groupings can only have single heads. But instances of a man giving bonds of manrent to more than one lord are rare, which makes bonds of manrent different from – and much stronger than – their precursors, especially those of the early feudal era when men were usually the vassals of several lords. It also makes them appear even more obviously a substitute for kinship, in which the lord's exclusive relationships with his followers are the same as those between the head and members of a family.

But while it was assumed in bonds of manrent that the lord, like a father, would maintain his followers' interests, in practice the institution possibly favoured the lord more than the followers. Not only did it require exclusive loyalty, but the legal contract was commonly just one-way, from follower to lord, and lords (while promising protection and patronage) rarely granted material rewards of land or money in return. It is hardly surprising that the institution became so popular with fifteenth-century magnates. Moreover, bonds of manrent were not necessarily given to lords voluntarily: they are sometimes found at the culmination of disputes between neighbouring landowners, being exacted by the victor from the loser.

These points suggest that the emergence of bonds of manrent in the mid fifteenth century was connected with the territorial reordering of that period. The disappearance of the old pattern of provincial earldoms and lordships must have caused local tension and strife – in the north-east competition to fill the vacuum left when the earldom of Mar came into crown possession in 1435 was an important aspect of James II's reign. In addition to the battle of Brechin (see chap. 7:vii), there were several cases of local violence elsewhere. More commonly, perhaps, local landowners simply faced up to each other – and then the weaker (with the smaller resources, kindred and following) backed down peaceably. But whether or not violence took place, whoever emerged as the dominant lord in a particular area generally formalized his position by obtaining bonds of manrent. Thus the institution did not simply evolve by chance from the earlier social ties; it was probably consciously developed – perhaps even invented – to fulfil a particular function. This is akin to the near-simultaneous emergence of the lordships of parliament (again marks of social superiority) developed by the same magnates who employed the early bonds of manrent. Both were consequences of the transformation of the top layer of Scottish noble society during the middle years of the fifteenth century.

What happened when a region contained two or more equally powerful nobles? One possible consequence was local feuding – which was certainly not absent from late-medieval Scotland. But there are also several instances of bonds of friendship between magnates, in which they agreed that disputes between them or their kindreds and followers should be settled jointly and amicably. One early example is an indenture between the duke of Albany and the fourth earl of Douglas in 1409. Similar agreements are quite common after the mid fifteenth century; they include bonds between the earl of Errol and the eldest son of the earl of Huntly (potential rivals in the north-east) in 1466, and Lords Graham and Oliphant in 1500. Such bonds indicate that local rivalries did not cause insurmountable problems. Perhaps the magnates were content to parcel regions out among themselves rather than challenge each others' spheres of influence (as seems more common a century later, when demographic expansion among noble kindreds may have made demarcation disputes harder to avoid).

The significance of these points is highlighted by a comparison with late-medieval England. There lord–man relationships were almost entirely based on the indenture of retinue, which was a two-way contract, was generally supported by a money-grant from the lord, and did not provide such exclusive loyalty, for a man could have indentures with more than one lord. Agnatic kinship ties never developed so strongly in England (except possibly in the far north), and kinship was an ineffective force outside the immediate family. And magnate power, in general, was not so regionalized; in most areas interlocking and conflicting interests are evident, rather than clear-cut spheres of influence – partly the result of long-term fragmentation of estates, accentuated by the effects of frequent succession by heiresses. Therefore although individual English magnates were very powerful, their local positions were often insecure. They needed gentry support, as all medieval magnates did everywhere, but were often unable to insist on it unequivocally. Moreover it could be fairly easy for gentry to play off one magnate in a region against a rival – thereby increasing the instability of local power structures and the tension of local politics.

For later medieval Scotland – although the argument remains theoretical at present – it appears that there was less likelihood of such instability and tension. It would be wrong to say that local lairds were generally under magnates' thumbs, or that magnates usually rode roughshod over lairds' interests. Yet the balance of power in the mutual relationships seems to have tilted towards the magnates, whereas in England it tilted towards the gentry. As a rule, Scottish lairds would probably have found themselves with little alternative but to accept the regional dominance of a particular magnate; if they quarrelled with him, there was rarely anyone else they could turn to to uphold their interests – let alone protect them in their quarrel. Thus despite the personal, institutional, and territorial upheavals within the higher nobility, the exercise of fairly clear-cut, unchallenged regional power by most magnates continued to be the most important characteristic of the Scottish nobility throughout the late Middle Ages. It was, indeed, not until the Reformation introduced the additional, disruptive, factor of personal religious beliefs into the lord–man relationships that the highly regionalized power structures of Scottish noble society started to disintegrate.

III

Government and Politics

6

The Machinery of Government

I

How was late-medieval Scotland governed? In its institutions –
largely introduced from England in the twelfth century – it was
a fairly typical west-European kingdom. At the very centre there
was the king – both a charismatic figurehead providing the essential focus for the national community, and a personal ruler to
whom all the kingdom's inhabitants owed loyalty and obedience.
Although some Gaelic traditions survived, Scottish kingship had
conformed reasonably closely to the Anglo-French model since the
twelfth century. And when in 1328 the pope granted Scottish kings
the right of ecclesiastical anointment or unction (previously denied
because of English pressure), which signified the bestowal of God's
grace, they were recognized as having unquestionably equal status
to their fellow monarchs elsewhere. They were independent sover-
eign rulers in all but English eyes.

In practice, of course, medieval kingship depended rather more
on the support of the kingdom's political community than on the
concept of divine grace. So long as the majority of the political
community respected and upheld the king's position, it was relatively easy to exert royal authority over recalcitrant individuals.
For Scotland, this is clear from its twelfth- and thirteenth-century
history, when good relations between crown and magnates enabled
institutionalized royal authority to be extended throughout the
entire kingdom. Moreover, as the following chapter shows, good
crown–noble relations continued as the norm in Scotland during
the late Middle Ages. Consequently, for all the nobility's regional
power, the authority of the crown continued to be maintained.
There were remarkably few rebellions against late-medieval

Scottish kings, and those that did take place were usually swiftly crushed.

Besides the office of king, Scotland's supreme institutions were the parliament and the council-general (similar to parliament but less formal; see section vi). In many respects the Scottish parliamentary institutions were like the English: they emerged in the thirteenth century; they contained clergy, nobles, and, from the fourteenth century, burgh representatives; they met irregularly but roughly once a year on average during most of the period; and they constituted the highest legislative, judicial and administrative forum. But no Scottish House of Commons developed: the Scots parliament always met in one body, and Scots lairds (unlike English gentry) belonged with the greater nobles to the second of the 'three estates'.

While the kingdom's major affairs were the concern of parliaments and councils-general, day-to-day business was carried out by the king and his secret or privy council – generally called 'the council'. Although extensive council records only begin to survive in Scotland from the 1470s, there is enough evidence to show that earlier it was similar to its counterparts elsewhere. Probably fewer than 10 persons usually attended its meetings: one or two bishops, earls, barons and clerical administrators (much the same pattern as in England). Its competence, however, was all-embracing: as the king's right-hand men, councillors acted in every aspect of government. All they could not do was sentence people to death or forfeiture, and settle lawsuits concerning landownership (functions reserved to the formally constituted common-law courts).

Beyond parliament and council Scotland had four sets of specialized central institutions (central in an administrative sense, that is; until James III's reign there was no fixed capital, and Perth and Stirling were as prominent as Edinburgh). Although individual Scottish institutions were less developed than their English or French counterparts, this was the normal medieval framework. First there was the secretariat. Formal documents – for instance for diplomacy, summoning parliaments, and conveying land – were issued from the king's 'chapel' (like the English chancery), which apparently was usually in Edinburgh castle; they were authenticated with the great seal, one of the main symbols of independent sovereignty. Brieves for initiating lawsuits (like English writs) and royal pardons were also obtained from the chapel; in the 1360s it charged 6s 8d for a charter conveying land and 3d for a routine brieve. But instructions for producing important great seal documents, and most other essential but ephemeral administrative materials, were issued under the king's privy seal. The privy seal office, the hub of the country's bureaucracy, seems to have been peripatetic with the king and council. The whole secretariat was headed by the chancellor. He was responsible for the great seal, but, being invariably a council member, did not keep it with him; instead he sent instructions for its use via the privy seal office. Under the chancellor, the privy seal was initially held by the king's secretary; then in the fifteenth century a separate keeper of the privy seal appeared, while the secretary looked after an even more private royal seal, the signet.

Next there was the household, or king's private staff, which ran the royal court. Various departments under special clerks saw to its food, drink, clothing, furniture and housing. Above them, for much of the period, were the steward of the household and the chamberlain – originally the person responsible for the royal bedchamber, but effectively the king's chief of staff. Between 1382 and 1424, however, the earl of Fife (duke of Albany after 1398) and his son the earl of Buchan were chamberlains, and they, while drawing the salary, left the household duties to deputies. Then (perhaps as a consequence) James I reorganized the household, downgrading the chamberlain and creating a new chief of staff, the master of the royal household.

Central finance was mostly the household's concern. Money collected by local agents was usually either spent on the spot in accordance with instructions, or forwarded to various household officials. Until the 1420s the chamberlain was the chief financial officer; but with James I's reorganization new officers, the treasurer and comptroller, took over most financial duties, leaving the chamberlain merely responsible for the burghs (though not for their customs). Yet despite the appearance of a treasurer, late-medieval Scotland did not have a separate treasury. The only distinct financial institution was the exchequer, which was purely an accounting office convened at approximately yearly intervals. In it the chancellor, together with some royal councillors and clerks, spent two or three weeks auditing the financial agents' accounts, finishing up with those of the chamberlain or treasurer and comptroller.

Finally there were the judicial institutions. As in England, parliament was the supreme law court – a point reflected in an

ordinance of 1399 'that ilke [each] yher the kyng sal halde a parle-
ment swa that his subiectis be servit of the law'. It 'falsed dooms',
that is heard appeals, dealt with petitions and complaints about
common-law affairs, and had sole jurisdiction over treason; and it
also declared the law, in other words legislated. Below parliament
the only regular central courts were those of the justiciars. There
were normally two justiciars, usually great magnates, responsible
for north and south of the Forth respectively. Theoretically they
made twice-yearly circuits round each sheriffdom. The practice fell
well short of that, but recent research shows that their courts were
held reasonably frequently. Justiciars had exclusive competence
(except within regalities) over major crimes – murder, rape, arson
and robbery with violence – and for remedying the illegal seizure
of land. In addition they heard appeals from local courts, and
investigated complaints against local officials, especially sheriffs.
There were also two types of supplementary central court. First,
special temporary justiciars were sometimes appointed for individual cases, presumably to deal more quickly with important affairs.
Secondly it was possible to petition the royal council. Although the
council's jurisdictional competence was limited, it did arbitrate in
quarrels (especially between powerful lords), fine or imprison
individuals who broke the peace, and right obvious wrongs (what
English law calls equity). In the 1420s so much judicial business
was coming before the council that James I ordered the chancellor
to hold special tribunals or sessions. These continued fitfully in
various forms under James's successors, and led eventually to the
creation of the Court of Session in the sixteenth century.

II

In the localities, as we have seen, the regional magnates usually
enjoyed much political power. But with respect to everyday
administration, the linch-pin of Scottish local government was the
sheriff (another twelfth-century import from England). Sheriffs
were generally important nobles, who increasingly often during the
late Middle Ages possessed the office hereditarily. They ran the 25
or so sheriffdoms – Scotland's main administrative divisions from
the twelfth century to 1975 – on the king's behalf. Their main task
was holding courts to deal with lesser crimes (chiefly theft and
unpremeditated killings), to investigate other breaches of common

or statute law, to settle disputes over landownership, and to publicize recent legislation. They arrested accused criminals and sent them to the justiciars if necessary; helped administer justiciar courts (to which appeals against sheriff-court judgements in civil cases could be made); held inquests concerning land inheritance; supervised local military equipment and helped recruit and lead the sheriffdom's forces in war; and (until James I's reign) collected revenues from crown lands and occasional direct taxation. To assist them in these wide-ranging duties they naturally had subordinate officials: chiefly sheriff-deputes (especially when the sheriffdoms were held heritably), but also clerks, bailies, sergeants, mairs and crowners. Most of these (except the clerks) were drawn from local landowners; among other things they delivered brieves and summonses, assisted with inquestions, and searched for criminals.

These were not the only agents of local government. The burghs had their aldermen (later provosts) and bailies; burgh courts looked after internal affairs and maintained commercial privileges against outsiders; and 'custumars' levied and accounted for the vitally important export duties. In the rest of the country, James I transferred most of the sheriffs' financial duties to officials called *ballivi ad extra*; the increasingly extensive crown lands were their special responsibility.

Then there were the local barons. In the hundreds of baronies of late-medieval Scotland, barons exercised similar functions to the sheriffs. Their most striking power was to execute thieves caught in possession of stolen goods; but settling disputes (including property disputes among their tenants) and upholding government regulations were probably the most common tasks of barony courts. Since the sheriffs were supposed to supervise their administrative activities, hear appeals against civil judgements and investigate accusations of negligence in criminal affairs, the barons – and their bailies and sergeants – count as subsidiary government agents within the sheriffdoms. In practice, however, they probably were left alone to run their baronies – within which (since baronies commonly corresponded to local communities) they would have presided over most of the ordinary government and justice experienced by most of the people of Scotland.

That applies particularly to the largest baronies: the estates belonging to bishoprics and abbeys and the old provincial earldoms and lordships. Most earldoms and lordships predated the sheriffdoms. Indeed the sheriffs' original responsibility seems simply to have been the areas outside them: the Latin for sheriff, *vicecomes* (vice-earl), can probably be taken literally in twelfth-century Scotland. The sheriffdoms subsequently came to include the earldoms and lordships (that helps explain why some Scottish sheriffdoms were much bigger than others), but it is hard to see the sheriffs ever having much more than a formal impact within them; as we saw in the previous chapter, earldoms and lordships survived as virtual provincial governorships well into the late Middle Ages.

Many, moreover, were regalities. As the fifteenth-century phrase 'royalty and regality' indicates, regalities were practically a separate part of the kingdom. A lord of regality had jurisdictional and administrative powers equal to the justiciars', including complete criminal jurisdiction, while civil appeals from regality courts went only to parliament. Justiciars and sheriffs had no authority in a regality; brieves and other administrative documents were issued in its lord's name from its own chancery; and any of its inhabitants brought before other courts could be 'repledged' back to the regality court for trial. Some regalities existed before 1306, but the fourteenth and fifteenth centuries were their heyday. Among them were Thomas Randolph's great provincial earldom of Moray, the vast Douglas possessions of the earls of Douglas and Angus, the Stewart lands, the earldom of Strathearn, the Douglas of Dalkeith estates, the lands of several abbeys and bishoprics, and many baronies.

To hold land in regality was a major status symbol, and so grants of regality were an important form of crown patronage, usually restricted to the royal family, leading magnates, and prominent royal councillors. Such grants have often been seen as seriously weakening Scottish government, but that is probably mistaken. The principle that regalities were subject to royal authority was maintained in Scotland just as it was, with similar institutions, in England and France. As has been said, appeals to parliament from regality courts were always possible. With 'repledging', a pledge had to be given that justice would be done; if it was not, the case would be tried elsewhere. Similarly, the 'police legislation' of the period (see section iv) always covered regalities; it was stated in 1372 that royal officers would act within regalities if the lords did not, and in 1398, that negligent lords of regality 'would have to answer before the king, concerning the loss of their lands and privileges of regality'. In at least one case a regality was cancelled; David II deprived Thomas Fleming earl of Wigtown of his privileges.

The reason was not Fleming's excessive power, but probably his lack of control over the turbulent western half of Galloway. The lands of Wigtown eventually went to Archibald Douglas 'the Grim', who already had eastern Galloway, and who ruled the province firmly from his great tower at Threave; 'Off justice he bare gret renown', wrote Wyntoun. Contemporaries clearly believed that the effective exercise of regality powers did not undermine but upheld the national system of government – as no doubt mostly happened in practice. And it should be added that when Archibald 'the Grim's' grandsons, the eighth and ninth earls of Douglas, came into conflict with James II, then despite the vast lands and privileges of the earldom, the Douglas power was resoundingly crushed by the crown.

III

Did these institutions enable late-medieval Scotland to be governed satisfactorily? Past generations of historians thought not, largely because at first sight they seem a weaker, less sophisticated version of England's. Emphasis was placed on the low level of crown revenue, the delegation of judicial responsibility to the nobility, and the general absence of the strong centralizing drive so characteristic of medieval English government. But although comparisons with England are instructive, the cause of the contrast should be considered. It is, broadly speaking, that Scotland never suffered the same pressures for institutional development. The emergence in England of medieval Europe's most centralized monarchy was largely stimulated by the need in the twelfth century for a system which could operate when the king was absent in his French possessions, and also by the constant need to finance expensive foreign wars. In addition, an atmosphere of distrust between crown and magnates in the twelfth and thirteenth centuries (also largely caused by the problems of English possessions in France) and the scrambled nature of most English nobles' estates, led to a steady decline in their judicial and administrative roles. None of these pressures was present in Scotland – so Scottish institutions did not have to be so highly developed and centralized.

Yet that does not necessarily mean the country was inadequately governed; government should be judged by results, not by institutions. It must also be remembered that most medieval people would not have shared many historians' enthusiasm for powerful central-ization, which could easily be oppressive; medieval English government has been aptly described as 'predatory',[1] and the absence of anything like the sequence of English constitutional crises from Magna Carta onwards is a striking corollary of Scotland's less centralized government. Most medieval people just had one basic – if vital – requirement of government: to ensure that they could live their lives in peace, with a minimum of trouble and interference. Therefore in the Middle Ages the crown's essential functions were to provide systems of defence and law and order: 'to make justice be done and uphold the laws, and to defend the realm with whatever royal power is needed against the enemy's invasion attempts', as the earl of Fife's tasks were described when he became guardian in 1388. As we shall see, both these functions appear to have been satisfied reasonably well within late-medieval Scotland's system of government.

The argument is straightforward with respect to defence. Scottish military records are scanty, and at first sight make unimpressive reading. Yet behind them can be discerned what was probably in practice an effective, well-oiled system. It was based on a scorched-earth policy which avoided battles – Robert I's strat-egy. When invasion was threatened, the major strongpoints, espe-cially Edinburgh and Stirling, were fortified and garrisoned at government expense, but lesser castles were not. Small forces were sent to places in the borders (at least in the fifteenth century), not to resist a major onslaught, but to delay it if possible, and to provide intelligence. Chains of beacons were prepared, to give speedy warning of 'the incumming of ane gret Ingliss hoist': a simple but effective form of communication. Meanwhile local military leaders were ordered by royal letters to recruit troops, and bring them to a muster or have them ready to march when the beacons were lit. An army could thus be raised swiftly. It would not fight (unless the Scots were over-confident, or the attacking force was small), but would harass the invaders, stop them mounting sieges, and threaten their communications and supplies.

As was stressed earlier, Scottish troops were summoned through the fundamental obligation on all able-bodied men to defend their homeland, and they served without pay. Probably the crown

[1] R.W. Southern, 'King Henry I', in his *Medieval Humanism* (Oxford, 1970), p. 231.

usually reimbursed the commander (if he were not the king) for his costs. But all troops were supposed to bring or buy their provisions; each lord had to come '*stuffatus*' with victuals or cash, according to Robert I's legislation of 1318. Armies were, naturally, forbidden to live off the country they were defending; and while it would be unrealistic to expect modern standards of discipline, the violent reaction by Lothian peasants to French foraging in 1385 suggests that this prohibition was generally heeded.

The sheriffs and barons were key figures in the system. Among their tasks was conducting 'wapinschaws' (weapơnshowings) to check equipment – horses, body-armour and swords for the better off, bows and spears for the rest – and presumably to select the best warriors. They also brought the local levies to the muster, and served as subordinate commanders. But they were not the only military leaders. The most important were the wardens of the east and west marches – offices created in the fourteenth century – who were responsible for the borders. The earls, too, had an important military function: in early-medieval Scotland they led the armies of their earldoms, and this practice survived after 1300. Other magnates were given formal rights of leadership, like the earls of Douglas in Lanarkshire and Tweeddale, and James Douglas of Dalkeith over the inhabitants of his estates. Less formally, prominent nobles generally brought their own followers with them when answering the royal summons to arms; indeed later sources depict sixteenth-century Scottish armies virtually as collections of noble followings.

The *levée en masse*, the delegation of responsibility to local nobles and the absence of regular wages all make late-medieval Scotland's military system appear rudimentary, especially by comparison with England's. Yet in practice 'wapinschaws' were like English commissions of array; the arms requirements echoed English legislation (to promote archery, football was banned in both countries, and golf too in Scotland); late-medieval English armies were raised through noble retinues, and the obligation of service in a national emergency was normal in medieval societies.

Thus the only significant difference comes over the payment of troops. Here the absence of Scottish paid armies is not necessarily a sign of backwardness; it could be suggested that Scottish governments were fortunate, for Scottish troops served without wages, while English would not! More importantly, the circumstances in which English paid armies evolved – persistent warfare in France since 1066 – differed sharply from those determining the evolution of Scottish armies. In Scotland the relative expense was a major factor: Scottish defensive armies were generally comparable in size to those of the English invaders, and if paid would have cost similar amounts – which would have meant proportionally far heavier taxation, given Scotland's much smaller population and resources. Obviously, therefore, the Scots crown (whether or not the point was consciously recognized) needed a system using unpaid troops – just as the English crown needed one in which they were paid. And once the Scottish system had been refined in the early-fourteenth-century crises, the subsequent reduction in the English threat made further developments unnecessary.

Perhaps the main conclusion that emerges from this is that in the late Middle Ages the English people mostly contributed indirectly to their country's war effort through taxation which paid for troops, whereas the Scots contributed directly – not through taxes but by supplying the actual fighting men (a higher proportion of the smaller Scottish population) and presumably most of their provisions. Thus – under the nobles' leadership, of course – the people of Scotland can be said to have provided their defence themselves, within the framework maintained by the crown. Their efforts were not in vain, for during the late Middle Ages Scottish armies were put in the field when needed, and, in the long run, Scotland was successfully defended.

IV

For justice, the evidence makes the argument more complex, but similar conclusions can be reached. The framework of royal government is evident in the hierarchical structure of courts, and in the law which they administered. The latter was the Scottish common law – detailed fairly reliably in the fourteenth-century handbooks *Regiam Majestatem* ('the royal majesty'; *c.* 1320) and *Quoniam Attachiamenta* ('with respect to procedures . . .') – and the parliamentary statutes which modified it. The nobility had an obvious judicial responsibility, both in parliaments and councils, and as justiciars, lords of regality, sheriffs and barons. But the most striking aspect of medieval Scotland's legal system is probably the role of the people; in practice they seem generally to have dispensed their justice themselves.

First, most disputes and crimes did not come before formal law courts, but were settled out of court. This was generally true in medieval and early-modern European societies; among the reasons were the cost and delays of litigation, and the fact that the person who brought an unsuccessful case risked a fine. Hence *Regiam Majestatem*, although chiefly concerned with law courts, included a section on arbitration. The Albany–Douglas indenture of 1409 stated that disputes between them or their followers should be settled by arbitrators from their councils; similar later agreements sometimes added that courts should only be used if arbitration failed. In 1385 Andrew Mercer arbitrated in one noble dispute, in 1400 William Keith and his council settled another, and so on – at that level evidence for out-of-court settlements is relatively abundant. Among the peasantry they were perhaps even commoner, on informal and semi-formal bases. The parish priests' function in settling disputes has already been mentioned earlier. Also, most importantly, there were 'birlaw men': members of local communities who acted 'by the consent of neighbours' (*Regiam Majestatem*) to maintain what Coupar Angus abbey's leases of the 1470s called 'good neighbourhood'. They appear in all the later barony records, and were doubtless equally prominent within medieval communities. Their function perhaps extended beyond simple neighbourliness, judging by a reference from thirteenth-century Lancashire to 'birelegia' men mediating between tenant and landlord.

Next, when cases did come before courts, the justiciars, sheriffs and barons who presided were conveners rather than judges: they (or their deputies) made the parties appear, supervised proceedings, profited from fines and forfeitures, and upheld decisions with their authority and power, but they neither initiated nor dispensed the justice. That was done by the members of the communities for which the courts were held. Civil cases started when one party approached a baron, sheriff or justiciar, or obtained a brieve ordering a hearing. With crimes, the victim or his kin normally brought a prosecution before a baron or sheriff, who either had the case heard or transferred it to a justiciar. Also, local communities could act collectively: they had to compile lists of alleged criminals for trial before the justiciars; while 'every baron may purge his lands of malefactors and men of evil fame thrice annually, by an assize of faithful men' (*Quoniam Attachiamenta*), with the accused being banished unless they agreed to stand trial. Moreover the actual justice was always the community's (except in occasional judicial combats). Decisions were made by the suitors of the court, that is the tenants of the territory for which the court was held, or by sworn juries selected from 'the good and faithful' men of the neighbourhood, who were presumed to know the truth about particular issues. And judgement was invariably pronounced by a 'dempster', one of the suitors appointed to declare his court's 'dooms'.

Another 'popular' aspect of Scottish justice is that in criminal affairs, great emphasis was laid on restitution and compensation – 'assythment' is the late-medieval term – by the perpetrator to the victim or his kin. This practice, a means of pacifying blood-feuds, was common in early European societies. But whereas in England it was obliterated by the royal principle that crimes were public, not private, affairs, within Scotland's judicial system 'kinship justice' survived and indeed flourished. Thus with murder (defined from the mid fourteenth century as deliberate, 'forethought-felony', and normally reserved to justiciar and regality courts), the usual death penalty could be escaped by purchasing a royal pardon – but only if assythment was also made to the victim's kin. If, however, a preliminary inquest found a killing was accidental or 'in hot blood', this lesser matter would (if assythment could not be arranged privately) come before a baronial or sheriff court. There, the main object would be to ensure assythment, and only if that was refused would a serious public penalty – probably, in practice, outlawry and forfeiture – be pronounced. *Regiam Majestatem*, following an archaic source, gives fixed amounts of compensation (mostly in cows); other material indicates that in late-medieval Scotland assythment was either negotiated in private settlements or assessed during court hearings.

This judicial system was highly localized – reflecting the importance of local communities in Scottish society. Within the local communities, everyone doubtless knew everyone else's business; so the rights and wrongs of disputes and the perpetrators of crimes would have been well known. Crime may have been less common than nowadays, because people would have had few goods (apart from livestock) to steal. These points apply to all pre-industrial societies, but for Scotland, with the close correspondence between baronies and local communities, they are particularly germane (one reason why Scottish seignorial courts remained viable). At a higher level, the regional power structures of noble society probably meant that landowners' quarrels were often settled through the efforts of local magnates and heads of kins, rather than in the courts. And even serious crimes may not have come before the justiciars very frequently. Judging by general studies of pre-industrial crime, the preliminary inquests would commonly have declared that killings were accidental or in hot blood. Also, accused persons were usually allowed bail, and many who anticipated being found guilty probably fled – incurring outlawry, preferable to death but nonetheless a severe punishment, since outlaws lost lands and goods and could be killed without penalty.

This system of criminal justice probably worked fairly well for most crimes, which would have been local. We must not, however, be too sanguine: there would have been great opportunity for victimization by dominant local groups, and the rule that only justiciars should deal with serious crimes and accusations on suspicion was probably intended to prevent lynchings. On the other hand that rule, and the fact that accused persons could miss several hearings before judgement went against them, while exhibiting an understandable anxiety for fairness towards defenders, caused serious delays in justice, and indeed could be exploited by criminals.

That applies chiefly to crimes committed by men who were not locals, from whom assythment was difficult to obtain, and against whom outlawry pronounced locally long after the event had little force. Most late-medieval Scottish criminal legislation concerned such mobile criminals – especially criminal gangs who, according to a statute of 1397, were committing 'grete and horrible destruccions heryschippis brynyngis and slachteris [i.e. harryings, burning and slaughters]'. Highlanders seem to have been particularly blamed. Under successive kings from Robert II to James II, various acts attacked the problem; all provided for summary justice at the hands of the local sheriff or baron if the accused was caught, and for immediate outlawry to be enforced countrywide if he fled. This subordinated the common-law principle of fairness to the desire for faster, more effective measures. There is a perennial dilemma here, about which parliament was concerned under Robert II and Robert III, for their acts were only temporary measures. But James I had fewer scruples: from 1432, summary justice executed by sheriffs and barons was prescribed permanently for all violent crimes found to be 'forethought felonies'.

In civil justice there was a similar desire to stop defenders stalling court hearings by exploiting procedures. The main solution was found in petitions to the royal council for immediate action. In Robert II's and Robert III's reigns there is considerable evidence of the council's acting as an alternative law court, and by James I's reign the sessions (comprising representatives of the three estates) were needed to relieve its judicial burden. During the fifteenth century the scope of conciliar jurisdiction expanded through the action of 'spuilzie' – a suit for damages following the despoiling of property – which could be heard before the council and sessions. Since spuilzie covered not only removal of goods but also wrongful occupation of land, it gave the council a way of dealing with land-ownership. By an act of 1458, when spuilzie of land was alleged the session (or presumably the council) was empowered to order the local sheriff to determine by immediate inquest who was the last lawful owner of the land, and restore possession to him. That could be challenged in the ordinary law courts, but with little likelihood of success. Spuilzie thus provided a quick, effective method of settling land disputes.

These procedural changes were accompanied by an increase in the number of advocates and public notaries. The notaries are connected with a growing desire for written records of all sorts of transactions (for instance bonds of manrent). After about 1400 conveyances involved more and longer documentation – to the disgust, according to Bower, of the Governor Albany. In general, late-medieval Scotland was experiencing 'a "quickening" of legal development'.[2] But, it must be stressed, this development was in a continuous line from earlier periods; the main characteristics of Scotland's judicial system were firmly established before 1300.

Legal historians of past generations were therefore wrong to believe that after the Wars of Independence Scots law stagnated in a 'dark age'. Their sweeping condemnation of late-medieval Scottish justice should also be challenged. Admittedly standards of law and order are notoriously difficult to assess. But (if the lurid preambles to statutes, probably reflecting political bias, are disregarded) the legislation's pragmatic measures never imply any real breakdown. Moreover, contrary to past assertions, they can be shown to have been put into effect. Also contemporaries did not believe that the nobility's judicial responsibility caused problems; much of the legislation actually increased it. Landowners would not normally want lawlessness on their estates, and although they did not give judgements, they organized and stimulated the local

[2]J.J. Robertson, 'The development of the law', in J.M. Brown, ed., *Scottish Society in the Fifteenth Century* (London, 1977), p. 142.

crime-prevention processes. James I (reputedly no friend to noble power) enacted that in the north lords were to maintain and live in their castles, 'for the gracious governance of their lands by good policing'. But contemporaries would have agreed that the justiciar courts were inadequate; hence the changes in criminal procedure and the growth in conciliar jurisdiction. Yet many matter-of-fact references to justiciars throughout the parliamentary records show the office still remained important – perhaps especially as an institution for supervising local sheriffs and barons.

The condemnations of late-medieval Scottish justice stemmed partly from the contrast with England, where the great twelfth and thirteenth-century expansion of central courts stimulated the proliferation of professional lawyers and judges, who made English law increasingly sophisticated. The fact that Scotland retained a system of amateur judges is obviously an important difference. Also, Scottish lawyers continued to be clerics, not laymen, trained and practising as much in the church courts as in the common-law ones. And because Scotland had no equivalent to the law school which developed at the Inns of Court near Westminster, there was no alternative to the traditional ecclesiastical education. Not until the late sixteenth century did Scotland have a legal profession comparable to England's; when it did, one consequence was the disappearance of private settlements and assythment.

Yet centralization and professionalization did not necessarily benefit the English legal system. Whereas Scots law remained flexible and pragmatic, English became obsessed with technicalities, procedures and precedents. In late-medieval England the difficulty of concluding common-law cases was notorious, while out-of-court settlements were also hampered by the system. Recent studies demonstrate that in practice, late-medieval English justice fell well short of the theory; there is no reason to believe that it worked any better than in late-medieval Scotland. Among the peasantry, local juries probably maintained similar standards in both countries; but crime among English landowners (a striking feature of the period) may have been worse than in Scotland, where inheritance and territorial patterns perhaps meant there were fewer occasions for quarrels and more likelihood of their settlement, especially out of court.

This discussion of Scottish justice should not, however, end by stressing contrasts with England. In fact Scottish trends fit the late-medieval English and European patterns quite well. For example England also experienced an expansion of conciliar justice, and the Scottish action of spuilzie closely resembles the English action of trespass, which flourished after 1400. There was a significant movement away from the English central courts; increasing judicial responsibility fell on the justices of the peace – who as local landowners were just like Scotland's barons and sheriffs (except that Scottish barons dealt only with their own estates, whereas English JPs could interfere in other people's). In Continental Europe, too, the growth of central conciliar and local summary justice is evident. Also, there was generally what historians see as a changed conception of crime (perhaps reflecting social dislocations following the demographic slump) shown in a new consciousness of collective crimes and conspiracies, which were blamed on criminal gangs and, more widely, on groups like vagabonds and witches. That is what the Scottish legislation suggests. Although Scotland's witch craze came later, there were several acts condemning vagabonds, while the awareness of criminal gangs has already been stressed. And there is also a clear theme (discussed below, in chapter 8) associating criminality with the Highlands. If the search for collective scapegoats for societies' ills was a general phenomenon of late-medieval Europe, then can it be suggested that in Scotland the Highlanders came increasingly to take the blame?

V

If, to medieval people, defence and justice were the most important aspects of government, to their kings there was another: finance. In late-medieval Scotland, however, the needs of royal finance affected the people less than in other countries, because the revenue mostly came from the rents of crown lands (including royal burghs) and from the customs introduced in the late thirteenth century on wool and leather exports. In the first case the burden was limited to the tenants, who paid what they would have to any landlord; in the second it probably fell chiefly on the foreign purchasers. The only impositions on the mass of the population were the 'contributions', direct taxes of a shilling or so in the pound on the assessed value of their property. But these were probably just levied in some 22 years between 1306 and 1469.[3] The only heavy taxes were those for the

---

[3]1326–30, 1341, 1358–60, 1365–66, 1368, 1370, 1373, 1399, 1424–25, 1442, 1447, 1455, 1464 and 1468. For references to taxation after 1424, see

1328 'payment for peace' (£20,000 over three years) and for James I's ransom (about £13,000 sterling over two years); otherwise yields seem to have been around £2,000. On the whole, therefore, fiscal demands were relatively slight – which is obviously connected with the way the tasks of royal government were carried out. The judicial system was self-financing, with the costs of organizing and supervising courts being met from fines and forfeitures; that is typical of the whole administration. And, of course, because Scotland could be defended without the need for paid armies, military costs were tiny by comparison with England's or France's – clearly a major reason for the scarcity of direct taxation.

Any financial emergency, however, could warrant taxation: David II's and James I's ransoms, the 1328 'payment for peace', the costs of important embassies and royal marriages (often thousands of pounds), and even difficulties with royal household expenses, as with the 'tenth penny' for life granted by the laity to Robert I in 1326. But such taxation was exceptional; despite the recent argument that in the 1360s David II had almost made it automatic, there was never much likelihood of that. Contributions were invariably individual taxes specifically negotiated with the three estates. In 1368 parliament stated that it was 'not expedient to the community to impose any contributions' the following year, which clearly shows it had the final say in determining whether there was an emergency that justified taxation.

The question of financial emergency largely depended on what the regular sources provided. Over the period revenue from land and customs fluctuated, but in a broadly complementary way. In the mid thirteenth century crown lands possibly yielded over £5,000 a year (at an informed guess), but grants to their supporters by Robert I and David II sharply reduced their net value, probably to around £2,000 a year in the late 1320s and only £500 or so after 1365. Conversely the customs' annual yield was about £2,000 in the late 1320s, when the main rate was 6s 8d per sack of wool; but because of David II's ransom the rate was trebled in 1358 and quadrupled (to £1 6s 8d per sack) in 1368, greatly increasing the revenue. In the 1360s it averaged around £7,000 a year, and after 1368 (when exports were booming; see Appendix B, Table I) it was over £10,000, with receipts of £13,414 9s $2\frac{3}{4}$d accounted for in

I.E. O'Brien, 'The Scottish Parliament in the 15th and 16th centuries' (Glasgow Univ. Ph.D. Thesis, 1980), pp. 403–4.

1372. Crown finance had come to be based almost entirely on the customs. But the subsequent export slump changed the situation. Early-fifteenth-century customs revenue averaged only £2,000–£4,000 Scots a year; during James I's personal rule it was £4,000–£5,000 Scots; and in the 1450s it was down again to around £2,500 Scots. That was offset, however, by a dramatic expansion in crown lands after 1424: James I and James II, giving revenue precedence over patronage, retained much of the vast territory which had come into their hands. An act of 1455 consolidated this reversal of earlier kings' policy by making large areas into permanent crown property, alienable only with parliamentary consent. By the mid 1430s land was probably producing about £4,000 Scots a year, and over £7,500 Scots by the late 1450s, when it was once again the major source of revenue.

Together, therefore, crown land and customs generally provided between £4,000 and £10,000 a year, with sums of £6,000-£8,000 (at fourteenth-century values) probably being most common. Such amounts, while small by English or French standards, apparently usually sufficed for the Scots crown. There were difficult periods, like the mid 1320s, the years when David II's ransom consumed large sums (1358-9, £6,667 a year; 1366-9, £4,000), and much of the earlier fifteenth century. Yet in the 1320s, although £4,000 (roughly) a year from land and customs was insufficient, another £2,000 from the 'tenth penny' made Robert I's finances quite healthy. In the fifteenth century, Albany's government was financed, ultimately, from his private purse, so the situation was better than the accounts show (see chap. 7:v). After 1424, while James I felt short of money, he did keep half the massive £26,000 Scots raised for his ransom (eventually spending it on luxuries), and devoted thousands of pounds to building at Linlithgow and Edinburgh. As for David II, in 1360 ordinary expenditure was little over £3,000 and, in 1366-7 £1,100 was owed for household supplies. But in 1361-5 (when the ransom was unpaid) and after 1369 (when instalments were lower and the customs were booming) there was plenty of money. Indeed after 1369 the accounts show lavish expenditure (by Scottish standards) and surpluses of £1,000-£2,000; neither David II nor Robert II, apparently, could use all the available cash. That indicates an upper level of about £8,000 for ordinary crown spending, and implies that at the more common levels of £6,000-£7,000 essential needs could usually be adequately financed from regular revenue.

What was the money spent on? Most – £2,000–£5,000 a year, depending on financial circumstances – went on 'household expenses', to provide for the kings, queens, immediate royal families, and their attendants and courtiers. Thousands of pounds were spent on food, drink, clothing and furnishings, while well over £500 a year usually went to the king's private expenses. Then there was patronage: grants of cash and annuities to magnates, lesser laymen and the Church. Again the amounts depended on the financial situation. The most lavish payments – at times totalling over £2,000 a year – were under Robert II and Robert III, naturally enough since (unlike their predecessors) they had far more money than land available for patronage. In the 1360s, conversely, David II's patronage only consumed around £500 a year. Under other kings, patronage levels were between these extremes, but generally over £1,000 a year – even under James I (though that mostly went on long-standing payments to the Church). Finally, there was expenditure on the country's actual governance. Usually £500 or so went on maintaining castles, another few hundreds on routine diplomacy and on salaries for officials like the chamberlain and clerk of the rolls, about £100 on the exchequer audit itself, and various small amounts on miscellaneous items – but that was all. In normal years around £1,500, and often less, seems to have been spent on running the country as opposed to maintaining the royal household. This brings us back to the point that it cost very little to carry out the tasks of government in late-medieval Scotland.

Yet that does not mean that government was inadequate. It must be reiterated that Scotland was defended successfully, while justice was provided and the laws maintained at least as satisfactorily as elsewhere. The common assumption of historians, that high revenue and expenditure can be equated with effective government, simply does not apply to Scotland. Nor would more revenue necessarily have strengthened the crown politically. It would have facilitated more lavish patronage – but that would have stimulated competition among the nobility to share and control the crown's money, as happened elsewhere. It could hardly have enabled Scottish kings to deal more effectively with magnate opponents, for (as we shall see in the following chapter) between 1306 and 1469 rebellions were invariably crushed – while in 1488 James III, with some £25,000 Scots in ready cash at his disposal (probably acquired from currency manipulation) was defeated and killed by rebels! And, as English medieval history shows, efforts to maximize royal revenue could easily provoke dangerous political opposition.

The main point about late-medieval Scottish crown finance, in fact, is not the size of the income and expenditure, but that generally they roughly balanced. There were as many overall surpluses as deficits, and the latter never grew out of control; the accumulations of debts and unpaid bills often found in England (Henry VI owed some £370,000 in 1449) were avoided by the Scottish kings. This solvency is probably what mattered most to contemporaries; it meant, for instance, that household extravagance and requisitioning only occasionally became contentious issues, and, in contrast to England, never caused bitter political conflict. And it was achieved, it must be remembered, without imposing heavy fiscal pressure on the country's people.

VI

Finally, we must return to the subject of parliament. In Scotland, as in England, parliament evolved in the thirteenth century from the kings' great councils. But the latter – known by the 1360s as councils-general – also continued. Together, these institutions lay at the heart of Scottish government. They provided the essential links both between the centre and the localities, and between the crown and the community of the realm, or (in the terminology adopted after 1357) the three estates of the realm.

On behalf of the national community, parliaments and councils-general enacted statute law, ratified treaties, supervised defence, justice and crown finance, authorized direct taxation (it has been claimed that councils-general could not tax, but the 1399 contribution was agreed in one), considered petitions on individual or general problems, and did whatever else the national interest required. Parliament, moreover, was the supreme common-law court, able to hear appeals from justiciar, regality and other subordinate courts, and (alone) to try cases of treason against the king and kingdom. That is one distinction between parliaments and councils-general; it meant that (as with other major courts) parliaments needed 40 days' notice, whereas councils-general could be convened more quickly. Another distinction is that the king's presence was not essential for councils-general, but it was (at least from the 1350s) at parliaments; thus, for instance, only councils-general were held during James I's captivity.

Only prelates, earls, barons and royal councillors attended the earliest Scottish parliaments, but because for taxation purposes fuller community involvement was required, under Robert I lesser landowners and burgess representatives were summoned too, and by the 1360s this had become automatic. This is broadly similar to the English practice, but there was one striking difference. In England two local gentry were elected in each shire and sat with the burgesses in the House of Commons. In Scotland, after some experiments, it became the practice to issue collective summonses through the sheriffs to all tenants-in-chief, and the lesser ones who attended belonged with the magnates to the second estate. The theory presumably was that when all lay tenants-in-chief were summoned with the ecclesiastical landowners and burgesses, the entire land of Scotland – and so in a sense all its inhabitants – was represented. All three estates – clergy, nobility and burgesses – assembled together; that was so even after the parliamentary peerage (whose members were entitled hereditarily to the status symbol of a personal summons) emerged in the 1440s.

The absence of separate houses of Lords and Commons in Scotland is explicable in various ways. The different methods of representing the two countries' landowning classes reflect simpler tenurial structures in Scotland and stronger communities of county gentry in England, while the segregation of the English knights of the shire and burgesses was probably due to greater social and political divisions. Also, in English parliaments the knights and burgesses acquired specific subordinate functions – organizing taxation and processing petitions about grievances – which strengthened their separate identity. Moreover, although in the thirteenth century the English magnates acted for the whole community over taxation, during the fourteenth they stopped doing so, because the taxes were now spent on paid armies largely composed of their own retinues; responsibility for taxpayers' interests therefore devolved upon the knights and burgesses. And, during the political crises stimulated by expensive foreign wars and oppressive domestic government, these gradually developed the technique of linking taxation arrangements with redress of grievances, which gave the House of Commons its strength. Such developments did not happen in Scotland: taxation was not used for armies, and so magnate interests did not diverge from the rest of the community's; petitions were handled by committees containing members of all three estates; and warfare and oppressive government did not cause such crises. The unity of the Scottish parliaments and councils-general was therefore maintained, whereas in England parliamentary divisions widened.

When the three estates met, however, few tenants-in-chief below the earls and barons attended. This was no doubt partly due to the cost, partly to the overwhelming prominence of magnates, prelates and royal councillors inevitable in a unicameral assembly – and it must also be stressed that because of Scotland's highly regionalized power structures the local communities were generally dominated by magnates, who were actually better able to represent them than the lesser landowners. In the 1469 parliament, the first for which an attendance list survives, there were 25 clerics, 54 nobles (mostly magnates), and representatives of 22 burghs; attendance was probably no higher at earlier parliaments. Two acts relating to this can be found in 1426 and 1428 (probably connected with James I's efforts to raise taxation); the first required full personal attendance, the second allowed 'smal barounis and fre tenandis' to elect shire commissioners instead. Neither was effective; the lesser landowners' attendance continued to be low and haphazard. But that did not vitiate the theory of representation, because it is likely that non-attenders employed the common medieval device of proxies. It was the summons, giving the option of either personal appearance or the delegation of responsibility, that mattered, not the actual attendance.

Those who did appear were not necessarily involved in all the business. Judicial committees appointed to hear common-law appeals date from at least 1341, and several *ad hoc* committees are also recorded. Most importantly, the 'general purposes committee' later known as the Lords of the Articles developed. This was usually a body of around 20 prominent persons, elected from all three estates to discuss the items on parliament's agenda, consider petitions, and draft legislation for parliament's approval. The business was often completed in a few days; but sometimes it took longer, and then the rest of those attending parliament went home, with instructions to reconvene later. When surviving registers of minutes begin, in 1466, the procedure appears well-established. Its origins go back to the late 1360s, when committees were elected to 'hold the parliament' while everyone else departed because of the harvest (1367) and bad weather (1369). Something similar happened in 1370, 1372, 1424, 1426 and 1431, and is implied in the records of other parliaments. The purpose was probably simply to reduce the inconvenience and expense of long parliamentary sessions. In some ways the committee is the Scottish equivalent of the English House of Commons; but precise details of its evolution, especially concerning the final report stage (obscurely indicated in 1370 and 1372) remain unclear.

Regardless of the use of committees, the low attendance, and the dominance of magnates, prelates and royal councillors, the Scots parliaments always maintained a striking concern for the whole community. It is never possible to deduce from a parliament's legislation who the actual legislators were, and although the king and council introduced many acts, probably as many were initiated by members of the three estates and may often have started as individual petitions. Apparently the only legislation upholding sectional interests is that against burgh craftsmen, but there was no complementary restriction of rural wages and employment, as in the English statute of Labourers. Admittedly acts against vagrants and beggars were harsh, but those were a common popular concern in late-medieval Europe. In times of dearth there were acts against hoarding, in times of plague acts to restrict the spread of disease. Among other things, parliament dealt with weights and measures, close seasons for salmon-fishing, wolf hunts, and the weed marigold. Legislation on land law attempted to curb sharp practices, and if anything favoured lesser landowners and even (slightly) the peasantry: thus, 'for the sauftie and favour of the pure pepil that labouris the grunde', sitting tenants were not to be evicted when estates changed hands (1450). Many parliaments wrestled with insoluble currency problems; some reinforced military arrangements; and most attempted to improve the judicial machinery. Attitudes and conventions were of course different from today's, but the whole corpus of legislation gives the impression of an all-pervading utilitarianism, and there seems little reason not to take it at face value.

The parliamentary concern for the whole community was partly, no doubt, due to the clergy. Yet it would be wrong to imagine that the magnates, collectively, were significantly less concerned. Over taxation magnate interests did not diverge from the rest of the people's, as happened in England; that is probably true of most other issues, too. After all the magnates were not only closely involved in making the legislation, but as earls, lords of regality, sheriffs and barons were largely responsible for implementing it in the country – especially with respect to military and judicial matters. Even in high politics, the common good is usually as evident as individual rivalries; the compromises and efforts to limit the consequences of acts of violence, which (as is shown in the following chapter) characterize late-medieval Scottish politics,. tended to take place when the magnates assembled together in parliaments and councils-general.

Parliament was also, of course, the forum through which royal authority was ultimately upheld against individual magnates (most obviously the Douglases in the 1450s) on the community's behalf. But it is clear that Scots parliaments would, if necessary, place the community's interests above the king's. This is indicated in the Declaration of Arbroath, and is found in the prohibition of orders by David II contravening common or statute law, in the dismissal of Robert II's favoured son Alexander from the office of justiciar because he was 'useless to the community', and in the resistance to James I's efforts at direct taxation (see chap. 7:ii, chap. 8:ii, chap. 7:vi). It is also, perhaps, implied in the 1458 parliament's 'humble' exhortation to James II to maintain its statutes, now that all rebels and law-breakers had been dealt with.

Thus, contrary to what has sometimes been stated, medieval Scotland's parliamentary institutions were far from powerless. In theory, indeed, they had the same constitutional position as England's. Yet late-medieval Scotland never suffered conflicts between crown and parliament on the scale found in England. The point is that the need for the Scots parliament to exercise its constitutional power hardly ever arose, because the general nature of Scottish government and society limited the areas of potential conflict so much. The use of unpaid armies, the strength of 'popular' justice, the normal ability of the kings to live within their regular revenue, and the extensive but not uncontrolled delegation of local administrative responsibilities, all meant that late-medieval Scotland could be governed without heavy pressure being placed on the people. That is why there was so little tension over constitutional issues, and why the Scots crown and parliament were almost always able to work together effectively in directing the machinery of government.

7

Kings and Magnates

I

As we saw in the first chapter, in the early fourteenth century Scotland's domestic politics are inextricably woven into the war with England. After David II's return in 1341 and the lessening of the English and Balliol threat, however, domestic and foreign affairs start to diverge. From then on late-medieval Scotland's domestic politics have their own separate history.

According to traditional accounts, it is an extremely uninspiring history. From the eighteenth to the mid twentieth century successive generations of historians described late-medieval Scottish politics in the gloomiest terms. They concentrated on outbreaks of violence and turbulence, and depicted a long, inconclusive power struggle between weak kings and selfish, overmighty magnates, coupled with a sorry sequence of royal minorities, incapacities, and captivities in England. One early Victorian writer remarked that the fifteenth century in Scotland contained 'no events of marked or decided character, to distinguish the age in any philosophical retrospect. We have the usual amount of feudal tyranny, violations of law and outrages on humanity.'[1] This is the opinion of late-medieval Scottish political history that has prevailed until quite recently.

At first sight the facts seem to support this opinion (as a glance at the Chronological Table of events in Appendix A will demonstrate). Adult kings ruled personally in Scotland for just 62 of the 128 years between 1341 and 1469. There were several rebellions,

[1]P. Fraser, *Tytler's History of Scotland examined* (Edinburgh, 1848), p. 103; cited in M. Ash, *The Strange Death of Scottish History* (Edinburgh, 1980), p. 119.

23 magnates met violent deaths (not counting those killed in battle against the English), James I was murdered by dissident nobles, and James II assassinated the eighth earl of Douglas. Yet this violence should be placed in perspective by comparing it with events in late-medieval England. Between 1341 and 1469 no Scottish king was overthrown by political opponents, whereas two were in England; England experienced twice as many rebellions and three times as many civil war battles; and three times as many English magnates met politically-related deaths, although the Scottish and English magnate classes were much the same size. During the fourteenth and fifteenth centuries as a whole, the only Scottish kings to lose their thrones were John Balliol and James III (in 1488), while James I and James III were the only ones deliberately killed; English kings lost their thrones on seven occasions, and five were killed. Only ten Scottish magnates were executed during these two centuries (again excluding deaths at English hands), compared with 46 English ones. And even James II's hot-blooded stabbing of the earl of Douglas hardly compares with Henry IV's cold-blooded execution of the archbishop of York. Although this analysis oversimplifies, it does demonstrate strikingly that, contrary to the opinion that was current for so long, Scottish domestic politics were far less turbulent and dangerous for the participants than in England – at least once the Bruce–Balliol civil war had died down. From the mid fourteenth century, indeed, they were quiet by European as well as by English standards, for comparison of Scotland with France, Spain or Italy would give roughly similar results.

Also, there is absolutely no evidence to support the idea of a continuous crown–nobility power struggle. At times kings did find themselves at odds with some (though never all) of the magnates: David II in the 1360s, James I in the 1420s, James II in the 1450s. But it is impossible to argue that there was any sustained general conflict; cooperation was the norm, not confrontation. As for the periods without active adult kings, these did cause some tension and difficulties, but the problems never got out of hand (as happened in France and England during the illnesses of Charles VI and Henry VI), reasonably effective government was maintained, and even the critical transitional periods when adult kings regained power only caused brief upheavals.

Furthermore, whenever one of the relatively rare acts of political violence did take place, it hardly ever had violent repercussions. As we shall see, after outbreaks of rebellion, as in 1363, 1411 and 1452, the rebels simply submitted and were pardoned (the final Douglas rebellion of 1455 is an exception, but even there the point partly applies); after incidents like the death of the duke of Rothesay in 1401 or the killing of the earl of Douglas in 1452, parliamentary enquiries exonerated those responsible; the coups by Carrick in 1384, Fife in 1388, Livingston in 1439 and Boyd in 1466 all received parliamentary sanction. The only example of immediate, strong counter-action was the exceptional case of James I's assassination, when the assassins were hunted down and executed. Otherwise the consequences of violence were remarkably low-key. The political community usually tried to halt violence – even if that sometimes meant condoning it; it did not encourage more through retaliation and revenge. Indeed the most striking feature of Scottish politics was what can be called 'the acceptance of the *fait accompli*': recognize what has happened and avoid fresh disturbance. There is a clear contrast with late-medieval England, where violence tended to beget violence, and reaction to the *fait accompli*, rather than acceptance, was more the norm.

Therefore the gloomy traditional accounts of late-medieval Scottish politics should be rejected. But in that case, what were the general political themes? One fundamental point is that (as was demonstrated in the previous chapter) constitutional affairs were hardly ever a major political concern in late-medieval Scotland – certainly not in the way they were in England. Instead, the main political theme of this period appears to be simply the importance of the king's personality. Because medieval kingship was intensely personal, the characters, policies and circumstances of individual kings (or their deputies during minorities or other regencies) obviously had a huge influence on domestic politics – indeed in the opinion of several recent historians of late-medieval England they were the major determinant.

Concentration on kings, however, can result in a one-sided portrayal of medieval politics – that is one of the problems about many older accounts of Scottish and also English history. It must be remembered that individual nobles had their own policies and characters, and that medieval politics always involved a number of interests, not just the crown's. For Scotland between 1341 and 1469 there are four noble family groupings to whom it is particularly important to pay attention: the three leading families of Robert I's reign, the Stewarts, Douglases, and Randolphs (including their heirs the Dunbars), together with the Drummonds, who were the kinsmen of David II through his second marriage to Margaret Logie, née Drummond (see the Genealogical Table, Appendix C). The varied fortunes of these family groupings, their relationships with one another, with the crown and with the wider political community, and the significance of the disappearance of their senior lines in the middle years of the fifteenth century, all had a great importance for Scotland's political history – just as much as that of the kings. They also help to provide it with a continuity and coherence which would otherwise be missing from studies of the individual reigns.

II

For the first few years after David II's return from France in 1341, however, the generalization about the low-key and stable nature of late-medieval Scottish politics does not apply. Scotland was apparently suffering from the internal dissensions and strife which are common within victorious independence movements, exacerbated by the disruption of Robert I's territorial settlement by deaths in the 1330s. The top of the nobility was particularly unstable: the Douglases were in eclipse because the lord was well under age, while the Stewarts and the Randolphs were headed by young men who were bitter personal rivals (see chap. 1:vi). The hostility between Robert Stewart and John Randolph earl of Moray seems to have polarized other antagonisms within the nobility – for instance the violent and ambitious William Douglas of Liddesdale can be associated with Stewart, his enemies Alexander Ramsay and David Barclay with Randolph. David II (who was only 17 in 1341) probably intensified rivalries by favouring the dashing Randolph against the staider Robert Stewart, his heir-presumptive; and, although Stewart acquired the earldom of Atholl in 1342, David did not make him an earl. David's kingship at this time appears distinctly partisan, a dangerous sign when coupled with the connections between central rivalries and local feuds; the combination of these factors was a major cause of civil wars in late-medieval England.

Scotland, however, did not explode into civil war. The battle of Neville's Cross, a turning-point in domestic as well as foreign affairs, defused the situation. John Randolph was killed, along with several other magnates; David II and William Douglas of

Liddesdale were captured. Robert Stewart (who led the retreat) was left as the leading Scottish noble, and, as before 1341, became lieutenant for the absent king. The records suggest, possibly misleadingly, that Stewart's lieutenancy was an administrative failure. Politically, however, it was a success; although he increased his own territorial power by taking over the vacant territories of Strathearn and (perhaps) Badenoch, he did not challenge other magnates, and thus ensured that partisan tensions would not disturb the 1350s. Moreover, although the head of the main Douglas family, another William Douglas, had now reached manhood, he (in contrast to Randolph) cooperated with Stewart; together with Randolph's brother-in-law and heir, Patrick Dunbar earl of March, they formed an extremely powerful political alliance. The only major domestic problem was caused by the return of William Douglas of Liddesdale, but he was killed in a personal quarrel by the lord of Douglas in 1353. While outrageous (the lord of Liddesdale was the lord of Douglas's godfather), this deed must have greatly increased Scotland's political stability.

After David II's release in 1357, the men who had run Scotland during his captivity obtained their rewards: Robert Stewart became earl of Strathearn, William Douglas became first earl of Douglas, and Patrick Dunbar earl of March was recognized as earl of Moray. But by 1360 the king's attitude towards the great magnates had changed – so much so that Stewart, Douglas and March rebelled in 1363. David took swift, decisive action (including hiring troops at a cost of at least £618), and the rebellion collapsed. From then until his sudden death, aged only 47 in 1371, 'nane durst welle wythstand his will', as 'Wyntoun' put it. A tough, energetic ruler, David maintained firm control of his kingdom, and (with the excuse of the ransom) greatly increased royal revenues both through the customs and, in some years, through direct taxation.

David's kingship, however, was not without faults. His abandonment of the hostages and default on the ransom, contributory factors in the 1363 rebellion, have been mentioned earlier. Another aspect of his rule is illustrated by an act of the 1370 parliament forbidding royal officers from carrying out commands under the great or privy seal or under the signet (the king's personal seal) which broke the normal law of the realm. Then there is the bitter complaint written in 1371 by the earl of Ross. David had insisted that Ross's daughter and heiress marry Walter Leslie, one of the king's close associates; refused to allow Ross to entail the earldom on his brother; forced Ross to let Leslie have some of his lands, and grant some to the king's stepson John Logie; rejected Ross's complaints at his illegal treatment with a list of Roman law authorities; and finally made Ross give in by confiscating the earldom, although Ross's imprisonment, which the queen, Margaret Drummond, had demanded, was not actually carried out. Ross was far from blameless, and his complaint was no doubt biased, but the points it raises – the hostility to the great magnates, involving the temporary confiscation of earldoms and imprisonment of earls; the favouring of less important nobles drawn from the middling baronage; the use of Roman law principles, which tended to set the king above the law; and the excessive influence of Margaret Drummond and her kin – are all recurring themes throughout the 1360s, both before and after the 1363 rebellion.

That was the kind of kingship that brought several English kings to grief. Why then were the problems of the 1360s not much worse? The answer is probably that by then the characteristic feature of late-medieval Scottish politics, the general reluctance throughout the political community to take disputes to extremes, had come into operation. The 1363 rebellion was a more-or-less selfish demonstration against royal policies, not a serious attempt to overthrow the king, and was bound to collapse once David acted firmly. But then David did not proceed with treason trials and executions; he simply made the rebels formally submit and swear future loyalty. Subsequently the king's attitude towards many of the great magnates can be described better as temporary strictness to individuals rather than general vindictiveness. Therefore in the 1360s Scottish politics never became a matter of life and death.

Some credit for this must go to the king; while his policies can be criticized, they did not extend to destroying his opponents. The behaviour of the great magnates is also significant: Stewart, Douglas and March not only cooperated with each other (avoiding the rivalries of the 1340s), but were also prepared to cooperate with David's regime after 1363. The impression given by witness lists to royal charters is of the great magnates doggedly maintaining their presence at court in the face of royal indifference to them. Because of that, David's policy of favouring lesser nobles was not as divisive as it might have been.

Three other factors, however, probably carry greater weight. The low level of centralization in Scottish government meant that the damage royal policies could inflict on magnates' local interests was limited. Secondly, domestic politics still took second place to foreign affairs and the pressure from Edward III; the knowledge that earlier in the century Scottish civil wars had greatly aided the English possibly reduced internal tensions. Thirdly, the lesser nobles favoured by David were not a homogeneous group. Some were exclusively king's men – like his stepson John Logie, his wife's nephew Malcolm Drummond, or Walter Leslie, William Dishington, John Herries and David Annan – whose prominence ended with David's death. But others, for instance Robert Erskine, Hugh Eglington, John Danielston and Archibald Douglas 'the Grim' (illegitimate son of the 'good Sir James') had close ties with Robert Stewart and the earl of Douglas. The role of such men was probably crucial. Their recruitment by David doubtless undermined the great magnates' strength and contributed to the 1363 débâcle. On the other hand their presence within the regime would have stopped it from being totally partisan; after 1363 they probably formed a bridge between the crown and the great magnates, helping prevent the latter's isolation.

Bridges were also built by two important marriages. The queen's nephew Malcolm Drummond married the earl of Douglas's only daughter, and her niece Annabel Drummond married Robert Stewart's eldest son John. The latter marriage is especially significant. David had already made Robert Stewart transfer Atholl to John, and following the marriage John became earl of Carrick. That was the only creation of an earl in the 1360s; moreover Carrick had been Robert Bruce's earldom and had been given to David himself as heir to the throne. The grant implies that David, who presumably expected to outlive Robert Stewart (eight years his senior), was recognizing John as the real heir-presumptive. It suggests that John can be linked politically with the king – significantly, in 1378 John named his eldest son David. The other main Bruce estate, Annandale (no longer held by the Randolphs) was given to the king's stepson, John Logie. Thus in the later 1360s the members of the queen's immediate family, her son, nephew and niece, were climbing into the top ranks of the nobility, forming a Drummond family grouping which probably rivalled the Stewarts and Douglases, especially when connections like Walter Leslie were included. If, as might have been expected, Robert Stewart had died before the king, then with the earl of Carrick inheriting the Stewart lands and with John Logie having Annandale and Walter Leslie by then earl of Ross, David's associates would have virtually dominated the higher nobility. In fact that did not happen. In 1369 David quarrelled with Margaret Drummond and divorced her; then in 1371 he himself died. John Logie lost Annandale; but the Drummonds, because of the two marriages, continued to be a major factor in Scottish politics for the next half century.

III

Robert II's reign (1371–90) appears at first sight to have begun badly and ended worse. Before the coronation he was faced with a political demonstration by his erstwhile colleague William earl of Douglas. In his last years he relinquished his executive powers: first, in November 1384, to his eldest son John earl of Carrick, and then, in November or December 1388 (after Carrick had been incapacitated by a kick from a horse), to his second son Robert earl of Fife. During the intervening period little seems to have happened – that is, there were no events of any obvious domestic political significance – but a continuous parliamentary concern with law and order also gives the reign a bad image.

But in domestic politics, just as in foreign, the reign was in fact not so unsuccessful. The absence of striking political events is hardly a misfortune: in the 1440s Bower looked back to 'the tranquility and prosperity of peace' under Robert II. Between 1371 and 1384 political tension seems lower than at any time in late-medieval Scottish history. And what 'Wyntoun' called the 'royd harsk begynning' must not be misunderstood. Douglas's demonstration was not, as is sometimes stated, a claim to the throne, but (as in 1363) probably concerned royal patronage and favour. It can be seen as a warning to Robert II not to follow his predecessor's policies, and may have been aimed at Robert and Thomas Erskine, to whom David II had entrusted the castles of Edinburgh, Stirling and Dumbarton. The nobility as a whole, and particularly George Dunbar earl of March and his brother John, stood by Robert II; the incident shows Robert's strength, not his weakness. The outcome, too, is significant. Douglas's point was taken: he maintained a position close to King Robert, while his son received a substantial pension and married one of the king's daughters. John Dunbar was rewarded with the earldom of Moray. The Erskines lost their castles, but were compensated and proved firm supporters of Robert II. And the two great strongholds, Edinburgh and Stirling, finished up in the hands of Robert's eldest sons. Thus nobody lost from the incident - Robert II seems to have pleased all the parties involved, no mean feat - but his own family's position was immeasurably strengthened.

This episode epitomizes the reign. It was peaceful and stable, yet the Stewarts virtually took over the higher nobility. Robert II's eldest son John already had Carrick and Atholl, and in 1371 received the Stewart lordship of Renfrew; his second son Robert became earl of Menteith in right of his wife in 1371, and in 1372 acquired Fife from its countess; his third son Alexander was given the lordship of Badenoch, married the heiress to the earldom of Ross in 1382, and was made earl of Buchan; his fourth son David was made earl of Strathearn and later added Caithness; and his fifth son Walter was married to the heiress of the lordship of Brechin. These grants have been called a waste of royal resources, but it would have been shocking and dangerous if the king's sons had not been suitably endowed, and none of the endowments actually came from crown lands. They meant, however, that Robert II's sons eventually possessed eight out of 15 earldoms, plus other extensive estates.

This transformation of the higher nobility was achieved without trouble probably because the rest of the political community had little cause for grievance. In the other major families, the Dunbar possessions had greatly increased, with Thomas Randolph's lordship of Annandale and earldom of Moray going to his heirs George and John Dunbar respectively; and the earl of Douglas added Mar to his broad estates when his wife's brother the earl of Mar died childless in 1374. Another Douglas, Archibald 'the Grim', had also become a leading magnate; he acquired half of Galloway from David II, half in 1372, and was allowed by Robert II to take over the estates of his wife's first husband, the last Murray of Bothwell. The result was a broad stable balance at the top of noble society - even the Drummonds were included, through their ties with the earls of Carrick and Douglas.

In general, too, Robert II's patronage (although benefiting his own family) was more even-handed than David II's. Available land was distributed reasonably fairly, as were privileges like grants in free barony, regality and 'blench-farm'. David II's henchman Walter Leslie was allowed to inherit Ross on his father-in-law's death, despite the latter's complaint. Robert's seven daughters married prominent nobles. There was also considerable patronage in money. For a Scottish king, Robert II was well off; booming wool exports provided enough customs receipts for him to meet all his commitments, and still pay several hundred pounds (eventually over £1,000) in annuities to various nobles. While the total amount may not have been very high by the English or French crown's standards, these annuities made an important contribution to many Scottish nobles' revenues, and were a vital part of crown patronage.

What then happened in the later 1380s? When Fife became guardian in 1388 Robert II's age (then over 70) and Carrick's infirmity were the official reasons. But these probably conceal a power struggle within the royal family dating from 1384. Historians have generally linked Robert II and Carrick together, but kings' eldest sons often opposed their fathers. The record of Carrick's appointment as lieutenant in 1384 states cryptically that Robert II relinquished power 'for certain causes', and includes safeguards against his countermanding Carrick's actions; that suggests Robert was not regarded as senile, and hints at a *coup d'état*. The next council-general, in 1385, saw several outright attacks on Robert's third son, Alexander earl of Buchan, the notorious 'Wolf of Badenoch', and in one case it was declared that any royal action on behalf of Alexander should be reversed immediately. By 1384 Robert's favouring of Alexander had probably weakened his support within the political community (it would certainly have antagonized the Dunbars; see chap. 8:ii), thereby facilitating Carrick's takeover. The death of the first earl of Douglas in May 1384 was perhaps a factor, too: the new earl, James, wanted more aggression towards England than his father and Robert II had shown.

In 1388–9 the pattern is similar. After Earl James's death at Otterburn in August 1388 there was a dispute over the Douglas inheritance between his sister's husband Malcolm Drummond and the heir to the entailed estates, Archibald 'the Grim'. Fife supported Archibald Douglas, and in the first parliament after he became guardian Malcolm Drummond was accused of wrongly obtaining a brieve from the chancellor giving him possession of some of the entailed lands. This was cancelled; the chancellor was apparently censured; Archibald Douglas duly inherited the lands and title; and Drummond fled to England, where he placed all his possessions, including the entire Douglas inheritance, under Richard II's protection. The affair must have involved Carrick,

Drummond's brother-in-law. He probably appeared, rightly or wrongly, to have been implicated in this attempt to divert the Douglas inheritance – which would have weakened his own position. This reappearance of the Drummond family connection in the political limelight is significant. Other former members of David II's circle also seem more prominent during Carrick's lieutenancy; most strikingly, a long-running dispute between John Logie and the earl of Fife was settled in Logie's favour in 1385. Can the political changes of the later 1380s therefore be explained in terms of a re-emergence of the divisions of the 1360s? That does seem likely, although the fact that the Stewarts were now the royal family and the appearance of new issues like the 'Wolf of Badenoch' and the Douglas inheritance obviously changed the pattern.

Robert II is generally portrayed as a spectator of these events. But some hints to the contrary can be found; for instance, the move against Carrick late in 1388 and the decision that Scotland should join the Anglo-French truce in 1389 were both made, at least formally, by Robert II in person. Perhaps Robert II and Fife can be linked together against Carrick and Drummond; Fife's appointment as guardian may have been a counter-coup. But however Robert II's role is interpreted, the main point is that these political upheavals were remarkably limited. They affected only a few individuals, and did not split the political community. Power changed hands without violence, with the consent of the political community, and in a parliamentary context; Fife's appointment was subject to parliamentary approval of his actions. There is a clear contrast with England, where similar questions of limiting or transferring royal executive powers caused far worse crises under Richard II, Henry IV and Henry VI. Even in the last difficult years, therefore, the minimization of political tension remains the chief characteristic of Robert II's reign – as it probably was of most of his whole career.

IV

When Carrick became king he took the title Robert III (1390–1406); his own name, John, was apparently considered unlucky in a king. He was still infirm when he succeeded his father, and probably never recovered; his reign's politics were therefore dominated by the guardianship issue.

Initially Fife continued in office. He was very powerful: guardian, earl of Fife and Menteith, keeper of Stirling castle; his son Murdoch was justiciar north of the Forth. But Fife was no longer so strong as his brother, now that the latter was king. Robert III's illness did not prevent him from favouring his supporters, who included Malcolm Drummond (back from England, and now lord of Mar through his wife), the Dunbar earls of March and Moray, magnates like the Lindsays of Crawford and Glenesk, James Douglas of Dalkeith and David Fleming of Biggar, and several south-western barons connected with the Stewart lordships. These all received royal patronage, generally annuities in return for retinue service to the king and his son David. Robert III, like Richard II and Henry IV of England, used the practice of retaining to build up his own, royal, affinity. Although poor by English standards, he had far more resources than any Scottish magnate, and consequently his affinity was much greater. Then there was the third earl of Douglas. In 1398 Archibald 'the Grim' had added the main Douglas estates to his own lordships of Galloway and Bothwell, creating a huge territorial complex. But he had always been a loyal crown servant, and after 1390 had no reason to continue supporting Fife if that meant opposing the new king. Fife's gradual eclipse is therefore not surprising. He probably never formally relinquished his office, and was given the rank of duke of Albany in 1398; but his guardian's salary ceased in 1393, and in 1399 he had to accept the appointment of the heir to the throne, now of age and duke of Rothesay, as Robert III's lieutenant.

The appointment was again made by a council-general after an attack on the king and his ministers (aimed presumably at Albany and Murdoch Stewart). But this time it was limited to three years, and was subject not only to parliamentary approval but to a specially nominated council (including Albany) which looks like a cross-section of the political community. The council could monitor Rothesay's actions, but otherwise they were not to be countermanded, 'as sumqwhile has bene seyne'. The procedure seems designed to avoid the tensions and uncertainties at the centre of government evident in the 1390s. But when Rothesay's three years expired in 1402 he was arrested by Albany and the fourth earl of Douglas, and imprisoned in Albany's castle of Falkland, where he died. A parliamentary commission of enquiry exonerated Albany and Douglas; Albany was reappointed lieutenant-general.

Rothesay's fall was probably his own fault. Superficially his lieutenancy was successful: he was active over law and order, held a parliament which made important reforms in the land law, and (together with Albany) countered Henry IV's invasion. Yet behind the scenes his support evaporated. There is evidence of his tactlessness and arrogance, which probably angered the wider political community. He ignored most of the special council: a council meeting in November 1399 seems dominated by his associates. He appears close to his uncle Malcolm Drummond, and his private officials included a William Drummond and John Logie – thus the Drummond faction was emerging again, possibly alienating other supporters. Finally there were his female relationships: he was involved with a sister of the earl of Crawford; then apparently married the earl of March's daughter; then repudiated her and married a daughter of Archibald 'the Grim'. This incensed the powerful Lindsays and Dunbars; March defected to England, with disastrous consequences. The Douglas marriage did not have the desired effect, either. Archibald 'the Grim' died soon after, and his son the fourth earl was a man who always put personal advantage first. Once Rothesay's star was waning, his brother-in-law sided with Albany.

Rothesay's death was followed quickly by Malcolm Drummond's, in similar circumstances after kidnap and imprisonment. The culprit may have been Alexander Stewart, illegitimate son of the 'Wolf of Badenoch', who married Drummond's widow in 1404 and through her became earl of Mar; or it might have been Albany himself, whom Drummond had clearly feared in 1388. At any rate, no action was taken. Later in 1402 the battle of Homildon removed many other magnates from the Scottish political scene, including the earl of Douglas. By the end of that year, therefore, Albany's position within Scotland appears practically unchallengeable.

He did not, however, have everything his own way. On parliamentary insistence, his appointment had to be renewed after two years; he did not have sole control over patronage; and the exchequer auditors were not afraid to question his accounts. Robert III, although virtually in retirement on Bute, engaged more retainers for his surviving son James, and also had all the vast Stewart possessions, including Renfrew, Cunningham, Kyle and Carrick, created into a regality for the prince – thereby removing them from the ordinary administrative machinery, which Albany ran. The Robert III–Albany power-struggle had not finished.

Its culmination came with the king's decision to send Prince James to France. Presumably Robert intended to protect James from a fate like Rothesay's. Albany, if he learnt of the arrangements (could they have been kept secret?) would hardly have objected publicly. On its return from despatching James in February 1406, however, the escort was attacked and its leader David Fleming killed by James Douglas of Balvenie, brother of the fourth earl. The quarrel may have been personal – but Douglas was Albany's son-in-law, and a year later Albany called him 'my lieutenant', while Fleming was probably Robert III's closest councillor. Is there perhaps something to the mid-fifteenth-century *Book of Pluscarden's* statement that Fleming was killed 'because he had been one of the chief actors in the seizure of King Robert II', which recalls the events of the 1380s? Certainly it is striking how three prominent opponents of Albany – Rothesay, Drummond and Fleming – all met sudden deaths. Prince James, too, temporarily vanished from the scene; English pirates intercepted his ship, and he spent the next 18 years in England.

James's capture was apparently a death-blow to the 69-year-old Robert III. According to Bower, he described himself as 'the worst of kings and the most miserable of men'. It is difficult to disagree, although we can sympathize with his obvious sense of frustration: in the Middle Ages kings' adult brothers (fortunately rare in Scotland) frequently caused political problems. But while Robert III was probably Scotland's least impressive king, it is significant that his reign was not more disastrous. In England and France, by contrast, weak and partisan kingship – not to mention the illnesses of Henry VI and Charles VI – caused far more unrest and violence. Judging by what happened elsewhere, Robert III's Scotland might have been expected to dissolve into civil war; but, as in the later 1380s, the political struggle was confined to the royal family and its close associates, and did not bring general strife to the political community.

V

On Robert III's death the duke of Albany became governor for the captive James I (1406–37). We shall never know whether Albany helped cause or prolong James's captivity. But for the next 14 years he was at last supreme within Scotland – even issuing crown charters in his own name, dated by the years of his governorship. Some historians have regarded that as sinister, but it simply reflects the fact that James I had not been crowned. What is more important is that Albany, as James's nearest relative, had every right to be governor. The central power struggle, intermittent since 1384, therefore ceased, and the whole political community, even former retainers of Robert III, apparently accepted his rule without question.

Albany however was not king, and could not grant away the crown's possessions or rights. His surviving acts as governor contain no grants of lands or annuities, and only one creation of a barony. After 1406 normal crown patronage, which adherents of the regime could reasonably have expected, completely dried up. Instead we find unofficial agreements and favours. For example Albany let his nephew the earl of Mar act as virtual lieutenant in the north. He also made a bond of friendship with the earl of Douglas in 1409, to provide a means of settling quarrels between their followings: hardly the act of an all-powerful ruler, but one that made considerable political sense. Even more sensibly the earl of March was allowed to return from England without suffering any penalties beyond having formally to surrender Annandale, which had been taken over in 1400 by the earl of Douglas.

Another aspect of Albany's unofficial patronage is his turning a blind eye when certain nobles helped themselves from the customs. Chief among them were the earl of Douglas, his brother James, and several of their retainers; they took over £7,000 Scots between 1409 and 1420. Douglas could have claimed this was owed him to supplement his £133 Scots fee as warden of Edinburgh castle, granted in 1400 (the earl of Carrick's fee, in the pre-inflation 1370s, had been £333); to offset the cost of redeeming his hostages, abandoned in England in 1409 (having led the Scots army at Homildon, he could have expected help with his ransom); and to meet his March Warden's expenses on raids and negotiations. These points, together with the fact that receipts were usually given, perhaps make the customs plundering appear less heinous. It was, admittedly, highly irregular – but perhaps Albany wanted to ensure that responsibility for such large payments rested with Douglas rather than himself.

The customs plundering followed the sharp reduction in government income caused by the export slump in the early fifteenth century. The Exchequer Rolls record a mounting deficit: £4,397

Scots by 1420. But the immediate financial situation was probably not so bad as it appears. For instance Albany stopped many heritable annuities granted before 1406 when the original recipient died. And he met the government deficit from his own pocket by not receiving his full annual £1,000 Scots fee as governor. In effect, he subsidized his public purse from his private purse. In this way, he was probably able to meet the costs of his government, such as they were, and even to afford the customs plundering. But this was at the ultimate expense of the crown, because the steadily mounting deficit was mostly owed to Albany himself.

It will have become obvious that the main beneficiary of Albany's governorship, apart from Albany, was the earl of Douglas. That perhaps suggests Albany's weakness. Yet the remarkably persuasive Douglas also did well out of Henry IV, Henry V, John duke of Burgundy, and Charles VII. He exhibited an acute sense of his own importance, but if that was satisfied posed no political threat. Albany had doubtless understood him ever since their joint action against Rothesay. Moreover, Douglas never dominated Scottish politics; offsetting him were Albany, the earl of Mar, and his long-term rival the earl of March (probably allowed back from England for that reason). During Albany's governorship the Stewarts, Douglases and Dunbars give Scotland's political society a fairly well-balanced appearance.

Another reason for not regarding Albany as weak is that, when he wanted, he could act firmly. After the earl of Strathearn was murdered in 1413, the killers were quickly dealt with. In 1411–12, following Harlaw, he led armies north and made the lord of the Isles submit (see chap. 8:iv). It is clear, indeed, that all his actions – whether conciliatory or ruthless – were carefully and usually well calculated. Unlike Rothesay, he never gave needless offence to the political community, and there are several instances of his courting popularity. One example is when he presided over a court case in which he was a party – and allowed the case to be lost. His whole career, from the late 1360s, shows all the characteristics of the successful politician. When he died in 1420 at the age of 80 (he was past the modern retiring age when he became governor), it was the end of one of the least eventful regencies in Scottish or English history.

Albany's achievement is highlighted by the change which occurred when his son Murdoch succeeded him. Duke Murdoch seems to have been an amiable person, but lacked his father's political grasp. In particular he could not control his sons, whom Bower described as insolent and lawless, and they probably alienated support for his regime. For example, while Murdoch continued his father's agreement with the earl of Mar, his eldest son Walter allied with a rival claimant to the earldom. Moreover 'the excellent prince Walter Stewart of Fife, Lennox and Menteith', as one document styled him, actually gave an undertaking to the French to continue the war with England when he became king or governor, and to prevent 'his subjects' from helping the English. Murdoch's sons eclipsed the successes of his governorship – the 1423 treaty ending a commercial war with Holland, and the negotiation of James I's ransom – and were completely counterproductive. After 1420 the earl of Douglas started working for James's return, while Walter Stewart's aggressive support for France no doubt helped persuade the English government to release the Scottish king in 1424.

VI

Shortly after his return, James I arrested Walter Stewart and two other nobles, all probably notorious troublemakers – demonstrating his intention to be a different ruler from his immediate predecessors. His toughness is reminiscent of David II, and also Margaret Drummond: perhaps he took after his mother's family. At any rate the Drummond–Albany feud reached its climax. By March 1425 Duke Murdoch and his father-in-law the earl of Lennox had been seized. James probably planned to send Murdoch as hostage to England for his ransom; but Murdoch's youngest son revolted in Lennox. In May an assize of 21 nobles sitting in parliament sentenced Murdoch, his two eldest sons and the 80-year-old earl of Lennox to death. This was carried out in the first state executions in Scotland since 1320. Walter Stewart's crime was armed robbery, but Murdoch and the others were probably condemned as accessories to the Lennox revolt. Since parliament had recently legislated against rebellion and helping rebels, the assize was bound to find them guilty. But James doubtless had other motives. He presumably remembered his brother Rothesay's death and his own captivity, and was obviously aware of the value of the Albany estates and of the last words in the last Exchequer roll before his return: '£3,809 15s 8d, owed to the lord governor'.

This affair, the bloody culmination of the past 40 years' politics, encapsulates the main domestic themes of the rest of James I's reign: crown–noble relations, law and order, and finance. Finance is the most important. Even when James had improved the financial situation – by stopping annuities, cancelling Duke Murdoch's debt, increasing the customs through encouraging trade, and extending the crown lands – his annual revenue was probably around £8,000 Scots, considerably less (after inflation) than David II's and Robert II's, chiefly because of the decline in the customs. Then there was his ransom: £33,333 sterling (£66,666 Scots), promised over five years. For this a 5 per cent tax on lands and goods was imposed in 1424. Bower, one of the collectors, said it raised over £18,000 Scots the first year, but far less the second, and it was then abandoned. Yet over £26,000 Scots was collected in all, a huge amount for Scottish taxation. Only about £12,000 Scots, however, went to the ransom. Initially James probably hoped to negotiate smaller instalments, and also to overcome taxpayers' resistance by introducing into parliament a system of shire representatives, who as in England would commit local communities to taxation. But by 1429 he had decided to stop the ransom altogether; the rest of the tax was mostly spent in Flanders on artillery, jewellery, and luxuries for the court, while much of his regular revenue went on building, especially at Linlithgow.

Compared with what he had seen at the English and French courts, James was not spending heavily. But it would have made a bad impression in Scotland, since he had abandoned his hostages to be redeemed by their own families, and was not generous with patronage to the nobility. There was, moreover, a point of principle. James had tried to distinguish between 'private' expenditure, met from his 'own' revenues (including, contentiously, the customs), and 'public' – on the ransom, warfare, and so on – for which taxation was required. Yet he then spent much of the 1424–5 tax privately. Parliament's reaction can be seen in 1431. It insisted that a tax agreed for a Highland expedition should be kept in a locked chest and spent only on the expedition or 'the commoun profit and use'; and when the expedition was called off, the tax was cancelled. Other attempts to raise taxation were unsuccessful; by 1436 James was instead pressing wealthy individuals for 'benevolences' or gifts. Thus James's financial difficulties lasted through the reign. They probably dominated his dealings with parliament, producing medieval Scotland's only constitutional struggle over taxation – which perhaps culminated, according to a recent analysis,[2] in a serious confrontation in autumn 1436 following the unsuccessful Roxburgh campaign.

It is sometimes stated that James's desire for money – even his admirer Bower called him acquisitive – also determined his policy towards the magnates. But cupidity was not the only reason for the Albany family's destruction. And with respect to the other magnates, James was more concerned with political advantage. He had a useful lever in his 1424 enquiry into the fate of crown lands since Robert I's time, which revealed irregularities in the transmission of several estates, including March (should Albany have pardoned the renegade earl?), Strathearn, Mar, and the Douglas lordships of Wigtown and Selkirk. That gave James legal grounds for confiscating Strathearn in 1427 and March in 1435 (when border tension was rising). But Strathearn was given for life to James's uncle Walter Stewart earl of Atholl (Robert II's youngest son) – who was actually the under-age earl of Strathearn's guardian, and doubtless instigated the whole transaction. The question mark over the Douglas lordships was probably used to benefit James's sister, the fourth earl's widow, who received Galloway (including Wigtown) for life; while Selkirk was apparently confiscated, possibly in connection with the fifth earl's temporary imprisonment in 1431. And James agreed that Alexander Stewart could keep Mar, and even transmit it to his illegitimate son, regardless of the claims of collateral heirs – on condition that if his line died out it should revert to the crown (as was to happen in 1435). James's policy was not simply to enrich the crown at the nobility's expense; with Strathearn and Mar, indeed, legitimate heirs were set aside for the benefit of powerful magnates.

This raises questions about James's famous zeal for law and order. He made firm statements on the subject, and was not likely to ignore blatant lawlessness in others. A cynic, however, might suggest a fiscal side to his concern; in 1434 he threatened to punish the sheriffs for not making as much money as possible out of law enforcement. Also, when he started the sessions (see chap. 6:iv), he was probably hoping to reduce his judicial load. And while Bower called him 'our lawgiver king', almost all his judicial legislation merely repeated or modified measures enacted by his predecessors;

[2] A.A.M. Duncan, *James I* (University of Glasgow, Scottish History Department, occasional papers, 1976).

the idea that James's return in 1424 marks a turning-point in the development of Scots law is an exaggeration.

The reign ended abruptly in February 1437, when James was killed in Perth by assassins led by Robert Graham of Kinpunt and Robert Stewart of Atholl, grandson of the earl of Atholl. Atholl, next in line to the throne after James's six-year-old son, was also involved. He apparently expected to become governor, and (perhaps his grandson's plan) even king should anything happen to James's son; but historians' arguments for a claim to the throne based on the superior legitimacy of Robert II's second marriage, to Atholl's mother, can be discounted. The conspirators also had personal grievances. David of Atholl, Earl Walter's son and Robert Stewart's father, had died a hostage in England in 1434, which presumably offset James's favours to Atholl. Robert Graham, similarly, was the uncle of the former earl of Strathearn, who having lost the earldom also became a hostage, remaining in England until 1453. Graham, moreover, seems to have been a political idealist and a prominent opponent of royal taxation (perhaps especially in 1436), who viewed James as a genuine tyrant.

The assassins expected their deed to be welcomed. James was probably never popular; as early as 1425 seditious talk causing discord between king and people had been made punishable by death. Bower's eulogies are balanced by Aeneas Sylvius' description of him in 1435 as short, fat, passionate and vindictive. Some of his dealings suggest he was 'too clever by half' – an impression possibly given also by his extravagantly complex poem the *Kingis Quair*. His relations with the earl of Douglas in particular seem cool. In addition to David of Atholl, at least 15 of his hostages died in England. And the Roxburgh fiasco must have seriously damaged his public image of strength and masterfulness – especially if it was followed by a conflict over taxation.

In the event, however, although Graham and Stewart thought the time had come for direct action, they received absolutely no support, but were quickly rounded up and executed. James had never antagonized the political community, and although many individuals may have disliked him, they were certainly not going to condone the horrific crime of regicide. The most powerful individual, the earl of Douglas – whom his brother-in-law Graham may have hoped would side with the assassins – was the new king's closest male relative after Atholl, and duly became lieutenant of the kingdom. James I's murder – the first killing of a Scottish king since the eleventh century – was thus the work of a small. isolated band of dissidents who completely misjudged the attitude of the political community. It was in no way part of any general crown-noble conflict.

Among its results, however, was the completion of a remarkable upheaval within the higher nobility. We have seen that James confiscated the earldoms of Fife, Menteith, Lennox, Strathearn and March, while escheats to the crown included not only Mar but Buchan and Ross in 1424 (when Albany's second son died at Verneuil), and Moray in 1429 (when the male line of the Dunbar earls died out). James did grant Strathearn to the earl of Atholl, and the title and part of the lands of Menteith to the former earl of Strathearn (who was then sent to England). But in what was a radically new policy he kept possession of the rest. Then in 1437 Atholl, Caithness and Strathearn also came to the crown, on the execution of the regicide Earl Walter. Thus between 1424 and 1437, partly by design and partly by accident, the main branches of the houses of Stewart and Dunbar disappeared from the political arena. And since the Drummonds had merged with the crown in the person of James I, the Douglases alone remained of the major family groupings of the fourteenth and early fifteenth centuries. Moreover Scotland was virtually denuded of earls. The only ones left were Douglas, Angus, Crawford, Menteith (a hostage in England), and Sutherland (also a hostage, 1427–47). This was an even greater transformation of the upper levels of Scottish political society than that under Robert I, and is by far the most important consequence of James I's reign.

VII

This transformation left the earls of Douglas with unrivalled power, a fact which dominates James II's reign (1437–60). It produced Scottish history's most famous crown–magnate conflict, which reached its climax in February 1452 when James II murdered William, eighth earl of Douglas,[3] and ended with the family's destruction three years later.

[3] There were five earls of Douglas in James II's reign.

(A) Archibald, 5th earl: became lieutenant in 1437; died of plague in 1439.

(B) William, 6th earl, son of (A): under-age; put to death in 1440, partly at least to benefit (C). *[cont. overleaf]*

Because the Douglases had been steadily amassing territory since Robert I's reign, the conflict with James II has traditionally been portrayed as the consequence of over a century of excessive royal generosity. But although Earl William was probably the most powerful Scottish magnate ever, his predecessors in fact had had almost as extensive estates; Earl William's greater power was due to the disappearance of so many other magnates between 1424 and 1437. Moreover no previous earl of Douglas had posed a serious threat to the crown: indeed the Douglases had a remarkably well-maintained tradition of loyalty and service. Historians currently argue that the eighth and ninth earls did not intentionally break that tradition. They stress that James II was invariably the aggressor: in 1450-1, when he twice overran Douglas lands by force; in 1452, when he summoned the eighth earl to Stirling and killed him; and in 1455, when he suddenly attacked the ninth earl. James's motives are explained as a mixture of fear, jealousy and acquisitiveness.

James's actions, however, must be related to Earl William's during the king's minority. In the power vacuum after the fifth earl's death in 1439, James had been siezed by a Lothian baron, Alexander Livingston, who persuaded a council-general to give him custody of the young king. The seventh and eighth earls maintained a close association with Livingston, and hence with James. Earl William appears as the king's lieutenant in 1444, which gave him royal sanction for his actions – including armed attacks on his rivals. His dominance was demonstrated in a parliament which he (technically James) held in 1445. Two brothers became earls of Moray and Ormond respectively, several henchmen became lords of parliament, and other important barons were wooed with titles; one opponent, Bishop Kennedy of St Andrews, was threatened with deprivation, another, the earl of Angus, with forfeiture, and a third, Lord Crichton, was besieged in Edinburgh castle. And Douglas's famous alliance with two of the remaining earls, Crawford and Ross

(C) James, 7th earl: formerly James Douglas of Balvenie, the 4th earl's brother; died in 1443.

(D) William, 8th earl, son of (C): dominated later years of James II's minority; murdered by James II in 1452.

(E) James, 9th earl, brother of (D): finally forfeited by James II in 1455, but lived on until 1491.

See also the Genealogical Table, Appendix C.

(the lord of the Isles, recognized as earl in 1437), probably dates from this time.

James therefore grew up amid Douglas power and manipulation. Even when he followed his marriage in 1449 (at the age of 18) by dismissing and punishing Livingston and his kin, the impetus probably came as much from Douglas – jettisoning the now dispensable Livingston – as James. In 1450 Douglas had royal charters issued confirming his ownership of Galloway and Selkirk, which the Douglases had repossessed after 1437, disregarding the grant of Galloway to the fourth earl's widow (Earl William even alienated part of Galloway in regality) and James I's confiscation of Selkirk. This directly challenged James I's policy – and since James II's councillors (several of whom had served James I) were trying to continue it, thereby challenged James II himself. James probably came to believe (and his councillors probably argued) that unless he made Douglas recognize royal authority, his minority would never really end.

This explains James's actions in 1450–1: the lands he attacked were Galloway and Selkirk. But in parliaments in July and October 1451 he had to back down and regrant them to Douglas, notwithstanding the fifth earl's surrender of them to James I or any offences by the fifth or eighth earls. James must have been bitterly humiliated – and Douglas made things worse by adding 'earl of Wigtown' to his title. However no king would back down permanently; not even Robert III had done that. James found new grounds for confronting Douglas: the Douglas–Crawford–Ross bond, now probably an issue because the earl of Ross had revolted in 1451 (see chap. 8:v). But again Douglas refused to give way, and James, in a temper, killed him.

With hindsight it seems inevitable that one of these young men would have killed the other. Had Douglas killed James, however, he would have suffered the same fate as James I's assassins. That is because James strictly speaking had not acted illegally against Douglas, nor had he antagonized the political community in other ways. Therefore despite the obvious sympathy for Douglas in 1451, no one would have condoned regicide. James's hot-blooded killing of Douglas was less heinous. Moreover few people would have wanted openly to question James's justification of the deed; and few risked opposing him in arms when he twice marched through southern Scotland in force. When the murdered earl's brothers retaliated, only their kinsman Lord Hamilton and some 600 men followed them. The crown's advantages in such conflicts are also seen in the north-east, where Douglas's ally Crawford was defeated at Brechin by the earl of Huntly. Huntly, although created earl in the Douglas-dominated 1445 parliament, was Crawford's rival in the north-eastern vacuum left by the earl of Mar's death in 1435, and sided with the king. The *Auchinleck Chronicle* stated 'thair was with the erll of huntlie fer ma than was with the erll of crauford because he displayit the kingis banere and said It was the kingis actioun and he was his luftennend'. The eighth earl of Douglas had used the royal banner to his own advantage in the 1440s; now it was used against his ally.

That is one reason why James II got away with murder. Another concerns patronage. James distributed land, titles, privileges and offices to his own supporters and to landowners, especially many southern lairds, who might otherwise have been neutral. It was rarely lavish, but meant as few people as possible were positively hostile. Douglas's position, again, was weaker. His estates, although vast, could not be used to reward followers indefinitely – and previous earls had already made many grants from them. Also the Douglas following may have grown so large that individual ties were diluted; of the major cadet branches, the earl of Angus and most of the Douglases of Dalkeith supported James. Moreover traditional Douglas followers may have had second thoughts after 1440, when the sixth earl was killed partly to benefit James Douglas of Balvenie. At least one of those who helped James II kill Earl William was from a family with a long record of Douglas service.

Thirdly, James used propaganda skilfully. In the June 1452 parliament he accused Earl William of conspiracy, causing rebellions, and refusing help against rebels. Thereafter he appeared to show clemency. The Douglas brothers and Crawford were pardoned, their forfeitures were cancelled, and the eldest brother became the ninth earl. In 1453 James agreed to hand over Wigtown in return for the earl's bond of manrent – a formal acknowledgement of superiority. Such bonds were demanded by victors in disputes between nobles, but it was most uncommon for a king to do so. James's purpose was probably to demonstrate his fairness: seemingly all he wanted was the acceptance of his authority. And with the submissions and reconciliations, the 1452 affair appeared to have followed the normal course of Scottish political crises.

But, for the king, too much had happened for the reconciliation to be sincere. In March 1455 James attacked the ninth earl, and had his resistance condemned as rebellion. The same factors worked for the king as in 1452. Also, despairing of Scottish support (Crawford had died in 1453), the ninth earl looked to England – thus confirming the accusations of treason. When Douglas's allegiance to the English king was demanded, even Lord Hamilton decided to submit to James. Only the earl's brothers fought, and they were easily defeated by some border lairds at Arkinholm, near Langholm; Moray was slain, Ormond captured and executed. In parliament in June 1455 the Douglas estates were forfeited; Scotland's greatest magnate family had been destroyed inside three months.

After that, not surprisingly, James II ruled unchallenged. The concern for public relations was maintained: most of his former opponents were pardoned, and several gained royal favour – including Lord Hamilton. And although the royal finances benefited most from the Douglas forfeitures, James's supporters, five of whom became earls, were well rewarded. Yet they were kept in check; for instance while Huntly (who had received the lordship of Badenoch) arranged his son's marriage to the earl of Moray's widow three weeks after Arkinholm, James took over Moray himself. With Moray and Mar, indeed, James continued his father's policy. But although parliament in 1458 was perhaps not entirely enthusiastic with his rule, this was expressed in a flattering request that the statutes be kept, which indicates a different atmosphere from James I's reign or David II's. There were apparently no disputes over taxation, despite James's campaigns. And the contrast between James II and his father is best seen in their sieges of Roxburgh: James I's army dispersed, James II's continued the siege after his death.

With the Douglases' destruction the last of the predominant families of the fourteenth and early fifteenth centuries disappeared. After 1455 different names – which were to resound for three or more centuries – appear at the head of Scottish political society: Gordon (earl of Huntly), Hamilton, Erskine, Campbell (earl of Argyll, *c*.1458), and so on. They belonged to old, substantial baronial families, but until the later fifteenth century they had not been so consistently prominent as the Stewarts, Douglases, Randolphs, Dunbars and Drummonds.

This change was institutionalized by the development of the peerage rank 'lord of parliament' between 1445 and 1452, and is epitomized by one of the leading politicians of those years, William

Lord Crichton. Crichton was James I's sheriff of Edinburgh and warden of Edinburgh castle, became chancellor in 1439, and remained an indispensable figure in central administration until his death in 1454. In contrast to traditional magnates, Crichton's powerful position rested on government service, and was backed up by his kin (including Huntly, his son-in-law). Although he was eclipsed by the Douglases, he was one of the architects of their downfall, and foreshadowed the lords who replaced them.

Of course Crichton, Hamilton and the like had many precursors in earlier reigns – most notably Archibald Douglas 'the Grim'. Prominence in government service and relatively small estates do not in themselves indicate a new nobility. But before the 1450s, important barons like that had always been overshadowed by the very great territorial magnates. Moreover, because of the new crown policy of retaining land that came into its hands, and the remarkable production of sons by fifteenth-century noble families, it was much harder for the leading nobles of the later fifteenth century to amass great territorial complexes through crown grants and marriages to heiresses, as the greatest men of the fourteenth century had done. Consequently, although the day of the great magnate was certainly not over, after 1455 Scotland no longer contained men of the calibre of Thomas Randolph, Robert Stewart (before he became king), his son the duke of Albany, and the earls of Douglas. In James III's minority (to 1469), central politics consisted of the manoeuvrings of lords like Argyll, Huntly, Hamilton, Lord Kennedy, or Lord Boyd, who (emulating Alexander Livingston) seized James III's person in 1466. There was no one dominant magnate, unlike the two previous minorities. The change is typified in the fact that until the Boyd coup the major figures were the queen-mother and Bishop Kennedy of St Andrews. A new era in Scottish politics had begun.

VIII

For all the stress laid earlier on the low-key nature of Scottish politics, the account given does encompass several conflicts, culminating in the great crown–Douglas struggle. That, however, is because disputes are natural within all political societies, and it is impossible in a brief survey to avoid focusing on them. It is worth reiterating that, while the striking incidents inevitably take up disproportionate space, they were the exception not the rule. Serious political troubles were brief – even the worst, in 1452, was over inside four months – and infrequent – at most they disturbed 16 of the 128 years between 1341 and 1469. And the same point applies for most of the next 100 years; even during James III's personal reign, when royal policies greatly intensified political tensions and the king himself was killed by rebels in 1488, the periods of actual crisis were remarkably short. Not until the 1560s, when the Reformation and the reign of Queen Mary caused great upheavals, did political strife and violence become at all common in Scotland (and even then the earlier pattern was re-established well before 1600). Thus for more than two centuries after the ending of the Bruce–Balliol civil war, the main characteristic of Scotland's domestic politics was peace and stability – especially by contemporary standards in England and elsewhere.

Why was this so? The answer cannot be found in any special Scottish reasonableness, stability, or the like. Enough violent outrages are recorded by the dominant members of the political community, the magnates, to prove they were no more saintly than their counterparts in other countries. And despite the importance of individual monarchs' personalities and policies for explaining medieval political history, the answer probably does not lie there either. None of Scotland's kings from David II to James II was a model of perfect medieval kingship. There seems little to choose between them and contemporary rulers elsewhere; if anything, it is surprising they did not provoke more troubles.

But if less than first-class kingship provoked comparatively little trouble in Scotland, then that can be related to the power of the crown. The great paradox of late-medieval Scottish history is that the institutions at the Scots crown's disposal were relatively underdeveloped by contemporary standards, yet in the period covered by this book no king was defeated by rebellion, and the two apparently overmighty magnate houses were crushed. The paradox is resolved by stressing that because the crown was institutionally weak, it *had* to have the political community's support – so all the kings knew they could never risk being in conflict with more than a part of it. Kings were only challenged by combinations of magnates in 1363 and 1452. The 1363 rebellion was half-hearted, and David II had crucial support from many other important landowners. In 1452 James II had to concentrate on the Douglases, but was fortunate that Huntly, partly for personal reasons, tackled Crawford; Ross, however, had to be conciliated – which stopped him supporting Douglas effectively.

Scottish kings, in fact, could never ignore the principle 'politics is the art of the possible'. That may seem obvious – but in England, where so many kings came to grief, they invariably antagonized much more of their political communities than Scottish kings ever did, probably because the pressures encouraging provocative royal actions were far greater. The English concept of kingship was more exalted, the law of treason more draconian, the judicial system more centralized, and the royal revenues far higher. It was therefore easy in England to pursue the king's personal interests – and often the factional ones of his favourites – to extremes, regardless of political consequences. For instance a common form of royal patronage involved manipulating local administration and justice, which often upset vested interests, turning them against the crown. These factors had much less force in late-medieval Scotland. There royal patronage usually consisted of grants of land, money, titles, and privileges, benefiting the recipient but usually not antagonizing others; and royal favourites were never a serious issue. At its simplest, it was harder for Scotland's late-medieval kings to make enemies for themselves; so in crises few subjects were willing to disregard their fundamental obligation – and indeed instinct – of loyalty. This is even true of the unpopular James I, as his assassins discovered.

The nature of local power is also highly relevant. As we have seen (above, chapter 5), probably the most striking features of late-medieval Scottish noble society was the existence of clear-cut local or regional spheres of influence, within which local magnates were extremely difficult to challenge. There are, of course, exceptions – notably in Moray in the later fourteenth and fifteenth centuries (see chapter 8), and in the north-east during the 1440s and 1450s, where the earl of Huntly only replaced the earl of Mar as the dominant force after nearly 20 confused years. But in England local power structures were much more fragmented, and clear-cut spheres of influence were more the exception than the rule. Consequently demarcation disputes between late-medieval English magnates were quite common; and because local interests interlocked, disputes tended to escalate – some historians see this as the main cause of the Wars of the Roses. There was far less likelihood of that in late-medieval Scotland.

Moreover when we consider local and central power together, we find that in late-medieval Scotland local magnates were relatively insulated from the effects of central politics. Whereas in England changes at the centre often caused upheavals in the localities as new regimes rewarded their supporters, in Scotland new regimes were less able to do that; they were more likely to try and conciliate the important local lords. Therefore it probably did not matter much to local Scottish magnates who was in power at the centre. They would have had little interest in reversing Carrick's supplanting of Robert II, Fife's supplanting of Carrick, or Albany's supplanting of Rothesay – especially when ostensibly reasonable explanations for the changes were given. Nor did they need to risk defying James II on behalf of the Douglases, or to challenge the Livingston and Boyd coups during minorities. This no doubt is why the central power struggles never spread outwards to encompass the whole political society.

These arguments, of course, only apply to the period following the Bruce–Balliol civil war. But the civil war itself may provide a further explanation of the subsequent character of Scottish politics. It was to Scotland what, in the fifteenth century, the Wars of the Roses were to England and the Armagnac–Burgundian struggle was to France. Now after both those great civil wars, domestic politics in England and France became rather more low-key: both countries witnessed an increasing avoidance of dangerous political activity, a reduction in support for what rebellions there were, and a growing readiness to make compromises and live with political rivals. These are the phenomena evident in Scotland after the 1340s. It may be, therefore, that a period of relative political peace and stability is a normal feature of the aftermath of bitter civil war, at least in the Middle Ages. Moreover, the point is probably accentuated for Scotland by the connection between the Bruce–Balliol civil war and the Wars of Independence: the civil war almost brought about the English conquest of Scotland. Subsequently the threat to national independence posed by internal civil war must have been another factor helping to restrain political disputes. Thus the fact that domestic politics in later fourteenth and fifteenth century Scotland are characterized by the comparative absence of violence and turbulence is also, probably, partly the consequence of the civil and international strife of the period after 1306.

8

Highlands and Lowlands

I

One further aspect of late-medieval Scotland's political history needs consideration: the relationship of the Highlands to the kingdom as a whole. This was, as we shall see, largely a matter of high politics. It also involves broader themes, however, for it was in the later Middle Ages that the Highland–Lowland, Highlander–Lowlander divisions, which were to be such an important motif in subsequent Scottish history, seem first to have become apparent.

At the beginning of the fourteenth century, it has been demonstrated that the geographical 'Highland line' hardly constituted a meaningful divide at all. The main division in Scotland was the Forth. North of the Forth, the normal lay and ecclesiastical subdivisions generally included both Lowland and Highland areas, while the significant geographical subdivision was between the eastern and western Highlands. Gaelic was an everyday language from Sutherland as far south as Fife on the east, and in Carrick and Galloway as well as north of the Clyde on the west. Settlement patterns and agricultural practices were much the same over most of Scotland, and about half the population probably lived north of a line from Clyde to Tay. The country's lay landowners were a homogeneous class; for instance the 'Gaelic' Macdougalls and 'Norman' Comyns were closely linked. Lowland lords were happy to acquire lands in the Highlands or on the west coast. Travelling through the Highlands, or doing business in them, was not considered particularly difficult or dangerous. And in medieval Scotland's greatest crisis, the Wars of Independence, Highlanders and Lowlanders participated equally on both sides.

By 1400 the situation had changed; an awareness of clear-cut differences between Highlanders and Lowlanders was developing.

An early statement of this is given in a famous passage from Fordun's chronicle, written in the 1380s.

The manners and customs of the Scots vary with the diversity of their speech. For two languages are spoken amongst them, the Scottish and the Teutonic; the latter of which is the language of those who occupy the seabird and plains, while the race of Scottish speech inhabits the highlands and outlying islands. The people of the coast are of domestic and civilized habits, trusty, patient, and urbane, decent in their attire, affable, and peaceful, devout in Divine worship, yet always ready to resist a wrong at the hands of their enemies. The highlanders and people of the islands, on the other hand, are a savage and untamed race, rude and independent, given to rapine, ease-loving, clever and quick to learn, comely in person, but unsightly in dress, hostile to the English people and language, and, owing to diversity of speech, even to their own nation, and exceedingly cruel. They are, however, faithful and obedient to their king and country, and easily made to submit to law, if properly governed.

This passage has many echoes in later writings, and its points (except the final one) were still being made after 1745.

Fordun indicated three main areas of difference: geography, language and way of life. The geographical division is essentially that between mountains and plains; but as well as rugged terrain, the north and west have poor, acid soils, and even the flat parts tend to be relatively unproductive. The Highlands and Western Isles are thus doubly inhospitable. In the Middle Ages that did not prevent settlement or arable farming, but the population was more thinly spread than in the south and east, while the agricultural balance tilted more towards pastoral farming, and towards cattle rather than sheep. The contrast is one of degree, not kind, and is apparent throughout the Middle Ages. But it may have intensified in the fourteenth century, because of the demographic collapse after 1349. Reduced population pressure presumably halted the advances into the Highlands from the south and east which had been going on for centuries, and also meant that within the south and east there was less need to farm poor hilly areas. Thus differences between 'Lowland' and 'Highland' agriculture perhaps became more marked.

The linguistic division is rather clearer. Although Fordun called Gaelic 'the Scottish speech', the advance of English since the eleventh century had progressed to such an extent that in the four-teenth century Gaelic ceased to be the majority language of Scot-land, and became largely confined to the Highlands (including the sea-coast north of Inverness) and Western Isles. English was advancing socially, too: by the early fifteenth century it was the standard language of court, government and nobility. For much of the Middle Ages, vernacular English and Gaelic had probably had equally low status after official Latin and aristocratic French, but once English was the establishment language, Gaelic alone may have seemed second-rate. 'Glunton, guk dynynd dach hal mischy doch', was how the author of the *Buke of the Howlat* (written in Moray) satirically represented Gaelic poetry in about 1450.

Nevertheless the late Middle Ages were not altogether bad for Gaelic. In the 1490s James IV apparently found it worth learning, and the effects of its new inferiority to English were not really felt until the later sixteenth century. There was a lasting renaissance in Gaelic culture and literature in the fifteenth century, under the patronage of the lords of the Isles. Also Gaelic's geographical retreat came to a halt; the linguistic line established in the four-teenth century lasted for over four hundred years. Why that hap-pened is unclear, but again the easing of population pressure in English-speaking areas may be a factor. The result was that Gaelic was no longer a declining language, as it had been since the eleventh century; in fact it was still spoken by a substantial proportion of Scots – 'half of Scotland', thought John Major in the 1520s. Thus Gaelic survived the late Middle Ages in a relatively flourishing and vigorous state. But one consequence of its success in stemming the tide of English was its new, closer, association with the Highlands.

During the fourteenth century, therefore, linguistic and geographical divisions coalesced within Scotland. But by them-selves these divisions are probably not very significant; medieval governments generally found little extra difficulty in ruling geographically and linguistically divided countries. That was largely because they operated through the landowning classes, and medieval landowners were rarely choosy about where their estates were situated. In late-fourteenth-century Scotland the Stewarts of Innermeath (Perthshire) acquired the lordship of Lorn, and the Sinclairs of Roslin (Midlothian) took over the Norwegian earldom of Orkney. Many Scottish sheriffdoms, most of the earldoms, and several other large complexes of estates straddled the Highland line; about half the rents in the earldom of Strathearn in 1380 came from the Highland area, from Crieff to Balquhidder.

According to Fordun, however, the Highlanders were also 'savage and untamed', 'given to rapine', and so on. That adds a crucial extra dimension to the Highland–Lowland differences: not only could the Highlanders be identified with a separate language and culture, they were distinguished by violent and lawless behaviour. This perception of Highland savagery also seems to be a fourteenth-century development. Before 1300 there is no evidence that the Highlanders were regarded collectively as any worse than other Scots, but by the mid fourteenth century references to 'wild' and 'domestic' Scots – Highlanders and Lowlanders – begin to appear. Admittedly the Highland reputation for violence and lawlessness did not reach its full intensity until the sixteenth century; but it can, for instance, be seen in the chronicles of Wyntoun and Bower as well as Fordun. Also, most significantly, the belief that law and order (while a cause for concern everywhere) was a particular problem with respect to Highlanders occurs repeatedly in the parliamentary records from 1369 onwards. The development of this reputation for violence and lawlessness is probably what made the Gaelic-speaking, Highland areas really stand out from the rest of Scotland in Lowland eyes, eventually producing the idea of a country split into distinct Highland and Lowland halves.

Why did that development take place? Part of the answer doubtless lies in Fordun's statement that the Highlanders were 'easily made to submit to law, if properly governed' – which implies that their association with violence stemmed largely from a lack of satisfactory local government. That is also implied by parliament's requirement in 1369 that, for 'the pacification and rule of the higher regions', the major landowners in the Highlands should swear to maintain peace and justice within their domains. Certainly in the later fourteenth century problems of lordship caused serious disturbances, especially in the great central province of Moray; indeed the trouble in Moray was probably the most important single factor behind the Highlanders' increasingly bad reputation.

But it also seems possible to write in terms of a clash between two different kinds of society: in the Highlands, the clannish kin-based society of the traditional Gaelic world; in the Lowlands, the feudalized society predominant there since its introduction by the twelfth-century kings and their Anglo-French followers. The distinction between the two was far from absolute; it has been remarked that 'Highland society was based on kinship modified by feudalism, Lowland society on feudalism tempered by kinship'. There was much intermarriage among Highland and Lowland families, and considerable intermingling of institutions and influences. Nevertheless, some significant differences can be seen. For instance, a major principle of kin-based Highland society was that 'consequent upon the weakening of the ruling family a province becomes wide open either to a takeover by the kindred within its bounds that benefits most from the decline of the ruling family or to inroads by powerful neighbours'.[1] This indicates an important contrast in the means by which ambitious Highland and Lowland lords might set about extending territories and spheres of influence. In the Lowlands, such aggrandizement generally took place under cover of lawsuits, often based on claims by inheritance; but in the Highlands – at least in the most turbulent areas and periods of Highland history – less importance was attached to legal niceties, and territory was extended simply by taking over the desired area and levying its rents, by launching plundering raids against rivals, or by imposing 'protection rackets' upon them. The contrast is between disguised and naked aggression; but in the Lowlands, where following the letter of the law (if only superficially) was strongly emphasized, it probably seemed one between lawful and lawless behaviour.

In the twelfth and thirteenth centuries, however, perceptions of differences between kin-based and feudalized societies would not have caused much concern in Lowland Scotland. During those centuries royal authority was steadily extended northwards and westwards, regardless of geographical and racial divisions: initially into and beyond the province of Moray, once the base for the main internal challenges to the Scottish kings, and then from the 1230s into the remotest parts of Scotland, the West Highlands and the Western Isles (which were technically subject to Norway until their annexation in 1266). The process was carried out in the first instance through military campaigns, but was consolidated by establishing a reliable upper layer of feudal landowners (of Gaelic as well as Anglo-French descent) who acknowledged royal super-

[1]Quotations from: T.C. Smout, *A History of the Scottish People, 1560–1830* (2nd, paperback, edn., London, 1972), p. 43; and J.W.M. Bannerman, 'The Lordship of the Isles', in J.M. Brown, ed., *Scottish Society in the Fifteenth Century*, (London, 1977) p. 213.

iority, and who thus, while maintaining their own local power, simultaneously upheld that of the crown. This is typical of the operation of European feudal kingship. It means that, by the end of the thirteenth century, the whole of Scotland would have appeared to have been feudalized. In such circumstances Lowland alarm about the Highlands and Highland society in general would hardly have developed.

But, as we shall see, things changed in the fourteenth century. The crucial upper level of feudal lordship which seemed to have been established throughout the Highlands was seriously disrupted; first through the Bruce–Balliol civil war, and subsequently because several major families died out in the male line. Out of the upheaval, the Macdonald lordship of the Isles emerged in the western Highlands and Islands. It was a self-consciously and even aggressively Gaelic institution, which probably appeared at times to be challenging Lowland government and society; and while it brought internal stability to the west-coast region, it also (in accordance with the principles of Highland kin-based society) exhibited a forceful expansionist dynamic, especially towards the neighbouring regions of Moray and Ross. In Moray, meanwhile, the disruption of local lordship produced a power vacuum and then a major regional power struggle – in which the protagonists, although originally Lowlanders, acted in a way which, to Lowland eyes, would have been associated more with Highland chiefs. For instance, they imposed 'protection rackets' (a prominent feature of Gaelic lordship), and employed gangs of what contemporaries called 'caterans'.

The term cateran, which derived from the Gaelic for a lightly armed warrior (the kind used on plundering raids) is particularly significant. It indicates a Lowland perception of a particularly Gaelic, Highland, problem – which was so acute by 1384 that a council-general decreed that all caterans should be arrested or killed on sight. Since caterans were associated with the lordship of the Isles as well as with Moray, their activities can be seen as reflecting a breakdown in the top layer of feudalized society throughout the Highlands, and thus the reversal of the earlier trend of Highland, and indeed Scottish, history. Some sense of this was probably current in late-fourteenth-century Scotland. Moreover, contemporary alarm about caterans would have helped stimulate the general perception of Highland violence and lawlessness. It may be suggested, therefore, that the emergence of hostile Lowland

attitudes to the Highlands and Highlanders from the later fourteenth century onwards was not simply the result of political events,
but can also be explained, at least partly, in terms of a conflict of
societies.

II

Accounts of late-medieval Highland political history usually
concentrate on the lordship of the Isles – hardly surprisingly, for
the lordship was the most impressive creation of Gaelic Scotland,
after the kingdom itself, and by the mid fifteenth century the lords
of the Isles dominated the north. Nevertheless, the lordship was
essentially peripheral: northern Scotland's geographical hub and
political key actually lay in the province of Moray, which covered
most of the pre-1975 shires of Moray, Nairn and Inverness. The
lords of the Isles only became so important in Highland affairs as a
whole after regional authority had disintegrated in Moray. Moreover, parliamentary records indicate that the awareness of a 'Highland problem' was probably caused first by conditions in Moray
and only then, a few years later, by the lordship of the Isles. It is
best, therefore, to examine fourteenth-century Moray before turning to the lordship of the Isles.

In earlier centuries – indeed since before the time of Macbeth –
Moray had been the centre of opposition to the Scots crown. Its
conquest and distribution among southern, 'Norman' families who
brought feudal lordship to the local Gaelic, kin-based society is a
major theme of twelfth and thirteenth-century Scottish history. At
the beginning of the fourteenth century, Moray was at the centre of
Robert I's brilliant 1307–9 campaign – a campaign which clearly
demonstrates its strategic importance. The campaign destroyed the
province's most powerful family, the Comyns of Badenoch, but
Robert, aware of Moray's importance and of the danger of leaving
a vacuum there, replaced them with his nephew Thomas Randolph,
who was created earl of Moray and placed in charge of the whole
province. Robert also built up two other leading local families, the
Murrays and the earls of Ross, creating a tripartite power-structure:
the earls of Ross north of the Moray Firth and in Nairn, the
Murrays along its shores and in the lordship of Garioch (Aberdeenshire); and above all the Randolphs, holding the entire province
with the vice-regal powers of regality.

By the later fourteenth century, however, these families were all extinct in the senior male line. After the third Randolph earl's death at Neville's Cross (1346), Moray (which had been entailed on males) reverted to the crown. For part of the 1360s David II allowed the title to be used by the ninth earl of March, brother-in-law of the last Randolph earl; but March probably had little interest in the province, and in 1367 an important upland part of it, Badenoch, appears in the possession of Robert Stewart (the future Robert II). The Murray inheritance also went through a female to a southerner, Archibald Douglas 'the Grim'. None of these magnates was in a position to devote much attention to Moray, and a power vacuum probably developed there. David II's own policy was probably to control the region through his own men, notably Walter Leslie, whom he forced on the earl of Ross as son-in-law and heir (see chap. 7:ii); David himself spent some time in Inverness in 1369. Because of David's early death, it cannot be said whether or not this policy would have been successful. As it was, his reign almost certainly saw a serious weakening of regional power within Moray. And, during it, Robert Stewart's third son Alexander, later the notorious 'Wolf of Badenoch', first appeared in the province: in 1370 he bestowed his protection, which no doubt derived from a following of Highland caterans, upon the bishop of Moray.

When Robert Stewart became king in 1371, Alexander (perhaps his father's spoilt favourite) showed what he wanted by seizing the revenues of the earldom of Moray. But the Randolph heirs-general, George Dunbar, tenth earl of March, and his brother John (supporters of Robert II in the reign's initial crisis) also had a claim on Moray. What looked like a sensible compromise was worked out: John Dunbar became earl of a reduced Moray; Badenoch, with the castle and forest of Lochindorb, went to Alexander Stewart, and he also became royal lieutenant north of the Moray Firth; and Urquhart castle and barony were given to Robert II's fourth son, David. This settlement, however, proved to be disastrous. Without the castles of Lochindorb, Urquhart, and Ruthven in Badenoch, the earls of Moray could not control the Highland parts of the province; they were forced back, vulnerably, on the coastal plain. But while they held the Inverness area, the focal point of the Highlands, no-one else could exercise supremacy in the region. Thus the conditions were created for a power struggle in Moray between the earls and Alexander Stewart of Badenoch.

Alexander clearly won. His power grew steadily in the first half of Robert II's reign; he became justiciar north of the Forth, he leased Urquhart (which controlled the Great Glen) from his brother, and shortly after Walter Leslie's death in 1382 he married the countess of Ross (who was also heiress to the remnant of Buchan) and was created earl of Buchan. He used his vast authority, however, to undermine rather than maintain law and order. Although no account of Alexander's career survives, an impression of it can be gained by reading between the lines in the parliamentary records and the records of the bishopric of Moray (he had a long dispute with the bishops). For instance, after his father lost executive power in 1384, the next council-general saw a wide-ranging attack on him, which included orders to arrest three Highlanders who had killed men of the earl of Moray. In 1388 he was dismissed as justiciar, because he was 'useless to the community'. Perhaps encouraged by that, the bishop of Moray agreed to pay a substantial, yearly-increasing fee to the earl of Moray's son for protection. The contract was soon annulled as worthless – presumably because in 1390 Alexander Stewart demonstrated his superior power by taking a band of 'wyld wykkyd Helandmen' (Wyntoun) and burning Elgin cathedral!

Alexander had obviously been abusing his regional power in his own interests. And not only did he fail to prevent disorder, he actually led Highland caterans himself. The earl of Moray apparently followed suit – in one document he undertook not to employ caterans against the bishop, with whom he too was quarrelling. Now, as has already been mentioned, in their use of caterans and of 'protection rackets', both were acting like Gaelic chieftains (especially Irish ones, imposed protection being a prominent feature of traditional Irish lordship). Thus what the 1385 council-general described as 'the lack of justice in the higher and northern regions, where many malefactors and caterans are roaming', is more than just an unfortunate consequence of a local power struggle; it also probably reflects a collapse in the top layer of feudalized society in the central Highlands, and a resurgence of some of the least stable characteristics of Gaelic kin-based society.

The 'Wolf of Badenoch' (a nickname first recorded in Walter Bower's chronicle, from the late 1440s) is usually portrayed simply as an archetypal 'bad baron'. But he was certainly not typical of the mass of late-medieval Scottish nobles. Generally their regional power produced stability rather than disorder. Alexander Stewart is an exception to that; how great an exception is demonstrated by the fact that he was the only late-medieval Scottish magnate to be singled out for direct condemnation by the political community. And, in the present context, he is particularly significant. He was, as the 1385 council-general implied, largely to blame for the disorder in the north which produced some of the earliest parliamentary references to a general 'Highland problem'. Moreover, in the 1390s he can be linked, directly and indirectly, with three of the most notorious examples of late-medieval Highland violence: the burning of Elgin cathedral by his own caterans in 1390; his sons' great cateran raid into Angus in 1392, which culminated in a pitched battle at Glasclune; and the fight between members of two Moray clans at Perth in 1396, which stemmed from the absence of positive regional authority capable of preventing feuds. These were exactly the kind of lurid events which made the Highlands appear alien and violent to the rest of Scotland at the end of the fourteenth century.

III

If, during the thirteenth and fourteenth centuries, Moray went from stability to disorder, the reverse applies to the west coast region. In the earlier Middle Ages this had been very turbulent; there were constant power struggles, and raiding and plundering were common, both internally and across the sea in Ireland. Some cohesion was brought in the twelfth century by the local potentate Somerled, but after his death in 1164 his 'kingdom' of Argyll and the Isles split among rival branches of his kindred (ultimately the Macdougalls, Macruaries and Macdonalds), whose conflicts maintained a violent equilibrium. In the later thirteenth century, however, the region's integration into the rest of Scotland began: partly through royal pressure (including the annexation of the Hebrides in 1266), and partly through the decision of the chief of the Macdougalls of Argyll, the senior and most powerful branch of Somerled's kindred, to cooperate with the crown. With this, the process of feudalization which had taken place in the rest of Scotland seemed to be underway in the west. But then, as in Moray, the Bruce–Balliol civil war and the failure of male heirs among major families, seriously upset the top layer of regional society. The Macdougalls (who had become closely linked to the Comyns by marriage) were the greatest casualty: they were dispossessed by Robert I for opposing him implacably, were restored to much diminished lands by David II, and then died out in the senior line. And many other leading families, both natives and incomers (including most notably Macruaries, Comyns and Randolphs) also disappeared for one reason or another.

The vacuum which developed was filled by the two most famous Highland families, the Macdonalds and Campbells. The Campbells' well-known activities as government agents started under Robert I, when they received territory forfeited by the Macdougalls and probably the sheriffship of Argyll too; later, a royal lieutenancy over Argyll came in 1382, and the dignity earl of Argyll in 1458. Thus they apparently took over from the Macdougalls. But Macdougall prominence had derived from the fact that they were the senior branch of the greatest house of the west. The Campbells had no such status, and despite their close relations with the crown were really parvenus in the late Middle Ages, never effectively replacing the Macdougalls. Far from helping to assimilate the west to the rest of Scotland, their inexorable acquisition of territories and establishment of cadet branches in conjunction with their pro-government stance probably had the opposite effect, judging by the anti-Campbell sentiment of much west-coast tradition.

The Macdonalds, who dominated the west during the later Middle Ages, require fuller discussion. The original Macdonald share of Somerled's territories grew through grants to Angus Og Macdonald and his son John by Robert I and David II (partly from Macdougall land); and then through John's takeover of the Macruarie share, when the last Macruarie chief died in 1346 leaving no male heirs but a sister, Amy, who was John's wife. The result was that John Macdonald possessed all the Hebrides except Skye, and most of the west coast from Glenelg to Kintyre. This virtually recreated Somerled's twelfth-century kingdom, and from the 1350s John and his successors styled themselves lords (in Gaelic kings) of the Isles. In the early fifteenth century John's son Donald continued the expansion by claiming and probably taking over at least part of the earldom of Ross; his son, Alexander the third lord, was officially recognized as earl of Ross in 1437. That made the lords of the Isles the chief power not only on the west but in the Highlands as a whole, a position they maintained until the later fifteenth century.

The most important recent study of the lordship of the Isles portrays the growth of Macdonald power as a manifestation of the natural fluctuations within kin-based society: kindreds decline when their ruling families weaken or die out (the Macdougalls, Macruaries, and earls of Ross), and their territories are taken over by more fortunate rivals (the Macdonalds and to a lesser extent the Campbells). And, as it makes clear, at subordinate levels within the lordship kin-based society was flourishing. It would be an over-simplification, however, to portray the lordship purely in those terms. At the highest level, 'feudalized' concepts are visible in the lords' transactions and policies.

For example, although female landownership was not recognized in Gaelic kin-based society, John acquired the Macruarie lands after marrying the heiress by feudal rules. Later he established a jointure, or joint ownership, of some of his lands (including Kintyre, part of the original Macdonald territory) for his second wife, a daughter of Robert II. Donald's claim to Ross was through his wife, sister of the last earl. Succession to the lordship went by primogeniture, generally the rule in feudalized societies (except that Donald was the eldest son of John's second marriage). When Donald died, his son succeeded, although his nearest full brother had been designated *tanaiste* ('chosen successor'), following the practice of kin-based Gaelic society. John's eldest son by Amy Macruarie was bought off with a large endowment including his mother's lands, but that was done in a feudal transaction with a royal confirmation charter which established that the lands were to be held of the lords of the Isles; this reduced the dangers of frag-mentation inherent in kin-based society. Similar though smaller endowments were made to other younger sons (provoking an unsuccessful rebellion by Donald's brother the *tanaiste*), and the lords of the Isles also asserted superiority over the rest of the lord-ship's major landowners by issuing them charters of their lands. All this indicates a feudal attitude to land, which probably helped maintain the lordship's unity throughout the fifteenth century.

Unity brought internal stability and peace – reflected in the fact that the lords' main residence of Finlaggan on Islay was unfortified! The period of the lordship is a golden age in west-Highland history and Gaelic culture, between the turbulent thirteenth and sixteenth centuries. 'In thair time thair was great peace and wealth in the Iles throw the ministration of justice', a seventeenth-century Macdonald historian wrote of the lords. Justice was administered through the 'Council of the Isles', which consisted of the chiefs of the major kindreds under the headship of the lord of the Isles, and was the forum for arbitrating and enforcing settlements in disputes among powerful men and families. But the council could only function while the lordship was controlled by one unchallenged authority; otherwise, as happened later, parties in disputes could play off rival powers in the region against each other. This is similar to the nature of magnate power in other areas of Scotland, and in practice the council of the Isles was little different from magnate councils elsewhere. Moreover the power exercised by the lords of the Isles was the kind of regional authority crucial to Scottish feudalized society. In many respects, therefore, the Macdonald lords were clearly moving towards a fairly typical form of feudalized lordship over the west-coast region.

Nevertheless, in the lordship of the Isles the feudalized concept of society never became predominant. That is partly because the lords ruled against an intensely Gaelic background, which they themselves encouraged. Ensuring they were always the focus of west-coast Gaelic culture must have helped maintain their power and forestall reactions against any 'non-Gaelic' policies. The result is evident in later Gaelic tradition and poetry. While the Campbells were notorious for ruling through charters, the Macdonalds were upholders of the old heroic ways. Macdonald poets attacked the Campbells: 'The sharp stroke of short pens protects Argyll. . . . By falsehoods you deprived us of Islay green and lovely.' Of themselves they said 'The broadsword's charter is the birthright of that bold people; often without seal's impression do they impose tax or tribute' – a good evocation of traditional Gaelic kin-based society. Thus the fact that under the Macdonald lords charters and feudal tenure became common in the west-coast region was hidden by their image as Gaelic chiefs *par excellence*. But to the rest of Scotland, the self-conscious Gaelicness of the lordship, which included the glorification of heroic but violent behaviour, probably helped make it appear a frightening world apart.

Also, while the lords reduced feuding and violence within the lordship, they did not prevent turbulent elements from looking elsewhere; indeed they probably welcomed it as a safety-valve for internal tensions. Good opportunities for plunder were available in Ireland (where west-Highland mercenaries or 'galloglasses' were common) and in other parts of Scotland – for instance Lachlan Maclean of Duart was fighting in Lennox in 1439. Macdonald cadets, excluded from chances of accession to the chiefship by the lords' policy of primogeniture, were probably particularly active outside the lordship. After his unsuccessful revolt, the second lord's brother and *tanaiste*, John of Dunivaig and Antrim, was driven to acquire his own lordship in north-east Ulster. In 1452 his son Donald Balloch of Antrim attacked and pillaged in the Firth of Clyde. And, most significantly, in the 1390s Alexander Macdonald of Lochaber,[2] another brother of the second lord, took advantage of the disorder in Moray to move up the Great Glen and assert his own power in the central Highlands. In 1394 he extracted land and protection money from the earl of Moray for keeping his and other caterans out of the earldom for seven years – then eight years later he sacked and burned Elgin.

Thirdly, when the lords came to extending territory and power beyond the lordship, methods characteristic of kin-based society were applied. The technique was to exert armed pressure in areas where legal lordship was weak or missing, achieve *de facto* superiority over the inhabitants, and appropriate the rents; if successful, such takeovers could easily become permanent, and even receive government ratification. An excellent example is Alexander of Lochaber's activities in the area south-west of Inverness in the 1390s: the earl of Moray had to cede him land, and the bishop of Moray could not stop him granting out land which actually belonged to the bishopric. The 'Wolf of Badenoch', Alexander Stewart, was probably trying something similar when he seized the rents of Moray in 1371. And that is how Donald lord of the Isles set about acquiring Ross in the early fifteenth century; his claim through a female followed feudalized principles, but the way he pursued it, by imposing himself on the local landowners in the expectation that the government would recognize the *fait accompli*, is typical of the kin-based concept of society – as is his great plundering raid of 1411, which led to the battle of Harlaw. Later John, the fourth lord, used the same methods to try and extend his power and authority in the province of Moray.

Finally, any chance that the internal feudalizing trend might bring the lordship's integration into the kingdom was negated by

[2]Not to be confused with his (?) illegitimate son 'Alasdair Carrach': see A.B.W. MacEwen, 'Alexander de Yle, Lord of Lochaber, and his son Alasdair Carrach', *Notes and Queries of the Society of West Highland and Island Historical Research* 14 (1980). I am indebted to Mr W.D.H. Sellar for this reference.

the lords' relations with the crown. Scotland's 'feudal settlement' had been established by the magnates in cooperation with the crown, but this (although evident in the west in the later thirteenth century) did not happen with the Macdonald lordship. Initially Macdonald policy was anti-Macdougall and thus anti-crown; they opposed John Balliol, sided with Edward I in 1301, and only supported Robert I after 1306 because he was fighting the Macdougalls. Subsequently this tradition meant that the lords of the Isles never had the same commitment to the Bruce–Stewart regime as other magnates: their aim was to keep as much independence as possible. When necessary, they accepted royal sovereignty – but sometimes only after a full-scale military expedition. Their lukewarm attachment must have disturbed the crown, especially since the lordship's kin-based society provided the lords with far greater military strength than any other Scottish magnate. Moreover, ever since John Macdonald had sided with Edward Balliol the lords of the Isles were claimed as England's allies in Anglo-Scottish truces. The initiative was doubtless English, and nothing came of it until the 1460s, but the lords would hardly have objected to this expression of their independence, while it must have galled the Scottish kings.

In such circumstances two policies were open to the crown. It could accept the lords' practical independence and hope to keep their cooperation, or it could attempt to assert its theoretically superior authority. The first policy prevailed in the fourteenth century. Trouble did arise over John's support for Balliol (which was perhaps a reaction against the Randolph supremacy in the Highlands created by Robert I), and in the 1360s when John refused taxation contributions. But both times there were reconciliations, probably through the efforts of Robert Stewart, another rival of the Randolphs, who became John's father-in-law in 1350, and arranged John's submission to David II at Inverness in 1369. And when Robert II became king he maintained good relations with the lord of the Isles.

This *laissez-faire* policy (perhaps coupled with John's need to consolidate his position in the west) kept the lordship from impinging on the rest of Scotland for much of the fourteenth century. But the situation could hardly continue indefinitely. The turning-point came with John's death in 1387. John's widow quarrelled with her sons, probably because they were witholding her jointure lands (a concept unknown to kin-based society). Her brother the earl of Carrick raised the matter in parliament in 1389, and government action was ordered. This doubtless antagonized the new lord, Donald, and his brothers. Some 40 years of hostility followed, in which the government tried to impose its authority and the lords reacted violently. The period of hostility confirmed the separateness of the lordship of the Isles: by resisting the crown, the lords made their internal policies work towards its independence, not its integration. And the strength of their resistance naturally made the lordship appear a danger to the kingdom as a whole. Moreover the trouble in the western Highlands with the lords of the Isles which flared up after 1387 followed the outbreak of disorder in the central Highlands earlier in the 1380s – and in the 1390s Alexander of Lochaber's attacks on Moray linked the two regions. It is therefore hardly surprising that in the consciousness of the rest of Scotland the problems of the west and central Highlands were combined, producing by the end of the fourteenth century the Lowland perceptions of violence and lawlessness in Highland society.

IV

During the next four centuries, Highland political history was played out against that background. The major themes in the fifteenth century were the crown's efforts to deal with the 'Highland problem', and the continuing importance of the province of Moray. Government actions in the Highlands – contrary to the impression sometimes given – were not ineffective. During the main period of trouble, from 1385 to 1431, many expeditions were planned, and most were successful. The earl of Fife, with a large retinue, was settling disputes in Moray in 1389. A few years later, the 'Wolf of Badenoch' was brought before his brother Robert III and the royal council, and made to seek absolution and promise reparations for burning Elgin. His sons who led the cateran raid on Angus are last heard of incarcerated in Stirling castle. In 1398 the duke of Albany (or perhaps Rothesay) led an army to the west which forced the submission of Donald lord of the Isles; Donald even consented to imprison Alexander of Lochaber (though he soon released him). Donald was made to submit again in 1412 after Harlaw, following two expeditions mounted by Albany. And in 1428 James I summoned the third lord, Alexander, to Inverness, seized him and executed some of his followers; Alexander was then released, rebelled in 1429, and was hunted down and defeated in what Bower called 'a bog in Lochaber'. He was finally imprisoned in Tantallon castle. The Scots crown was thus far from powerless in the Highlands. But these expeditions show it reacting to crises, not forestalling them (and in James I's case, probably exacerbating the situation). Such actions could only be short-term solutions, with no guarantee of lasting peace; for that, cooperation with local magnates capable of providing stable regional authority was necessary.

Within the Highlands, the 'Wolf of Badenoch' was probably the most powerful figure until his death in 1405. The later stages of his career are obscure, but its immediate effect, the undermining of the earls of Moray, proved permanent. The Dunbars remained a pale shadow of the Randolphs, limited to the Moray coastal plain. Thus the conditions encouraging a power struggle within the central Highlands continued to exist. And with the death of the 'Wolf of Badenoch' most of the province of Moray was left vulnerable to peripheral pressure. The result was a competition for power in the central Highlands between magnates from the west and east.

From the west there was, of course, Donald lord of the Isles. The lordship included Lochaber, which opened up the Great Glen, and further north Donald had designs on Ross (which included the lands of Nairn). Walter Leslie's son Alexander earl of Ross had died in 1402 leaving a young daughter and a sister who was Donald's wife, and Donald's plan was to establish himself as *de facto* ruler of Ross in his wife's right, thus forcing the disinheritance of the Leslie heiress. The combination of the Isles, Ross and Nairn would have made Donald exceptionally powerful in the Highlands as a whole.

Donald's main rival, from the east, was another Alexander Stewart, the eldest son of the 'Wolf of Badenoch'. Reversing his father's career, this Alexander started as a leader of Highland caterans but eventually became a respectable figure in European noble society. The transformation started when he married Isabella countess of Mar, and was recognized as earl of Mar and lord of Garioch in 1404. Then after his father's death he was allowed (although illegitimate) to take over Badenoch and Urquhart. He thus controlled an impressive amount of territory, and unlike his father saw that his interests lay in cooperation with the government. He became its main agent in the Highlands, carrying out in different circumstances the role of Thomas Randolph a century earlier.

That is the background to the battle of Harlaw. In 1411 Donald lord of the Isles seized Dingwall and Inverness, and then led a large army through the north-east into Garioch. He was met at Harlaw (near Inverurie) by Alexander earl of Mar with a force drawn from eastern Scotland. After a bloody, inconclusive battle Donald retreated; government armies retook Inverness and Dingwall, and in 1412 the duke of Albany made him submit at Lochgilphead. Donald's aims and the significance of Harlaw have been much debated. The most reasonable assumption is that he decided – following the traditions of kin-based society – that the way to gain full control of Ross was to attack and defeat the government's strongest supporter in the north, the earl of Mar. That explains why the battle was fought in Garioch. Had Donald won, he would have proved himself the most powerful figure in northern Scotland, and could have expected to make the government give in to him over Ross (not to mention further expansion). But the drawn battle meant Donald's campaign was a failure; and in 1415 the claim to Ross was emphatically rejected, for Albany made the heiress resign it in favour of his own second son John earl of Buchan, and then enter a nunnery.

Buchan's interests lay elsewhere: he led the Scots in France and died without heirs in 1424. In the twenty years after Harlaw the earl of Mar remained the chief power in the Highlands: 'he successfully governed almost all the north beyond the Mounth', wrote Bower. His main responsibility was still dealing with the lord of the Isles, for instance during fresh hostilities in 1416. And after James I had provoked a major crisis in 1428–9 by attacking and imprisoning Alexander, the third lord, Mar was sent to the west in 1431 to start the process of bringing order. He was, however, defeated at Inverlochy by the forces of the lordship.

This battle was a turning-point in Highland history. It demonstrated that the west-coast region was a greater problem without the lord of the Isles than with him. The 1431 parliament, perhaps recognizing this, seems to have urged conciliation. That made raising and financing another army difficult, and James I gave in, either washing his hands of the west or accepting that only the lord of the Isles was capable of controlling it. Alexander was released, the hostilities stopped, and the *modus vivendi* between the crown and the lords of the Isles which had existed under Robert II and John Macdonald was re-established. The reversal of crown policy eventually went so far as to accept the Macdonald claim to Ross. The earl of Mar was probably sensitive about this, and while he lived Alexander Macdonald did not call himself earl of Ross. But Mar died in 1435; Alexander started using the title earl of Ross a year later, and it is found in government documents from 1437. The lords of the Isles had finally acquired Ross officially – and since Mar left no heirs and the Dunbar earls of Moray had died out in the male-line in 1429, they had also become easily the greatest magnates in the entire Highlands. Early in James II's minority the government recognized this by making Alexander justiciar north of the Forth.

In the 1430s, therefore, Highland politics were transformed, with the Macdonalds taking over the centre of the stage. Since the surviving documents relating to Alexander mostly concern Ross, Macdonald interests may have been reorientated. In his later years Alexander appears in the records as a fairly typical Scottish magnate, and in 1449 his career ended appropriately with his death at Dingwall and burial at Rosemarkie. Had Alexander's career come fifty or so years earlier, it might have paved the way for the assimilation of the lordship of the Isles within the rest of the kingdom, but the 1430s were too late for that. If anything the political union of the west-coast lordship of the Isles with the east-coast earldom of Ross may have served to reinforce the Lowland perception of a united, threatening Highlands.

V

Macdonald dominance of the Highlands continued until the 1470s. Thus the period covered by this book closes with the lords of the Isles at the height of their power. However their dramatic fall began a few years later, and with hindsight the factors behind the reversal of their fortunes can be seen emerging between 1437 and 1469.

Although they held Ross they were not unchallengeable within the province of Moray. A threat soon came from the Douglases. One brother of the eighth earl of Douglas married a Dunbar heiress, and another received the Douglases' former Murray lands along the Moray Firth; in 1445 they became earls of Moray and Ormond respectively. The Douglas–Ross–Crawford bond (see chap. 7:vii) may have been partly a reaction to this: it presumably safeguarded the Macdonald sphere of influence. Another reaction was probably John Macdonald's marriage to a daughter of James Livingston in 1449 – significantly, the Livingstons and the Macdonalds were both attacked in the *Buke of the Howlat*, written *c*.1450 for the Douglas earl of Moray. After the Livingstons lost power, John Macdonald revolted in 1451; he claimed he had been denied promised crown patronage, and seized the vital Moray castles of Inverness, Urquhart, and Ruthven in Badenoch – doubtless what he had hoped for from his marriage. The incident coincided with the start of James II's struggle with the Douglases, so John was allowed to keep control of Inverness and Urquhart. Not surprisingly he did not support the Douglases against James II, despite the bond and their pleas (though Donald Balloch's raid on the Clyde estuary may be connected). But although James II's victory in 1455 removed the Douglas challenge, it revealed another. Shortly after the Douglas earl of Moray was killed, his widow married the earl of Huntly's eldest son. That was ominous, because Huntly had already emerged as the successor to the earl of Mar in Aberdeenshire, and in 1451 had been granted Badenoch. James II checked Huntly's designs on Moray by annexing the earldom himself, but Huntly was clearly threatening Macdonald power in the central Highlands.

John reacted to this – and perhaps to the absence of royal reward for not helping the Douglases – with fresh efforts to expand his power once James II was dead. In the far north he quarrelled with the earl of Orkney; Islesmen attacked Orkney and Caithness. But his main interest was still in Moray. Between 1460 and 1464 he seized nearly £1,500 and a huge amount of grain and cattle from crown territory (mostly forfeited Douglas lands) near Inverness. It took a full-scale expedition by the royal council to make him stop – and then his men burned much of the land they vacated. At the same time he dreamt of far greater power. In 1462 ambassadors from Edward IV of England and the exiled earl of Douglas persuaded him to transform the vague English alliance the lords of the Isles had always had into something more concrete. The result was a secret treaty proposing that the lord of the Isles, his cousin Donald Balloch, and the earl of Douglas would become Edward IV's subjects, help him conquer Scotland, and share the land north of the Forth among them.

These efforts at expansion coincided with events which suggest that John's power was declining in its west-coast heartland. In the 1460s a violent family feud raged among the Macdougalls of Dunollie (near Oban). They were within the lordship's orbit, and John might have been expected to settle the affair. In fact it seems he could not, and Donald Balloch (probably the feud's instigator) backed one side while Colin Campbell earl of Argyll (with parliament's support) backed the other. The affair seems symbolic of challenges to John's position on the west coast: both from within his own family and from the Campbells, whose own power had been growing steadily. It is tempting to conclude, therefore, that the lords of the Isles had become increasingly concerned with the central Highlands at the expense of the west.

The themes of the 1450s and 1460s come together in later years when John Macdonald's power was collapsing. His treaty with England was made public in 1475, and for his treason Ross and Kintyre were confiscated. After the humiliation of his condemnation, submission, and forfeiture, his family turned against him. Other chiefs in the lordship supported him, but his son – who apparently wanted to regain Ross by force – and clan Donald defeated him in a sea-battle some time in the early 1480s. Fresh family problems in the 1490s – his nephew had been plundering part of Ross – caused James IV to declare all John's lands forfeit in 1493. The forfeiture was more in theory than in practice, but it led in the long run to the disintegration of the lordship and its final disappearance in 1545.

The ultimate beneficiaries of John's downfall were the Campbells under the earls of Argyll in the west, the Gordons under the earls of Huntly in the east, and the Mackenzies of Kintail in the north. But the transfer of power was slow, and the process caused much violence. Throughout the whole of the Highlands in the late fifteenth and sixteenth centuries the characteristics of kin-based society seem to be flourishing; this is the period of most of the stories of clan feuds and vendettas. In the end, therefore, the collapse of the power built up by the lords of the Isles had the effect of increasing the Highlands' reputation for violence and lawlessness. It thus greatly intensified the perception of Highland–Lowland divisions within the kingdom of Scotland – that perception which was to prove one of the most enduring legacies of late-medieval Scottish history.

A Note on Further Reading

Primary Sources

Until fairly recently Scottish scholars were apparently happier to print the available sources for Scottish medieval history than to study them in depth; a fascinating discussion of why that was so is given in M. Ash, *The Strange Death of Scottish History* (Edinburgh, 1980). The results of their labours are conveniently listed in the 'List of abbreviated titles of the printed sources of Scottish history to 1560', *Scottish Historical Review* XLII (1963), supplement. There are two excellent analytical guides to the printed and unprinted material: B. Webster, *Scotland from the Eleventh Century to 1603* (London, 1975); and G. Donaldson, *The Sources of Scottish History* (Edinburgh, 1978).

The records most used for this book are: *The Exchequer Rolls of Scotland*, eds. G. Burnett *et al.* (Edinburgh, 1878-1908) I-VII; *The Acts of the Parliaments of Scotland*, eds. T. Thomson and C. Innes (Edinburgh, 1882-1914) I-II; *The Acts of David II King of Scots*, ed. B. Webster (*Regesta Regum Scottorum* VI; Edinburgh, 1982); *Calendar of Documents relating to Scotland in H.M. Public Record Office*, ed. J. Bain (Edinburgh, 1881-8); *Registrum Honoris de Mortoun* (Douglas of Dalkeith documents), ed. C. Innes (Bannatyne Club, 1859); W. Fraser, *The Douglas Book* (Edinburgh, 1885); W. Fraser, *The Red Book of Menteith* (Edinburgh, 1880); *Statutes of the Scottish Church*, ed. D. Patrick (Scottish History Soc., hereafter SHS, 1907); *Calendar of Papal Letters to Scotland: Clement VII of Avignon*, ed. C. Burns, and *Benedict XIII of Avignon*, ed. F. McGurk (both SHS, 1976); *Rental Book of the Cistercian Abbey of Coupar Angus*, ed. C. Rodgers (Grampian Club, 1879-80); *Registrum Episcopatus Moraviensis* (Moray bishopric records), ed. C. Innes (Bannatyne Club, 1837); *Regiam Majestatem and Quoniam Attachiamenta*, ed. T.M. Cooper (Stair Soc., 1947).

The main chronicles for late-medieval Scotland are: John Barbour, *The Bruce*, ed. W.M. MacKenzie (London, 1909); John Fordun, *Chronica Gentis Scotorum*, ed. W.F. Skene, trans. F.J.H. Skene (Historians of Scotland, 1872-9); Andrew Wyntoun, *Orygynale Cronykil of Scotland*, ed. D. Laing (Hists. of Scot., 1872-9), or ed. F.J. Amours (Scottish Text Soc., hereafter STS, 1903-14); Walter Bower, *Scotichronicon*, ed. W. Goodall

(Edinburgh, 1759); *The Asloan Manuscript*, ed. W.A. Craigie (STS, 1923–5), vol.I, for the 'Auchinleck Chronicle'; John Major, *A History of Greater Britain*, ed. Ae. J.G. Mackay (SHS, 1892); Jean Froissart, *Chronicles of England, France, Spain . . .*, trans. T. Johnes (London, 1848).

In addition to *Barbour* and *Wyntoun*, the vernacular poems mentioned in the text (and many others) can be found in: *The Poems of Robert Henryson*, ed. D. Fox (Oxford, 1981); *The Poems of William Dunbar*, ed. J. Kingsley (Oxford, 1979); *The Kingis Quair*, ed. M.P. McDiarmid (London, 1973); *The Bannatyne Manuscript*, ed. W.T. Ritchie (STS, 1928–34) – vol.IV for 'The Buke of the Howlat'; *The Maitland Folio Manuscript*, ed. W.A. Craigie (STS, 1919–27) – vol.II for 'The Harp'; *Devotional Pieces in Verse and Prose*, ed. J.A.W. Bennett (STS, 1955) – including 'The Contemplacioun of Synnaris'; *Hary's Wallace*, ed. M.P. McDiarmid (STS, 1968).

Secondary Works

General: Pride of place among general studies of late-medieval Scotland must go to R.G. Nicholson's magisterial *Scotland: The Later Middle Ages* (Edinburgh, 1974); although I do not always agree with it, it is simply indispensable, and I owe it a huge debt. Shorter accounts of the period can be found in A.A.M. Duncan's masterly revision of W.C. Dickinson's classic *Scotland from the Earliest Times to 1603* (i.e. the 3rd edn, Oxford, 1977); G. Donaldson, *Scottish Kings* (2nd edn, London, 1977); *The Scottish Nation*, ed. G. Menzies (London, 1972); and, for an unorthodox but stimulating approach, John Foster's essay 'Scottish Nationality and the Origins of Capitalism', in *Scottish Capitalism*, ed. T. Dickson (London, 1980). There are no general works specifically on fourteenth-century Scotland, but for the fifteenth century there is the excellent collection of essays edited by J.M. Brown (now Wormald), *Scottish Society in the Fifteenth Century* (hereafter *SSFC*; London, 1977); also, in A.I. Dunlop, *The Life and Times of James Kennedy, Bishop of St Andrews* (Edinburgh, 1950), the examination of the 'times' is even more rewarding than that of the 'life' (which exaggerates Kennedy's importance). Four invaluable distillations of information must be recommended: *An Historical Atlas of Scotland*, eds. P.G. McNeill and R.G. Nicholson (St Andrews, 1975); D.E.R. Watt, *A Biographical Dictionary of Scottish Graduates before 1410* (Oxford, 1977); *The Scots Peerage*, ed. J.B. Paul (Edinburgh, 1904–14); and *Origines Parochiales Scotiae*, ed. C. Innes (Bannatyne Club, 1851–5); each one makes fascinating reading for anyone interested in Scottish history. Finally, of course, a wealth of learned discussion is published in the major Scottish historical journals, *Scottish Historical Review* (*SHR*), *Records of the Scottish Church History Society* (*RSCHS*), *Innes Review* (*IR*), and *Northern Scotland*.

Chapter 1: Bruce, Balliol and England: Robert I is the subject of a book worthy of the king: G.W.S. Barrow, *Robert Bruce and the Community of the Realm of Scotland* (2nd edn, Edinburgh, 1976); as A.A.M. Duncan said, it is 'the first modern book on medieval Scottish history'. But it should be supplemented by two of Duncan's own pieces: his review, 'The Community of the Realm and Robert Bruce', *SHR* XLV (1966), and his Historical Association pamphlet (G. 75, 1970), *The Nation of Scots and the Declaration of Arbroath* (which has a good translation of the Declaration). R.G. Nicholson's detailed account of *Edward III and the Scots, 1327-1335* (Oxford, 1965) deals with the end of Robert I's reign and the first part of David II's. The 1330s and 1340s are covered in J. Campbell's broader discussion, 'England, Scotland and the Hundred Years War', in *Europe in the Late Middle Ages*, ed. J.R. Hale *et al.* (London, 1965), which I have followed closely. Nicholson, *Later Middle Ages*, chaps. 4-6, is also most important. Other valuable studies of specific themes and episodes include: N. Reid, 'The kingless kingdom: the Scottish guardianships of 1286-1306', *SHR* LXI (1982); G.W.S. Barrow and P. Barnes, 'Robert Bruce's Movements in 1307', *SHR* XLIX (1970); G.W.S. Barrow, 'Lothian in the First War of Independence', *SHR* LV (1976); G.W.S. Barrow, 'The Aftermath of War: Scotland and England in the late Thirteenth and early Fourteenth centuries', *Trans. Royal Historical Soc.* (hereafter *TRHS*) 5th ser., 28 (1978); J. Scammell, 'Robert Bruce and the North of England', *English Historical Review* (hereafter *EHR*) LXIII (1958); R. Frame, 'The Bruces in Ireland', *Irish Historical Studies* XIX (1974); J.F. Lydon, 'The Bruce Invasion of Ireland', *Historical Studies* IV, ed. G.A. Hayes-McCoy (London, 1963); J.B. Smith, 'Edward II and the Allegiance of Wales', *Welsh History Review* VIII (1976-7); N. Fryde, *The Tyranny and Fall of Edward II* (Cambridge, 1979), chap. 9, 'The defeat in Scotland, 1322-3'; J. Dilley, 'German Merchants in Scotland', *SHR* XXXVII (1948); W. Stanford Reid, 'Trade, Traders and Scottish Independence', *Speculum* XXIX (1954); G.G. Simpson, 'The Declaration of Arbroath revitalised', *SHR* LVI (1977); G.W.S. Barrow, 'The Idea of Freedom in late medieval Scotland', *IR* XXX (1979); and S. Reynolds, 'Medieval Origines Gentium and the Community of the Realm', *History* LXVIII (1983).

Chapter 2: 'Auld Inemie' and 'Auld Alliance': I have generally followed the interpretations in Campbell, 'England, Scotland and the Hundred Years War', A.A.M. Duncan, *James I* (University of Glasgow, Scottish History Dept, occasional papers, 1976), and N.A.T. Macdougall, 'Foreign relations: England and France', in *SSFC*. The chapter's approach also owes much to J.J.N. Palmer, 'The War Aims of the Protagonists', in *The Hundred Years War*, ed. K. Fowler (London, 1971), though that is limited to England and France. Fuller details are given in Nicholson, *Later Middle Ages*, E.W.M. Balfour-Melville, *James I* (London, 1936), Dunlop, *Bishop Kennedy*, and C. Macrae, 'Scotland and the Wars of the Roses' (unpublished Oxford D.Phil. thesis, 1939) – a strangely neglected work. E.W.M.

Balfour-Melville, 'Papers relating to the Captivity and Release of David II', *Miscellany of the Scottish History Society* IX (1958), prints important documents. C.J. Ford's brilliant 'Piracy or Policy: the Crisis in the Channel, 1400–3', *TRHS* 5th ser., 29 (1979) opens up the subject of piracy. English policy towards Scotland can be followed from: J.J.N. Palmer, *England, France and Christendom, 1377–99* (London, 1972); A. Tuck, *Richard II and the English Nobility* (London, 1973), chap. 7; A.L. Brown, 'The English Campaign in Scotland, 1400', in *British Government and Administration*, eds. H. Hearder and H.R. Loyn (Cardiff, 1974); C. Macrae, 'The English Council and Scotland in 1430', *EHR* LIV (1939); R.A. Griffiths, *The Reign of King Henry VI*; and C.L. Scofield, *The Life and Reign of Edward IV* (London, 1923). There is little on Franco-Scottish relations, apart from the essays by Campbell and Macdougall and passages in the general works; but the Scots in France after 1419 are well covered in B. Ditcham, 'The employment of foreign mercenary troops in the French royal armies, 1415–1470' (unpublished Edinburgh Ph.D. thesis, 1978), and L.A. Barbé, *Margaret of Scotland and the Dauphin Louis* (London, 1917) is more than just the sad story of James I's daughter. Scotland's relations with Scandinavia deserve fuller treatment than it has been possible to give here. The starting-points are: B.E. Crawford, 'The Pawning of Orkney and Shetland', and K. Hørby, 'Christian I and the Pawning of Orkney', in *SHR* XLVIII (1969); and B.E. Crawford, 'Foreign relations: Scandinavia', in *SSFC*.

Chapter 3: Economy and Society: I.F. Grant, *The Social and Economic Development of Scotland before 1603* (Edinburgh, 1930), though still valuable, is very dated. Until it is replaced, the best introductions are: *Coinage in Medieval Scotland*, ed. D. Metcalf (British Archaeological Reports 45, 1977), essays by R.G. Nicholson, N.J. Mayhew, I.H. Stewart and J.M. Gilbert; R.A. Dodgshon, 'Medieval Rural Scotland', in *An Historical Geography of Scotland*, eds. G. Whittington and I.D. Whyte (London, 1983); S.G.E. Lythe, 'Economic Life', in *SSFC*; A.A.M. Duncan, 'Burgh Life', chap. 25 of Duncan and Dickinson, *Scotland from the Earliest Times*; and G.S. Pryde, *The Burghs of Scotland: A Critical List* (Glasgow, 1965). Then there is R.A. Dodgshon's extremely important but idiosyncratic book, *Land and Society in Early Scotland* (Oxford, 1981). T.B. Franklin, *A History of Scottish Farming* (London, 1952) is useful, but almost entirely limited to monastic landlords. J.M. Gilbert, *Hunting and Hunting Reserves in Medieval Scotland* (Edinburgh, 1979) deals with the less- and uncultivated areas; cultivation high on Lammermuir is the basis for M.L. Parry, 'Secular climatic change and marginal land', *Trans. Institute of British Geographers* 64 (1975). I.H. Stewart, *The Scottish Coinage* (rev. edn, London, 1967) is definitive; and see also W.W. Scott's forthcoming article on 'Sterling and Usual Money of Scotland: 1370–1415', in *Scottish Journal of Economic and Social History*. The complexities of foreign trade are illustrated in 'A Medieval Scots merchant's handbook', printed by A. Hanham in *SHR* L (1971).

Valuable studies of earlier and later periods include A.A.M. Duncan, *Scotland: The Making of the Kingdom* (Edinburgh, 1975), chaps. 12–16, M.H.B. Sanderson, *Scottish Rural Society in the Sixteenth Century* (Edinburgh, 1982), T.C. Smout, *A History of the Scottish People, 1560–1830* (London, 1969), and I.D. Whyte, *Agriculture and Society in Seventeenth-Century Scotland* (Edinburgh, 1975). J.L. Bolton, *The Medieval English Economy* (London, 1980) provides an excellent guide to the period's general economic trends; and the debate initiated by R. Brenner, 'Agrarian Class Structure and Economic Development in Pre-industrial Europe', in *Past & Present* 70 (1976), 78–80 (1978), and 97 (1982), has important implications for Scotland.

Chapter 4: Church and Religion: Apart from Nicholson, *Later Middle Ages*, the only up-to-date general account of the late-medieval Scottish Church is in the first chapters of I.B. Cowan, *The Scottish Reformation* (London, 1982); but cautious use may still be made of J. Dowden, *The Medieval Church in Scotland* (Edinburgh, 1910) and A.R. MacEwen, *A History of the Church of Scotland* (London, 1913–18). *RSCHS* XXI (1981) contains an excellent bibliography, compiled by I.B. Cowan. G.W.S. Barrow's important 'The clergy in the Wars of Independence', in his *The Kingdom of the Scots* (London, 1973) surveys the beginning of the period, and some of its themes continue in D. McRoberts, 'The Scottish Church and Nationalism in the Fifteenth Century', *IR* XIX (1969). There are two good biographies of fifteenth-century bishops in Dunlop, *Bishop Kennedy* and J. Durkan, *William Turnbull Bishop of Glasgow* (Glasgow, 1951). For Schisms and Conciliarism see R. Swanson, 'The University of St Andrews and the Great Schism', *Journal of Ecclesiastical History* XXVI (1975), J.H. Burns, 'Scottish Churchmen and the Council of Basle', *IR* XIII (1962), and J.H. Burns, 'The Conciliarist Tradition in Scotland', *SHR* XLII (1965). Ecclesiastical institutions are dealt with in: D.E.R. Watt, *Fasti Ecclesiae Scoticanae* (Scottish Record Soc., 1969); I.B. Cowan and D.E. Easson, *Medieval Religious Houses, Scotland* (London, 1976); I.B. Cowan, *The Parishes of Medieval Scotland* (Scot. Rec. Soc., 1967); G. Donaldson, 'Church Courts', in *An Introduction to Scottish Legal History* (Stair Soc., 1958); S. Ollivant, *The Court of the Official in Pre-Reformation Scotland* (Stair Soc., 1982); K.L. Wood-Legh, *Perpetual Chantries in Britain* (Cambridge, 1965), which is almost unique in covering Scotland as well as England; and I.B. Cowan, 'The Medieval Church in the Highlands', in *The Middle Ages in the Highlands*, ed. L. Maclean (Inverness, 1981). The universities are the field of D.E.R. Watt; as well as his *Dictionary of Graduates*, there are his articles on 'University Graduates in Scottish Benefices before 1410', *RSCHS* XV (1963–5), 'Scottish Student Life abroad', *SHR* LIX (1980), and 'Education in the Highlands', in *The Middle Ages in the Highlands*. See also D. Shaw, 'Laurence of Lindores', *RSCHS* XII (1954), and, for both schools and universities, J. Durkan, 'Education in the Century of the Reformation', in

Essays on the Scottish Reformation, ed. D. McRoberts (Glasgow, 1962). The main starting-points for literature and literacy are: J. MacQueen, 'The literature of fifteenth-century Scotland', in *SSFC*; D. Fox, 'Middle Scots Poets and Patrons', in *English Court Culture in the Later Middle Ages*, eds. V.J. Scattergood and J.W. Sherborne (London, 1983); G.G. Simpson, *Scottish Handwriting, 1150-1650* (Edinburgh, 1973), and M.T. Clanchy, *From Memory to Written Record: England 1066-1307* (London, 1979). J.G. Dunbar, *The Architecture of Scotland* (London, 1978) and G. Stell, 'Architecture: the changing needs of society', in *SSFC*, are the best introductions to ecclesiastical building; see also M.R. Apted and W.N. Robertson, 'Late Fifteenth-Century Church Paintings from Guthrie and Foulis Easter', *Proceedings of the Society of Antiquaries of Scotland* XCV (1961-2). Relatively little has been written on Scottish religion and religious life, with the following splendid exceptions: I.B. Cowan, 'Church and Society', in *SSFC*; A.A.M. Duncan, 'Religion and Society before the Reformation', Duncan and Dickinson, *Scotland from the Earliest Times*, chap. 27; D. McKay, 'Parish Life in Scotland', in *Essays on the Scottish Reformation*; A.I. Dunlop, 'Remissions and Indulgences in Fifteenth-Century Scotland', *RSCHS* XV (1963-5); and J.A.W. Bennett, *Poetry of the Passion* (Oxford, 1982), chap. V, 'The Scottish Testimony'. Chapter IX of J.A.F. Thomson, *The Later Lollards* (Oxford, 1965) deals with Scotland. For late-medieval religion in general see R.W. Southern, *Western Society and the Church in the Middle Ages* (London, 1970), and F.R.H. Du Boulay, *An Age of Ambition* (London, 1970), chaps. 8, 9; and in this part of the chapter I have been heavily influenced by the work of John Bossy: 'The Mass as a Social Institution, 1200-1700', *Past & Present* 100 (1983); 'The Social History of Confession in the Age of the Reformation', *TRHS* 5th ser, 25 (1975); and 'Blood and baptism', in *Studies in Church History* 10, ed. D. Baker (London, 1973).

Chapter 5: The Nobility: The only full-length studies of the late-medieval Scottish nobility are Jenny Wormald, *Lords and Men in Scotland: Bonds of Manrent, 1442-1603* (forthcoming, Edinburgh, 1985), and A. Grant, 'The Higher Nobility in Scotland and their Estates, *c.*1371-1424' (unpublished Oxford D.Phil. thesis, 1975). Parts of their arguments are developed in J.M. Brown, 'The exercise of power', in *SSFC*, J. Wormald, 'Bloodfeud, Kindred and Government in Early Modern Scotland', *Past & Present* 87 (1980), A. Grant, 'The development of the Scottish peerage', *SHR* LVII (1978), and A. Grant, 'Earls and Earldoms in late medieval Scotland, *c*1310-1460', in *Essays presented to Michael Roberts*, eds. J. Bossy and P. Jupp (Belfast, 1976). There is also the collection *Essays on the Nobility of Medieval Scotland*, ed. K.J. Stringer (Edinburgh, forthcoming), which includes papers by G. Stell on the Scottish medieval castle (supplementing his Architecture chapter in *SSFC*), B.E. Crawford on the Sinclairs, N.A.T. Macdougall on the Humes, and A. Grant on family extinctions and survivals. K.J. Stringer's own book, *Earl David of Huntingdon (1152–1219): A Study in Anglo-Scottish History* (Edinburgh, forthcoming) considers many of the themes of this chapter for an earlier period. Invaluable insights are also to be gained from K.B. McFarlane, *The Nobility of Later Medieval England* (Oxford, 1973) – the seminal work for all study of late-medieval nobilities – and R.R. Davies, *Lordship and Society in the March of Wales, 1282–1400* (Oxford, 1978).

Chapter 6: The Machinery of Government: The best introductions are in A.A.M. Duncan, *Scotland: The Making of the Kingdom* (Edinburgh, 1975), chap. 22 (for late-thirteenth-century government), and in B. Webster's survey of the records, *Scotland from the Eleventh Century to 1603* (London, 1975), together with his *Regesta* volume *The Acts of David II*. Much valuable detail and analysis can be found in J. Mackinnon, *The Constitutional History of Scotland* (London, 1924) and R.S. Rait, *The Parliaments of Scotland* (Glasgow, 1924), but their interpretations are very old-fashioned. For good modern discussions of parliament, council-general and council, see: A.A.M. Duncan, 'The early parliaments of Scotland', *SHR* XLV (1966); A.A.M. Duncan, 'The Central Courts before 1532', in *Introduction to Scottish Legal History* (Stair Soc., 1958); I.E. O'Brien, 'The Scottish Parliament in the 15th and 16th Centuries' (unpublished Glasgow Ph.D. thesis, 1980); and A.L. Brown, 'The Scottish "Establishment" in the later Fifteenth Century', *Juridical Review* new ser., XXIII (1978). T.M. Cooper, 'The First Law Reform (Miscellaneous Provisions) Act', in his *Selected Papers* (London, 1957), examines Robert I's 1318 legislation. The starting-point for local government is W.C. Dickinson's three great institutional studies of sheriffs, baronies and regalities, and burghs, in his introductions to *The Sheriff Court Book of Fife*, *The Court Book of the Barony of Carnwath*, and *Early Records of the Burgh of Aberdeen* (SHS, 1928, 1937, 1957). Apart from G. Dickinson, 'Some Notes on the Scottish Army in the first half of the Sixteenth Century', *SHR* XXVIII (1949), there is little specific on Scotland's military system; but details can be gleaned from the political histories and the parliamentary records. Similarly, finance has not attracted much attention, except for A.L. Murray's 'The Comptroller, 1425–1488', *SHR* LII (1973) and 'The Procedure of the Scottish Exchequer in the early sixteenth century', *SHR* XL (1961), and C. Madden, 'The Finances of the Scottish Crown in the late Middle Ages' (unpublished Glasgow Ph.D. thesis, 1975); but the *Exchequer Rolls* and their introductions are great mines of information. Justice, however, has fared much better (at least in the quantity of material). After the Stair Society's comprehensive *Introduction to Scottish Legal History* (1958) and B. Webster's illuminating comments in his book on the records, there is J.J. Robertson's useful general discussion of the fifteenth century, 'The development of the law', in *SSFC*. A.A.M. Duncan's 'Regiam Majestatem: a reconsideration', *Juridical Review* new ser., VI (1961) is an essential supplement to the

Stair Society text. For the workings of the formal judicial system, see: Dickinson's *Fife* and *Carnwath*; H. McKechnie, *Judicial Process upon Brieves* (Glasgow, 1956); I.D. Willock, *The Jury in Scotland* (Stair Soc., 1966); and, especially, H. MacQueen, 'The Brieve of Right in Scots Law', and 'Dissasine and Mortancestor in Scots Law', in *Journal of Legal History*, 3 (1982) and 4 (1983). The informal system has been brilliantly illuminated by J. Wormald, 'Bloodfeud, Kindred and Government in Early Modern Scotland', *Past & Present* 87 (1980), reprinted in *Disputes and Settlements*, ed. J. Bossy (Cambridge, 1983) – in which see also the chapter on English arbitration by M.T. Clanchy. Two other important studies of English justice are A. Harding, *The Law Courts of Medieval England* (London, 1973), and M.T. Clanchy, 'Law, Government and Society in Medieval England', *History LIX* (1974); and the introductory chapter of *Crime and the Law: The Social History of Crime in Western Europe since 1500*, eds. V.A.C. Gatrell *et al.* (London, 1980), is also most valuable.

Chapter 7: Kings and Magnates: Nicholson, *Later Middle Ages*, gives a full account of the politics of the period. I prefer J. Wormald's interpretation, however, from her 'Taming the Magnates?' in *The Scottish Nation*, ed. G. Menzies (London, 1972) (revised and reprinted in *Essays on the Nobility of Medieval Scotland*, ed. Stringer), and from her 'The Exercise of Power' in *SSFC*. Details of the careers of many of the nobles mentioned in the chapter can be found in *The Scots Peerage*. David II's reign has been studied in B. Webster, 'David II and the Government of Fourteenth Century Scotland', *TRHS* 5th ser., 16 (1966), and in R.G. Nicholson, 'David II, the historians and the chroniclers', *SHR* XLV (1966). No specific work has been published on Robert II, Robert III, or the dukes of Albany. A.A.M. Duncan's *James I* (University of Glasgow, Scottish History Dept occasional papers, 1976) is far superior to Balfour-Melville's detailed biography; it is summarized in chap. 19 of Duncan and Dickinson, *Scotland from the Earliest Times*. Similarly, the first two chapters of N.A.T. Macdougall, *James III: A Political Study* (Edinburgh, 1982) provide a better account of James II's reign than the fuller treatment in Dunlop, *Bishop Kennedy* (although Macdougall is probably over-critical of James); the third and fourth chapters give the definitive history of James III's minority; and the whole book should be read to see what can be made of late-medieval Scottish politics. For what happened in England see M.H. Keen, *England in the Later Middle Ages* (London, 1973), J.A.F. Thomson, *The Transformation of Medieval England, 1370–1529* (London, 1983), and R.L. Storey, *The End of the House of Lancaster* (London, 1966), which has influenced my interpretation considerably.

Chapter 8: Highlands and Lowlands: The best starting-point is G.W.S. Barrow, 'The Highlands in the Lifetime of Robert the Bruce', in his *Kingdom of the Scots*. Nicholson, *Later Middle Ages*, deals with the Highlands well. For

Gaelic, see also D. Murison, 'Linguistic Relationships in Medieval Scotland', in *The Scottish Tradition*, ed. G.W.S. Barrow (Edinburgh, 1974). J.W.M. Bannerman has written two admirable studies of the Lordship of the Isles; one on its society in *SSFC*, the other on its politics in the appendix to K.A. Steer and J.W.M. Bannerman, *Late Medieval Monumental Sculpture in the West Highlands* (Edinburgh, 1977); and in the latter, his historical notes on the inscriptions are also very important. *The Middle Ages in the Highlands*, ed. L. Maclean (Inverness, 1981), is an extremely valuable collection of essays, including J.M. Munro, 'The lordship of the Isles', J. Dunbar, 'The Medieval Architecture of the Scottish Highlands', and J. MacInnes, 'Gaelic Poetry and Historical Tradition'. The Lordship's earlier history is dealt with in A.A.M. Duncan and A.L. Brown, 'Argyll and the Isles in the Earlier Middle Ages', *Proc. Soc. Antiq. Scot.* XC (1956-7). A. Grant examines one later episode in 'The Revolt of the Lord of the Isles and the Death of the Earl of Douglas, 1451-2', *SHR* LX (1981). Little has been written on late-medieval Moray and the 'Wolf of Badenoch'. *The Scots Peerage* is useful, but the account given here derives chiefly from the government records and the *Register of the Bishopric of Moray*; the approach was stimulated by *The Hub of the Highlands: the Book of Inverness and District*, ed. L. Maclean (Inverness, 1975). For the Gaelic world beyond Scotland see the invaluable book by K. Nicholls, *Gaelic and Gaelicised Ireland in the Middle Ages* (Dublin, 1972), and R. Frame's illuminating article 'Power and Society in the Lordship of Ireland 1272-1377', in *Past & Present* 76 (1977).

Appendix A: Chronological Table

1296–1305	First phase of war with England. Scotland virtually conquered 1304–5; William Wallace executed 1305.
1306	Robert Bruce killed John Comyn; rebelled; was crowned Robert I (1306–29). Bruce–Balliol/Comyn civil war; Robert I defeated.
1307–9	Robert I won control of northern Scotland, following death of Edward I of England and accession of Edward II, 1307.
1309	St Andrews parliament; declarations acknowledging Robert I as king; relations re-established with France.
1309–77	Papacy's headquarters (Curia) located at Avignon.
1310–13	English-held strongholds in southern Scotland captured.
1312	Thomas Randolph made earl of Moray. Treaty with Norway.
1314	Battle of Bannockburn (23–4 June). Scots landowners who would not accept Robert I disinherited by parliament.
1315–23	Raids on northern England.
1315–18	Campaign in Ireland, led by Edward Bruce (and Robert I, 1317). Unsuccessful; Edward Bruce defeated and killed at Dundalk, 1318.
1318	Berwick captured. 'Robert I's Statutes', ? followed shortly by *Regiam Majestatem*.
1320	Following papal pressure, letters to Pope John XXII, including 'Declaration of Arbroath'.
1323	13-year truce with England.
1324	Treaty of Corbeil with France, established 'auld alliance'.
1326	'Tenth penny' tax for life granted to Robert I.
1327	Edward II of England deposed by Isabella and Mortimer; accession of Edward III. Attacks on north of England and Ulster.
1328	Treaty of Edinburgh; English recognized Scottish independence; Scots undertook £20,000 'payment for peace'. Papacy recognized Scottish independence; gave kings right to unction at coronations.

1329	Death of Robert I. Accession of five-year-old David II (1329–71).
1329–41	David II's minority; earl of Moray initially guardian.
1332	Earl of Moray died (July). Edward Balliol and 'disinherited' invaded; battle of Dupplin (August); Balliol crowned king (September); driven out (December).
1333	English siege of Berwick; battle of Halidon Hill; Edward III and Balliol overran Scotland.
1334	David II sent to France.
1334–7	Invasions by Edward III; Scottish resistance, led by Andrew Murray. Balliol forces defeated at Culblean, November 1335.
1337	Outbreak of Hundred Years War between England and France. Scots regained control of Scotland; David II returned, 1341.
1342–6	Raids on north of England. Rivalries among leading nobles.
1346	Battle of Crécy; French defeated by English. England invaded; battle of Neville's Cross; David II captured.
1346–57	David II's captivity. Edward III abandoned Balliol; Bruce–Balliol civil war finally ended.
1346–54	John Macdonald of the Isles combined Macdonald and Macruarie territory (after death of last Macruarie chief, his brother-in-law), which became basis of Macdonald lordship of the Isles.
1349	Bubonic plague reached Scotland. Beginning of population fall.
1350–5	Edward III's peace proposals rejected.
1355–6	Scots, with French encouragement, attacked Berwick (November); Edward III devastated Lothian (February: the 'Burnt Candlemas').
1356	Battle of Poitiers; French defeated by English.
1357	Treaty of Berwick: David II ransomed for £66,667; 23 hostages sent to England; long truce concluded.
1358	Customs rate raised from 6s 8d to £1 per sack of wool. 'Non-provincial' earldom of Douglas created.
1360	Anglo-French peace concluded. David II stopped ransom payments.
1361–2	Second general attack of plague.
1363	Abortive rebellion by Douglas, Stewart and March. David II married Margaret Drummond. Fresh negotiations with Edward III.
1364	Parliament rejected Edward III's proposals.
1365	Scots undertook to pay ransom at £4,000 a year.
1366	National land valuations reduced by almost half.
1367	Weight of silver in coinage reduced.

1368	Customs rate raised to £1 6s 8d per sack.
1369	Anglo-French war restarted. Ransom cut to £2,667 a year; 14-year truce confirmed. Margaret Drummond divorced. Beginning of parliamentary concern over Highland lawlessness.
1370	Parliament legislated against royal commands which were contrary to the law. Last record of a serf in Scotland.
1371	Death of David II. Accession of 55-year-old Robert Stewart, as Robert II (1371–90). Douglas demonstration. Beginning of Stewart dominance of higher nobility. 'Auld alliance' reconfirmed.
1371–84	Alexander Stewart 'Wolf of Badenoch' became dominant in north; disintegration of order in Moray.
1372	Peak year of wool exports: 9,252 sacks.
1373	Parity of English and Scots currencies ended; exchange rate 3:4.
1375	Barbour's *Brus*.
1377	Richard II succeeded Edward III. Scots stopped paying ransom.
1378–1417	Great Schism in papacy; French and Scots support Avignon popes.
1379	Third general attack of plague.
1384	Truce expired; Scots overran Annandale and Teviotdale; brief English invasion. Robert II surrendered executive power to earl of Carrick. Highland caterans to be arrested or killed.
1385	English invaded Scotland; Franco-Scottish army invaded England; both unsuccessful. War in Flanders damaged cloth industry there; beginning of long-term slump in Scottish wool exports. Parliamentary attack on 'Wolf of Badenoch'.
*c.*1385	Fordun's *Chronicle of the Scots' Nation*.
1388	Invasion of England, following 'Appellant' *coup d'état* there; battle of Otterburn; earl of Douglas killed. Dispute over Douglas inheritance. Earl of Fife replaced Carrick as guardian.
1389	Scots joined Anglo-French truce.
1389–1431	Hostility between crown and lords of the Isles.
1390	Death of Robert II. Accession of 53-year-old John earl of Carrick, as Robert III (1390–1406). Fife stayed guardian (? until 1393). 'Wolf of Badenoch' burned Elgin cathedral. Weight of silver in coinage reduced; English–Scottish exchange rate became 1:2.
*c.*1390–5	'Usual money of Scotland' replaced 'sterling'; inflation beginning.

1392	Cateran raid into Angus, led by sons of 'Wolf of Badenoch', repulsed at Glasclune.
1396	Clan fight at Perth.
1397	'Statute of Stirling': law-and-order procedures, enacted in Scots.
1398	Major Anglo-Scottish negotiations. Honorific dukedoms of Rothesay and Albany created. Donald lord of the Isles made to submit.
1399	Duke of Rothesay appointed lieutenant for Robert III. Richard II of England deposed by Henry IV.
1400	England raided; brief invasion by Henry IV. Earl of March defected.
1401	Channel piracy intensified; Scottish exports seriously affected.
c.1401	Weight of silver in coinage reduced.
1402	Imprisonment and death of Rothesay; duke of Albany became lieutenant. England invaded; battle of Homildon Hill; earl of Douglas, Murdoch of Fife, etc., captured. Scots confidence evaporated.
1406	Prince James captured at sea by English. Death of Robert III. Accession of 12-year-old Prince James, as James I (1406–37).
1406–24	James I's minority/captivity in England; Albany governor (to 1420).
1407	Burning of English Lollard John Resby.
1409	Jedburgh castle captured and demolished.
1411	Battle of Harlaw; lord of the Isles repulsed; made to submit (1412).
1412	St Andrews University founded.
1413	Henry IV of England succeeded by Henry V.
1415	Anglo-French war restarted; English victory at Agincourt.
1416	Henry V released Murdoch of Fife.
1417	'Foul' (foolish) raid on Berwick and Roxburgh.
1418	Scots followed rest of Europe in acknowledging Pope Martin V, whose election (1417) ended the Great Schism.
1419	6,000 Scots troops sent to France. Anglo-Burgundian alliance (to 1435) caused tension between Scotland and Low Countries.
1420	Death of Albany; succeeded as governor and duke by son Murdoch.
c.1420	Wyntoun's *Orygynale Cronykil*.
1421	Battle of Baugé.
1422	Henry V of England succeeded by Henry VI.
1423	Treaty with Holland.
1424	James I ransomed for £33,333; 27 hostages given. Scots

	army in France destroyed at Verneuil. Weight of silver in coinage reduced.
1425	Arrest and execution of Duke Murdoch, two of his sons, and his father-in-law earl of Lennox. Their estates went to the crown. Bishops required to conduct inquisitions into heresy.
1426	Treaty with Denmark. Beginning of 'sessions'.
1427	Default on ransom. Act against burgh craftsmen's 'conspiracies'.
1428	Agreement with France, not honoured by James I. Legislation to prohibit unauthorized purchase of benefices in Rome ('barratry'), and, ineffectively, to bring shire commissioners to parliament.
1429	Alexander lord of the Isles rebelled; defeated and imprisoned.
1431	Temporary imprisonment of 5th earl of Douglas. Government forces defeated by Macdonalds at Inverlochy; parliament urged conciliation; lord of the Isles released.
1433	Burning of Bohemian Hussite preacher.
1435	English repulsed at Piperden. Anglo-Burgundian alliance ended.
1436	James I committed himself to France; daughter married dauphin. Unsuccessful siege of Roxburgh.
1437	James I murdered. Accession of his six-year-old son, as James II (1437–60). Assassins plus earl of Atholl executed. With Atholl's forfeiture, crown had acquired 11 earldoms since 1425.
1437–49	James II's minority; 5th earl of Douglas initially lieutenant; lord of the Isles recognized as earl of Ross.
1439	5th earl of Douglas died. Alexander Livingston seized James II.
1440	'Black Dinner': 6th earl of Douglas executed, at instigation of uncle (subsequently 7th earl), Livingston and William Crichton.
1442	Earliest known example of a bond of manrent.
1444	8th earl of Douglas became king's lieutenant-general.
1445	Douglas-dominated parliament. Emergence of lordships of parliament and concept of Scottish parliamentary peerage.
c.1445	Bower's *Scotichronicon*.
1448	English raid on Annandale repulsed at battle of the Sark.
1449	James II married Mary of Gueldres; Livingstons fell from power; end (in practice) of James II's minority.
1450	Jubilee indulgence; made available in Glasgow. James II attacked Douglas lands in Selkirk and Galloway.
1451	Donald lord of the Isles rebelled. James II backed down

	towards Douglas. Glasgow university founded. Weight of silver in coinage reduced; English–Scottish exchange rate became 1:3.
1452	James II killed earl of Douglas. Douglas rebellion collapsed. Earl of Huntly defeated earl of Crawford at Brechin.
1453	English expelled from France; end of Hundred Years War.
1455	James II attacked 9th earl of Douglas, who fled to England; Douglases defeated at Arkinholm. Douglas lands forfeited; most (plus other lands) annexed to crown. English 'Wars of the Roses' began.
1455–7	James II attacked Berwick and Roxburgh, and raided England.
1458	Among many other measures, parliament established procedure for cases of 'spuilzie', but resisted the idea of feuing land; James II was 'humbly' exhorted to keep the statutes.
1460	James II killed at Roxburgh. Accession of his 10-year-old son, as James III (1460–88). Roxburgh castle captured and demolished.
1460–9	James III's minority; no lieutenant appointed.
1461	Henry VI driven out of England (by Edward IV); given asylum in Scotland in return for handing over Berwick.
1462	Secret treaty between lord of the Isles and Edward IV; its disclosure in 1475 helped cause the lord's eventual forfeiture.
1464	Henry VI sent back to England; long truce made with Edward IV. Lord of the Isles made to submit.
1465	Anglo-Scottish truce extended until 1519 (in theory); growing Anglo-Scottish rapprochement, leading to 1474 and 1502 treaties.
c.1465	*Auchinleck Chronicle* compiled.
1466	Lord Boyd seized James III.
1468	James III married Margaret of Denmark. Orkney (1468) and Shetland (1469) pledged for her dowry; neither were ever redeemed.
1469	End of James III's minority; overthrow of Boyds. With Shetland's acquisition, kingdom of Scotland reached its fullest extent.

Appendix B: Economic Data

Table I: Wool and Leather Exports

Wool exports include sheepskins (reckoning 240 skins to the sack) and are given to the nearest 10 sacks. Leather exports are given to the nearest 100 hides. The totals are yearly averages, generally for five-year periods, though with some variations caused by missing accounts and irregular accounting periods. Since accounts for individual ports are not totally complete, the figures often include estimates, and so must not be taken as being 100 per cent accurate. The figures derive from *The Exchequer Rolls of Scotland*, vols. I-VII.

Period	Wool (sacks per year)	Leather (hides per year)
1327–32	5,700	36,100
.....		
1341/2–42/3	2,450	17,900
.....		
1359–64	5,660	30,900
1365–9	5,460	38,000
1370–4	7,360	39,500
1375–9	5,140	35,600
1380–4	4,750	56,400
1385–9	3,090	48,300
1390–4	4,760	33,800
1395–9	3,910	34,200
1400–5	1,840	29,200
1406–9	2,590	23,300
1410–14	2,950	22,900
1415–19	2,350	23,800
1420–1/2	1,880	19,500
.....		

Period	Wool (sacks per year)	Leather (hides per year)
1424–9	3,760	21,300
1430–4	3,020	22,500
.....		
1440/1–4/5	1,580	14,300
1445/6–9/50	2,580	26,300
1450/1–4/5	1,330	35,200
1455/6–9/60	1,320	19,900
1460/1–4/5	2,110	18,200
1465/6–8/9	1,930	15,000

Table II: Food Prices

This table gives the prices for the main foodstuffs found in *The Exchequer Rolls of Scotland*, vols. I-VII. The figures are obviously inadequate for any detailed study, but do serve to indicate the broad trends during the late Middle Ages. Grain prices are given per boll (approximately 6½ bushels), animal prices per head. (*: 1424 prices are from the testament of Alexander Hume of Dunglass, in Hist. Mss. Comm., 12th report, appendix viii, p. 87.)

	Oats	Meal	Wheat	Barley	Malt	Cattle	Sheep
1326		1s 8d; 2s		2s		7s 10d	1s 6d
1327						9s 3d	
1328	6d; 6d		1s 8d				
1329	6d; 8d; 10d; 10d	10d; 1s 3d; 1s 9d	1s 9d	1s 3d; 1s 6d			
1330	11d; 1s 4d	1s 7d; 2s	2s; 2s 6d; 2s 11d		10d; 1s; 1s 3d; 1s 6d; 2s 1d; 2s 3d	5s; 6s 8d; 8s; 8s 4d; 8s 3d; 10s	1s 3d; 1s 6d; 1s 6d; 1s 9d; 2s
1331			1s 11d; 2s 10d	1s 3d; 2s 5d	2s 4d	7s	1s 8d
Averages, 1326–31	(10d)	(1s 9d)	(2s 3d)	(1s 9d)	(1s 7d)	(7s 10d)	(1s 7d)
1358			1s 8d				
1359			2s 7d				
1360				10d		5s	
1361				1s			
1362			2s	1s			

1365			3s 7d				
1366	7½d		2s 7d		2s 8d		
1367			2s 2d		2s 3d		
1368				11d	2s 1d	6s 8d	
1369	8d	2s 1d	2s 10d			5s	1s

1372		1s 8d	2s 6d; 2s 10d		2s 1d; 2s 5d	5s	1s; 1s 11d
1373			2s 11d		2s 7d; 2s 8d	5s	1s
1374		1s 9d	3s 5d		2s 6d; 2s 8d		

1380	1s	2s 2d	3s 4d; 3s 9d		2s 5d; 3s 4d	5s; 5s	1s; 1s 4d
1381							
1382			3s 4d				

1383 / 1384	1s 3d	1s 8d	2s 5d 3s 4d		2s 3d	6s	1s 2s–3s
1424*			3s 4d			13s 4d	
1341	3s 4d						
1432							
1433	2s		6s	6s 8d		10s; 12s	
1434				4s 10d			
1435							
—							
1438	2s			5s	5s	11s 10d; 12s	
—							
—							
1444			10s	3s 4d			
1445			12s				
1446	5s			6s 1d			
1447				5s			
1448				5s			
1449			6s 5d; 7s; 8s	5s; 3s 9d; 4s		16s	
1450	2s 6d	4s; 4s; 5s	9s	3s 9d; 5s	5s 6d	18s	
1451	3s; 4s 9d	4s 2d	8s				
1452	2s 6d		6s 8d				
1453	2s; 2s 6d				6s 8d	16s 9d; 17s; 17s 3d; 18s; 20s; 13s 4d	
1454	2s 8d				6s 8d		
1455	5s; 6s	5s	9s 6d				
1456	3s 4d; 5s 3d	8s; 10s	8s		13s 4d	18s; 20s; 22s; 17s 6d	
1457	4s 2d				6s	14s 9d; 15s; 13s	
1458	2s; 2s 6d	4s; 6s 8d					
1459		6s					
1460	5s	5s 9d; 6s 8d; 8s; 10s		3s 4d		14s 5d	
1461			9s	3s 4d			
1462	5s	5s; 8s; 10s		5s; 6s 8d; 8s		7s 6d; 15s; 20s	
1463	1s	4s; 4s 6d		3s 4d		15s; 15s 4d	
1464	4s	4s; 4s 6d	6s 8d; 8s	4s 2d; 5s		18s; 18s 1d	
1465		6s 8d	6s 8d; 8s	6s 8d	6s 8d	18s 6d	
1466			8s 4d	4s 2d			
1467	3s 8d	4s 2d				12s; 20s 4d	
1468	4s 2d				4s 2d	19s	
1469	4s						

Table III: Currency Changes
This table gives the weights in silver coins which made up one £ of account in Scotland and England (i.e. 240 × 1 silver penny, or 40 × 1 sixpenny groat, etc., as appropriate), together with the official exchange rates between English and Scottish currency. It derives from I.H. Stewart, *The Scottish Coinage* (revised edn, London, 1967); G.C. Brooke, *English Coins* (3rd edn, London, 1950), and J. Gilbert, 'The Usual Money of Scotland and exchange rates against foreign coin', in *Coinage in Medieval Scotland*, ed. D. Metcalf, British Archaeological Reports, 45 (1977).

Weight of £ in Scotland		Weight of £ in England	
To *c*. 1296	5,400 gr.	To 1279	5,400 gr.
		From 1279	5,340 gr.
c.1320 - 1333	5,143 gr.		
		From 1344	4,800 gr.
From 1351	4,320 gr.	From 1351	4,320 gr.
From 1367	3,680 gr.		
From 1390	2,764 gr.		
From *c*. 1400	1,680 gr.		
		From 1412	3,600 gr.
From 1424	1,440 gr.		
From 1451	1,178 gr.		
		From 1464	2,760 gr.
From 1470	780 gr.		

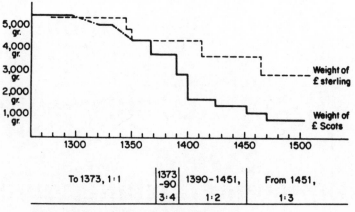

To 1373, 1:1	1373 -90 3:4	1390 - 1451, 1:2	From 1451, 1:3

Exchange Rates of English and Scots Currency

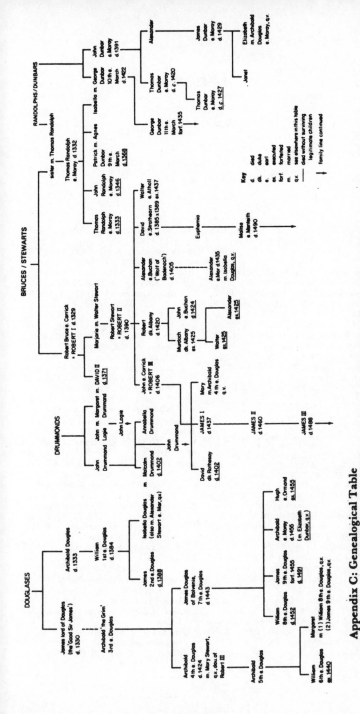

Appendix C: Genealogical Table

This table provides abbreviated genealogies for the four major noble families of late-medieval Scotland. For full details see *The Scots Peerage*, ed. J.B. Paul (Edinburgh, 1904–14).

Index